Praise for
Disciplined Entrepreneurship for Climate and Energy Ventures

"The energy system is challenged simultaneously to deliver reliably and affordably while minimizing emissions and serving the needs of investors. Technology and business model innovation are the essential tools for meeting this complex challenge, and MIT's Climate and Energy Ventures class has, from its inception, supported and developed entrepreneurs whose success we all depend on. This book captures the insights gained over fifteen years by faculty and students alike and, as such, provides an invaluable guide to those who will build the clean energy economy."

—Ernie Moniz, Former **US Secretary of Energy**

"Addressing the closely coupled Climate and Energy challenge is the moral imperative and economic opportunity of our generation. I have watched the MIT climate and energy entrepreneurial ecosystem from its start and as it has successfully grown well beyond MIT. I know that at the core of its success have been rigorous frameworks to bring research to market. This book describes the MIT model in ways that should be useful to all current and aspiring innovators in this field."

—Susan Hockfield, President Emerita, **MIT**

"There is no pathway or prescription to successfully address climate change, nor energy security, nor economic and environmental well-being without energy innovation. This book makes accessible to everyone proven, actionable, entrepreneurial strategies arising from one of the world's greatest epicenters of innovation. I highly recommend it to all."

—Andy Karsner, Former Under Secretary, **US Department of Energy**

Current Member of Board of Directors, **Exxon Mobil**

Managing Partner, **Emerson Collective**

"*Disciplined Entrepreneurship for Climate and Energy Ventures* is more than a guide—it's a catalyst for action. What sets this book apart is its tailored focus on the unique challenges and opportunities within the climate and energy sectors. It's an empowering blueprint for anyone committed to harnessing entrepreneurship as a force for meaningful, lasting change."

—Georgina Campbell Flatter, CEO, **Greentown Labs**

"Through my personal journey in building companies and supporting hundreds of entrepreneurs, I know that the learnings are hard won, and the journey can feel lonely. This book captures best practices that I hope every entrepreneur can benefit from to accelerate their progress and build world-changing companies."

*—Carmichael Roberts, PhD and **Serial Co-Founder of Multiple Deep Tech Companies***

*Co-Founder and Managing Partner, **Material Impact***

"What I learned in the Disciplined Entrepreneurship framework has helped me found and build two successful climate and energy companies. This framework has been my road map, and I can't recommend it highly enough as a reference book for climate tech entrepreneurs."

*—Alex Wright-Gladstein, CEO and Founder of **Sphere**, Co-Founder of **Ayar Labs***

"At Breakthrough Energy, we've learned that building and deploying reliable, affordable, and clean energy solutions takes more than just good technology. It also takes teams with focus, humility, and grit. This book distills hard-earned wisdom into a guide that is both practical and inspiring for anyone working to build the next generation of transformative energy ventures that the world will rely on for decades, even centuries, to come."

*—Rodi Guidero, Executive Director, **Breakthrough Energy***

"People often say that there is no 'playbook' for building new ventures in the climate & energy space. That changes today with the arrival of this singular new book that distills the hard-won lessons learned in the trenches over the last almost 20 years by the teaching team at MIT's Climate & Energy Ventures course. A bible for aspiring entrepreneurs who want to save the planet and make a lot of money while they're at it."

*—David Danielson, Former Assistant Secretary, **US Department of Energy***

*Co-Founder of **ARPA-E**, **MIT Energy Club** and **MIT Energy Conference***

"In my quest to address the dual challenge, I have looked far and wide to find the best methodology. I found it in this Disciplined Entrepreneurship approach, and we have successfully brought it to Texas. I strongly believe it should be adopted globally, and we intend to help facilitate this."

*—David Baldwin, Partner at **SCF Partners***

*Co-Founder of **OpenMinds** and **TEX-E***

"As a serial entrepreneur in the energy and climate space, co-founding five and successfully exiting four, I found that a lot of the conventional wisdom was wrong. There are first principles that you can learn to make your chances and magnitude of success much higher. While each page captures nuggets of this wisdom, the genius of this book is how it pulls them all together in a systematic way that entrepreneurs will find very useful. It gives you a fabulous, straightforward map of what you should do and how you should do it. Pure gold for any entrepreneur in this field."

*—Jonathan Hinton, **Serial Energy Company Founder***
$700M in Exits, EY Entrepreneur of the Year

"When I launched my energy startup Kurion—later acquired by Veolia—I faced countless challenges. The frameworks now clearly laid out in this book were my guideposts, giving me the confidence and structure to reach both success and impact. After years of working closely with founders from zero to exit, the authors have distilled their insights into this invaluable resource, tailored towards energy ventures. I can't recommend this highly enough."

*—Gaëtan Bonhomme, PhD, Co-Founder & CTO, **Kurion***
*Partner, **Breakthrough Energy Ventures Europe***

"It was the Climate and Energy Ventures class at MIT that showed me that there was a systematic way to build and evaluate these types of companies. These lenses, as well as the discussions in the classes, have been invaluable to me as a global investor with a focus on sustainability and impact investing for the last 15+ years."

*—Shahazwan (Juan) Harris, Head of Strategic Investments, **EPF Malaysia**,*
*Former Executive Director, Investments, **Khazanah Fund** (Malaysia)*

"I'm not sure my start-up company would have made it without these frameworks—but I know for certain it wouldn't have achieved the same level of success. The prescriptive, actionable guidance in this book is unmatched for anyone building a climate or energy company. For me, Disciplined Entrepreneurship was a true north star."

*—Oliver Stahl, Founder and CEO, **Entelios AG***

"Good thing entrepreneurship can be taught. Because energy needs entrepreneurs. If you would like to help accelerate the transition away from hydrocarbon fuels, learn how here, from the experts, step by step."

*—Bob Metcalfe, **Turing Laureate***
*Co-Inventor of **Ethernet**, Co-Founder and longtime CEO of **3Com***
*Research Affiliate, **MIT CSAIL**, Emeritus Professor, **The University of Texas at Austin***

"As a passionate government and then corporate advocate for sustainability, it is my fervent desire that a rigorous and systematic approach like this be adopted globally as quickly as possible. It will not just help preserve the planet but also create significant concurrent, economic prosperity. These two do not have to be at odds with each other as this book shows."

*—Brune Poirson, Former Secretary of State and Minister of Parliament, **Government of France***

"This book is a call to action for the next generation of innovators poised to lead the energy transition, and this book should become the Bible for all that want to join the crusade. In Houston—the energy capital of the world—the stakes are especially high. But so are the opportunities. We need leaders who can navigate both the technical and commercial challenges of building transformative solutions. At TEX-E, we've seen firsthand how critical it is to equip young entrepreneurs with the right tools, frameworks, and mindset to tackle these challenges. Whether you're in a university lab, a startup incubator, or a garage with a big idea, this book will help you translate your vision into venture. I recommend it to anyone serious about making a lasting impact in the energy space."

*—David Pruner, Executive Chairman, **TEX-E***

"At Powerhouse Ventures, we know that great entrepreneurship can be taught, and learned. This book is an invaluable resource for aspiring entrepreneurs to accelerate clean energy abundance and build enduring, high-growth businesses."

*—Emily Kirsch, Founder and Managing Partner, **Powerhouse Ventures***

24 STEPS TO BUILD SOLUTIONS
FOR PEOPLE AND THE PLANET

DISCIPLINED ENTREPRENEURSHIP FOR CLIMATE AND ENERGY VENTURES

BEN SOLTOFF

BILL AULET
TOD HYNES
FRANCIS O'SULLIVAN
LIBBY WAYMAN

WILEY

Library of Congress Cataloging-in-Publication Data

Names: Soltoff, Ben, author.
Title: Disciplined entrepreneurship for climate and energy ventures : 24
  steps to build solutions for people and the planet / Ben Soltoff
  [and four others]
Description: Hoboken, New Jersey : Wiley, [2026] | Series: Disciplined
  entrepreneurship series | Includes index.
Identifiers: LCCN 2025033020 (print) | LCCN 2025033021 (ebook) | ISBN
  9781394285518 (hardback) | ISBN 9781394285532 (adobe pdf) | ISBN
  9781394285525 (epub)
Subjects: LCSH: New business enterprises--Management. | Climatic
  changes--Economic aspects. | Entrepreneurship.
Classification: LCC HD62.5 .S67295 2026 (print) | LCC HD62.5 (ebook)
LC record available at https://lccn.loc.gov/2025033020
LC ebook record available at https://lccn.loc.gov/2025033021

Cover Design and Illustration: Marius Ursache

We dedicate this book and the learning herein to entrepreneurs—the people in the arena, past, present, and future—as well as to all our colleagues who add to the field of climate and energy entrepreneurship every day.

And to our families, and particularly to the children (and grandchildren) in our lives: Lily, Rose, Thomas, Clare, Carty, Jacklyn, Caroline, Avery, and Leon. The world is an amazing place. We wrote this book to educate and equip the people who will ensure that it stays that way for you and for the generations who come after you. Maybe you will become climate and energy entrepreneurs yourselves when you grow up, or maybe you will contribute in other ways, but whatever you do, we hope that you will espouse and champion the values found in these pages.

CONTENTS

FOREWORD

On May 6, 2005, then MIT President, Susan Hockfield, announced in her inauguration speech that climate was the moral imperative of our generation.[1] She committed to marshaling the vast resources of MIT to address this challenge. One of those assets was entrepreneurship, and it was to be combined with science, engineering, technology, and other interdisciplinary competencies, just as these competencies had been combined in the RadLab so successfully in World War II.

With this charge, I started to look into the area. After decades as an entrepreneur in the information technology (IT) sector, I was surprised by the lack of entrepreneurial activity in the energy sector. I thought it was going to be easy to change this. I would just take the refined principles I had learned and codified, apply them to the energy sector, and we would have this sorted out in a year or so. With that expectation, I set out to do my first solo, brand-new-from-the-ground-up course at MIT in the fall of 2007, then simply called "Energy Ventures".

Oh, was I wrong!

After a systematic analysis of the industry and the challenges, I realized that energy was fundamentally different. My former MIT colleague and later US Secretary of Energy, Ernie Moniz, summed up the situation brilliantly in two sentences: "The energy industry is a multi-trillion dollar per year, highly capitalized, commodity business, with exquisite supply chains, providing essential services to all levels of society. This leads to a system with considerable inertia, aversion to risk, extensive regulation, and complex politics."

The dynamics driving innovation in this sector are dramatically different than those in the IT sector.[2] Consistent with the Moniz description of the system we are looking to innovate, the end product is most often a commodity (such as a kilowatt-hour of electricity), and the requirements to produce this end product are much more capital intensive. As such, it takes decades for breakthrough innovations to be adopted in the market. Disintermediating the existing players is often not a feasible strategy; you have to work through them. Solutions must focus more on price than value, and they definitely need to scale to be meaningful.

Then, there is the additional dimension that energy is an essential service to society at all levels, and as such, it must have strong and direct links to policy and politics. At the micro level, it is often perceived as a right rather than a privilege, which has additional ramifications at the macro level. For governments, energy and climate are two of the strongest factors driving national security and economic well-being and growth. While "energy independence" is a term fraught with issues, it is still a powerful topic for political discourse and political leaders. There is no escaping regulation.

In this analysis, I realized that traditional venture capital, which had a terrific product-market fit for the IT industry, was ill-suited for energy. I wrote about this in my August and October 2007 articles "What's Wrong with Energy Investing?" (Parts I and II),[3] which I must say with some humble brag got criticized at the time but now hold up pretty damn well. This was near the height of the peak of Cleantech 1.0 investing. Venture Capital (VC) investors in this wave did not do well, but there were some who did well specifically in wind energy. Unfortunately, many VC investors ran away from this sector and blamed the sector, not the framework in which they were building and analyzing companies.

But the practical question I faced while designing an academic course was, what should the future climate and energy entrepreneur do to be successful? After a tremendous amount of thought and dialogue with many mentioned in the acknowledgements of this book, and then testing hypotheses, I realized along with my colleague (and course co-founder) Tod Hynes, that there were many key components of the battle-tested and proven Disciplined Entrepreneurship framework that did transfer. . . but we needed to add more and make adjustments.

This course has run continuously since its launch in 2007. Well over 600 students have taken it at time of this writing, and we have seen how they have done in the real world. It is profoundly satisfying and rewarding to see their success. Our teaching team expanded to include Francis O'Sullivan, who brought an incredible depth of expertise on the technical side to the team; Libby Wayman, who adds expertise based on her firsthand experience in government and large corporations; Jacquelyn Pless, who joined as an instructor and shared her wisdom on economics, policy, and innovation, as well as improving rigor from an academic research mindset; and finally, Ben Soltoff, who added a new perspective that included rich global experience and expertise in climate as well as being a thoughtful and highly productive writer (don't underestimate that when documenting what you have learned into a book!). A series of tremendously talented teaching assistants have also run the course and taken it to levels I could not have imagined at the beginning.

The result is a framework that we have found to work, and we have the evidence to back this up. Over 60 companies (and counting, as they increase at an exponential rate) have directly come out of the class, and they have raised at least $2.3 billion in funding and created more than 2,500 jobs. There have already been at least 116 CEOs and co-founders who have come through the course over the years to date. Several students have gone on to start a second or third company. These subsequent alumni companies have raised an additional $5 billion and created more than 4,500 additional jobs.

Is what we are presenting in this book an algorithm to guaranteed success? Is it perfect? Is it done? The answer to all these questions is definitely *no*. Consistent with the Disciplined Entrepreneurship brand, it is meant to be rigorous but accessible and very action-oriented guidance to dramatically enhance your odds of success and allow you to get started (which is often the hardest part of the entrepreneurial process). It is imperfect but very useful, and it will always be evolving. I am sure what we are offering in this book will significantly contribute to the corpus of knowledge about how to teach and do entrepreneurship in this crucial field to have real world impact. I should also note that calling it "entrepreneurship" might limit the impact, because this is not just about startups. Maybe "innovation" is a better word for some of you, because the structure will help you to be more innovative leaders in government, large corporations, non-profits, and financial organizations. We need many more new-generation leaders in these organizations (much more so than other industries), who can find ways to overcome the seeming intractable challenges we face as a society. These entrepreneurs in larger organizations, often but not always working in collaboration with startups, are essential for our future success as a society. And there are great economic opportunities here as well! Nothing wrong with using market forces for good.

Lastly, as we have seen with the foundational Disciplined Entrepreneurship framework, once we have clear frameworks, we can start to apply artificial intelligence (AI) to accelerate the process and support broader base adoption.[4] To leverage the power of AI, we must first have proven and clear structure. That is what we are offering here for the first time, and we intend to launch AI tools to support this in the near future.

The goal of our efforts over the past 20 years was to create an accessible, practical, rigorous, and even fun guide for building climate and energy ventures or solutions, and I believe we have achieved that here. I am very confident that you will find this helpful, but it is not sufficient. While this book will give you a great start, there is more that you must do to complement it. We also look forward to others building off this framework to solve the singularly most fundamental challenge of our generation, as President Hockfield laid out two decades ago.

— Bill Aulet

Notes

1. https://news.mit.edu/2005/inaug-speech-sh.
2. Generally, there are not trends driving exponential growth like Moore's law (the number of transistors on a microchip roughly doubles every two years) or Metcalfe's law (the value of a network is proportional to the square of the number of nodes), but there are some similar dynamics such as Wright's law, which predicts a consistent decrease in price for every increase in the volume of production.
3. https://www.d-eship.com/articles/whats-wrong-with-energy-investing-part-1/ and https://www.d-eship.com/articles/whats-wrong-with-energy-investing-part-2/.
4. https://news.mit.edu/2024/new-ai-jetpack-accelerates-entrepreneurial-process-0919.

INTRODUCTION

Tackling the Dual Challenge

Throughout history, energy has been interlinked with human progress. Coal, oil, and gas initially seemed like gifts from the gods. Their high-density energy-to-mass ratio allowed for rapid economic prosperity. If a scientist in a lab had invented any of them, they would have surely gotten a Nobel Prize. These energy sources fueled the Industrial Revolution and advanced society in unimaginable ways.

But like most things in life, this progress came at some costs. Many of our most prevalent energy sources emit greenhouse gases, which we now know cause warming and other changes to the climate. Since the Industrial Revolution, the average global temperature has gone up by more than a full degree Centigrade—closer to one and a half degrees if we look at the hottest recent years. That may not seem like a lot, but it is the fastest rate of temperature change on Earth in the last 10,000 years, and the world is now hotter than it has been in 100,000 years. We are facing a level and rate of warming that has not happened since the dawn of humanity.

The grand challenge of the 21st century will be to decouple energy use from emissions. We need to increase reliable and affordable access to energy while addressing detrimental effects on the climate, which includes removing the emissions and heat that we've added to the earth's system. This is what is known as the Dual Challenge.[1]

Solving the Dual Challenge is an urgent priority. When we started working on these issues, climate change was regarded as a future problem, but it is now clear that we are facing the impacts in the present. This is more apparent than ever in the United States, where we live. Just in the year we wrote this book (2024–2025), we saw floods that washed away entire communities in western North Carolina, as well as wildfires that burned huge swaths of Los Angeles, the second largest city in the country.

Much of the widely accepted social narrative on climate change focuses on grim prognostications about how these effects are getting worse. But we only get so far by fretting about what could happen, rather than rolling up our sleeves and doing something about it.

What Does This Mean for Entrepreneurs?

This is a book for entrepreneurs, and entrepreneurs don't see change as something scary; they see it as a source of great opportunity. The Dual Challenge is one of the greatest opportunities of our era. Does that mean we are advocating for entrepreneurs to exploit problems in the name of profit? Quite the opposite, actually. At its core, entrepreneurship is about solving problems, and it is about doing so in a manner that is not only financially sustainable but also financially successful, because that is a proven pathway to achieve both scale and impact.

The Dual Challenge poses a host of interesting and important problems to solve. For instance, there is the energy transition that entails moving away from an emissions-heavy energy system and toward one that is neutral or even beneficial for the climate. We need to provide a clean path for growth that works for countries across all levels of economic development.

We must also find ways to help people, institutions, and systems adjust to an altered environment. Our global economy was built on a stable climate that no longer exists. We need to adapt to the new changing climate and become more resilient at the local, national, and global level. This shift creates a tremendous opportunity for those who are willing to embrace and drive change.

Climate and energy problems create new markets, and entrepreneurs stand to gain immensely if they can figure out how to serve them and capitalize on transformative business models. They also get the added benefit of doing the right thing for current and future generations.

The Dual Challenge is often regarded, falsely, as a trade-off—we can either have better lives or we can have fewer emissions. Scalable climate and energy solutions must find a win-win. Entrepreneurs have many opportunities to create products that enhance user experience while solving pressing global problems.

We should note here that not all entrepreneurs are startup founders. Entrepreneurs can also operate in existing companies, organizations, and government institutions. Innovation in those places is essential for building solutions at scale where they can have meaningful impact in a short amount of time. We need companies with large balance sheets and capital-intensive infrastructure to be deeply involved, because they can handle scale and long timelines. We need entrepreneurs to thrive within large energy organizations . . . and even within government, nonprofits, and academic institutions.

If any of that sounds appealing, then you might just be a climate and energy entrepreneur, and this book is for you!

Yes, Climate and Energy Entrepreneurship Can Be Taught!

More than a decade ago, Bill Aulet began the first edition of *Disciplined Entrepreneurship* by posing the question of whether entrepreneurship could be taught. Over the course of that book, he answered that question with a clear and resounding *yes*. For over a decade, *Disciplined Entrepreneurship* has provided would-be entrepreneurs with a 24-step framework that is rigorous, accessible, and open source. Since the book was published, this framework has benefited hundreds of thousands of entrepreneurs and entrepreneurial thinkers, and it is now taught at hundreds of universities worldwide.

Disciplined Entrepreneurship (DE) also continues to be the backbone of much of MIT's entrepreneurship curriculum, as well as hundreds of other schools too. MIT is home to what may be the oldest US entrepreneurship course,[2] which is currently structured as a step-by-step run-through of the DE process, where students learn each step by actively working on a startup idea.

The DE framework is also a valuable resource for courses that focus on entrepreneurship within a certain industry or area. One of the most successful courses in that category is Climate & Energy Ventures (CEV), which Bill described in his Foreword to this book. The course solicits the most promising climate-related ideas or technologies from MIT and beyond, and students join interdisciplinary teams to explore the potential of these ideas and technologies as scalable climate ventures. You will find case studies from some of those companies throughout this book.

Over the years, we have observed and mentored hundreds of climate and energy startups. We have found not only that climate and energy entrepreneurship *can* be taught but also that it *should* be taught! We need as many bright minds and great ideas as possible addressing this challenge, and these concepts should be available to everyone. However, even with the best training and preparation, it is a hard road.

Why Is It So Tough to Be a Climate and Energy Entrepreneur?

Climate and energy ventures tend to be resource-intensive, tech-heavy, infrastructure-building businesses deeply intertwined with government and large corporations. They face excruciatingly long pathways to market and must build up a sophisticated capital stack, often to produce a commodity that's chemically or physically identical to incumbent products. On top of that, the founders bear the moral and emotional burden of dealing with the planet itself as a stakeholder—the weight of the world is on their shoulders.

Due to the long timelines and high capital needs, climate and energy ventures have what we call a high price of poker relative to other ventures. It costs more to play the game, which means that you need to make each move more thoughtfully and intentionally, including the decision of whether to play at all. The price of poker escalates over time. The longer you play, the pricier it gets, and if you cannot ante up for the next round, you fold.

The price of poker is much higher for climate and energy ventures than for other types of ventures.

Another way to think about the difficulty of climate and energy ventures is what's called the *valley of death*, which is the phenomenon where promising solutions fail to reach scale due to the challenges of funding, scaling, and deploying new technology. In practice, climate and energy ventures usually face multiple valleys of death, because each stage of technology development and commercialization requires a step change in the amount of time, money, and customer traction necessary to proceed. Each stage also involves different management skills and a different set of expectations from new funders and supporters.

Valleys of death are not unique to climate and energy. They exist across all *deep tech*, a term for ventures that aim to commercialize complex science or engineering innovations, usually requiring substantial research and development as well as large amounts of money.

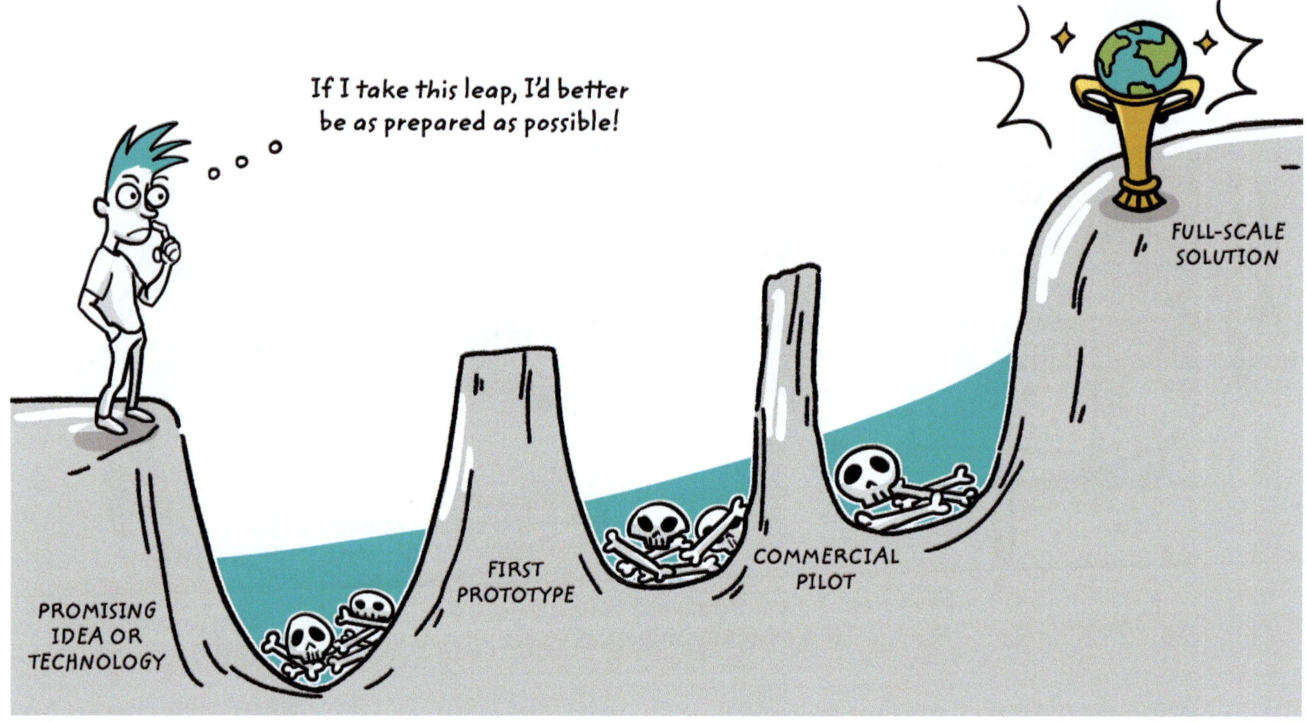

Climate and energy ventures face multiple valleys of death.

As we said, it is a hard road, but if you are up to the challenge, you are in luck. This book will break down the journey of starting a climate and energy venture, letting you know what to expect and how to navigate it. Like the original *Disciplined Entrepreneurship*, our framework will not guarantee a positive result, but it will vastly increase your odds of success.

To DE or Not to DE?

As we were writing this book, a few people asked us why climate and energy ventures would require their own book when there are so many great entrepreneurship books already out there, including the previous books in the DE series. Those volumes contain a trove of broadly applicable lessons and frameworks that can apply to entrepreneurs tackling the Dual Challenge of climate and energy.

However, when we spoke to the climate and energy entrepreneurs in our network, especially alumni of the MIT CEV course, they told us that the existing resources were useful, but they needed to pick and choose the relevant points, filtering carefully to figure out what was useful to them and what was not. They were not getting all the information they needed from the existing literature, and when we explored why, we could not find a single how-to book on entrepreneurship specifically for climate and energy ventures.

The purpose of this book is to fill that gap. We wrote this guide to distill the most valuable lessons of climate and energy entrepreneurship and share them directly with aspiring climate and energy entrepreneurs.

The original DE process helps entrepreneurs build a solution at the intersection of what the customer needs and what product they can develop to meet those needs (product-market fit). It also deals with the challenges of finding the right pathways and channels to reach scale (channel-market fit), and it lays some of the groundwork for building a financially successful venture. If we were to draw out these elements as a Venn diagram, it would look something like this:

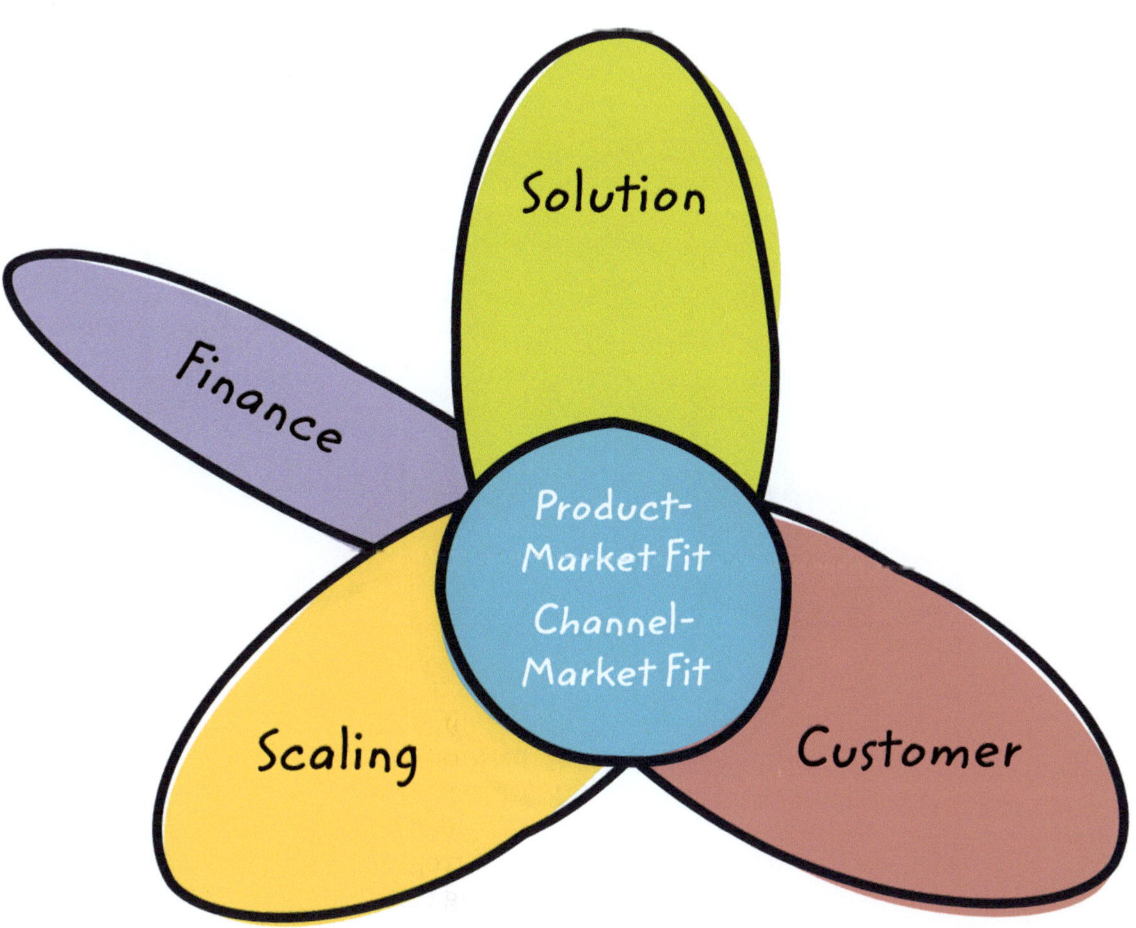

Climate and energy ventures need to find product-market and channel-market fit, but they also need to account for other factors that have been simplified in the original framework. They need a robust financial strategy to fund their ventures from multiple sources over a long time frame. They need to navigate the landscape of policy and geopolitics. They often need to figure out how to build solutions at a massive industrial scale. And they need to measure planetary impact in addition to customer value. As a result, the Venn diagram for climate and energy ventures looks more like this:

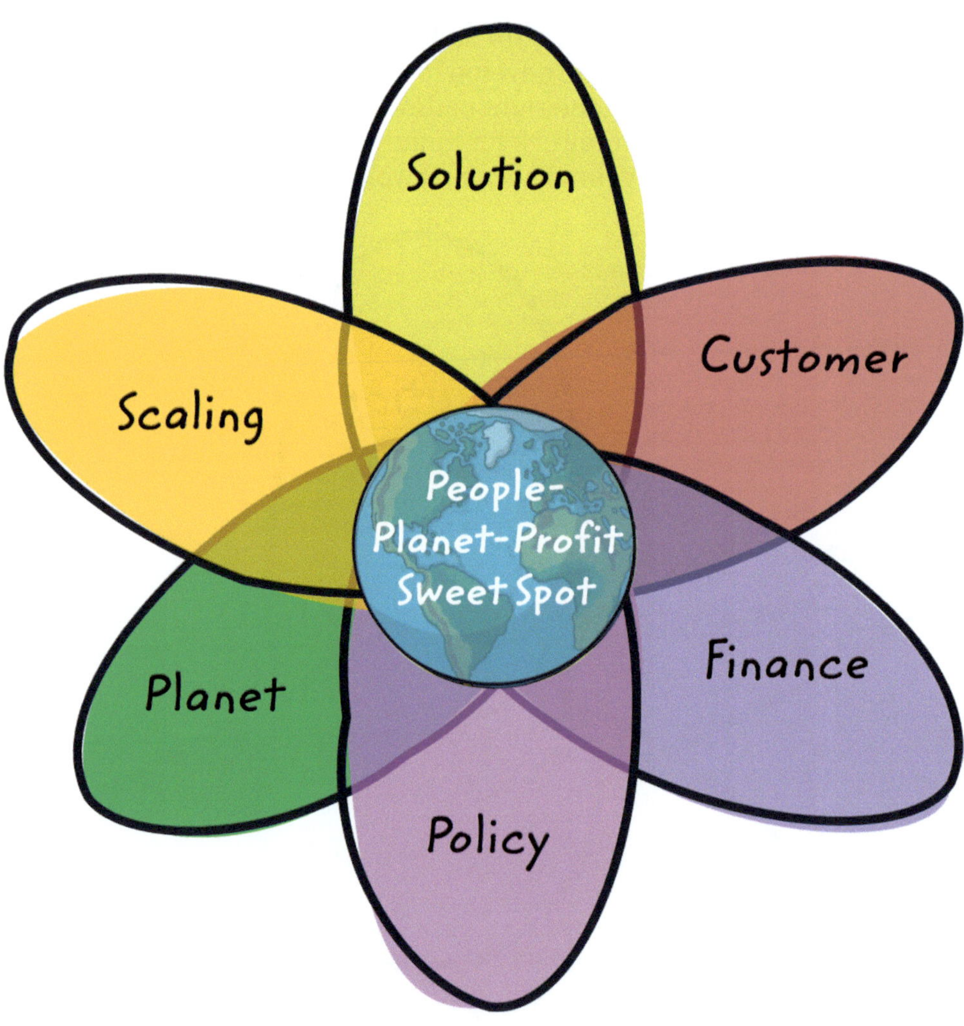

At the center of the Venn diagram is the sweet spot where a venture has a positive impact in terms of people, planet, and profits. This is sometimes known as the triple bottom line.

Because of the high price of poker in this game, climate and energy entrepreneurs also need to be particularly intentional about selecting which problem to solve in the first place. They need to understand the climate landscape and the dynamics of the energy industry, as well as their own personal skills and interests, in order to find a high-value problem or opportunity. You might be spending at least 10 years of your life on this new company, so take the time up front to find the right problem to work on. You might have noticed that the Venn Diagram looks a bit like a flower. We can think of problem exploration as the fertile soil from which the flower grows.

Adding problem exploration gives us seven elements that comprise the core themes of this book. We can summarize each of these themes with a driving question:

- **Problem exploration.** What problem should *you* solve?
- **Solution.** Is the solution fit for purpose?
- **Customer.** Who pays? For what? Why and how?
- **Finance.** How do you finance your solution?
- **Policy.** Is policy in your favor?
- **Planet.** If it works, does it matter?
- **Scaling.** How do you build it at scale?

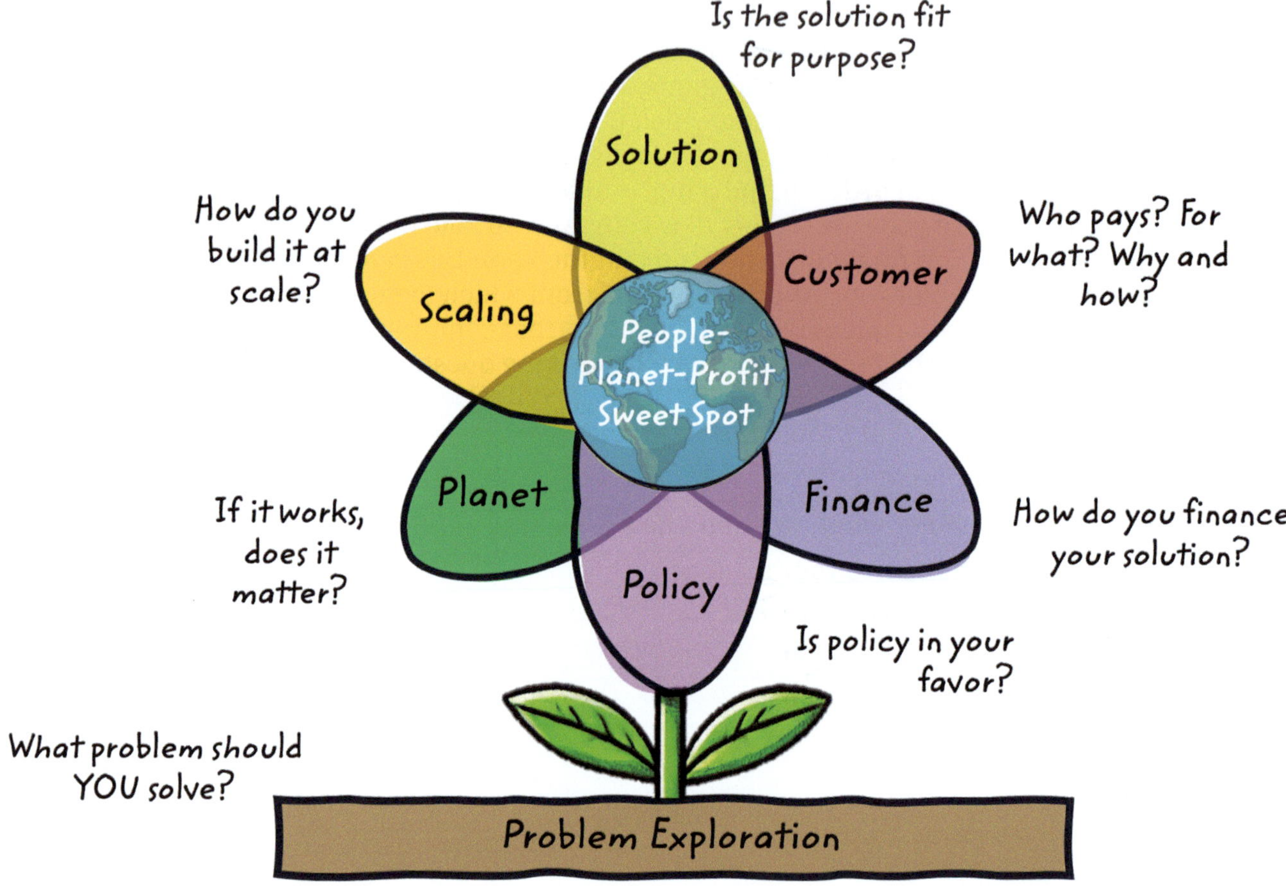

These themes guide a tailored set of 24 steps to building a successful climate and energy solution. We redesigned the entire DE process to more accurately reflect the unique journey of climate and energy ventures.

Here is a visual map of those 24 steps, color-coded according to their corresponding themes.

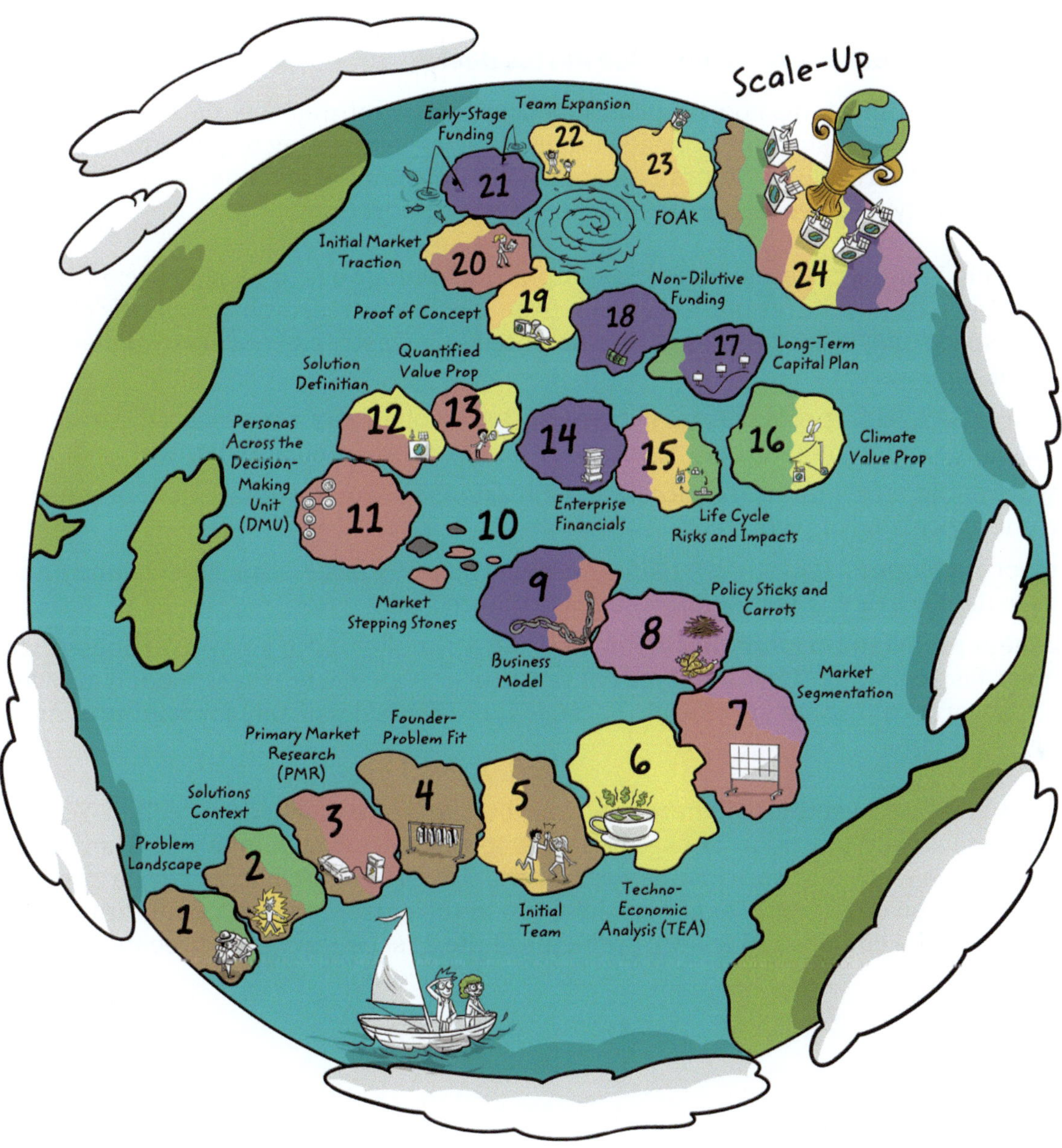

Scale-Up
Early-Stage Funding
Team Expansion
22
23
21
FOAK
Initial Market Traction
20
Non-Dilutive Funding
19
18
24
Proof of Concept
Long-Term Capital Plan
17
Solution Definition
Quantified Value Prop
12
13
14
15
16
Climate Value Prop
Personas Across the Decision-Making Unit (DMU)
11
10
Enterprise Financials
Life Cycle Risks and Impacts
Market Stepping Stones
9
Policy Sticks and Carrots
8
Business Model
Market Segmentation
7
Primary Market Research (PMR)
Founder-Problem Fit
Solutions Context
3
4
5
6
Problem Landscape
2
1
Initial Team
Techno-Economic Analysis (TEA)

What Type of Entrepreneurs Will Find Value in This Book?

While we realize the title of this book implies a focus on new ventures, the real focus is on entrepreneurs, whether they are in startups or inside other, often larger existing organizations. This book will be of value to all sorts of innovators who are addressing climate and energy challenges. Here are just a few of the types of ventures that this book can support:

- **Deep tech.** Ventures commercializing complex technology based on novel scientific developments. Deep tech ventures often originate from laboratory research, and in the climate and energy space, they often need to be implemented at infrastructure scale to achieve their full potential impact.

- **Hardware.** Physical products, not necessarily based on laboratory research. These solutions are usually smaller than infrastructure scale and faster to build and deploy.

- **Software.** Digital solutions that accelerate emissions reduction, adaptation, or other climate- and energy-related objectives.

- **Project developers.** Identifying, planning, and executing large-scale climate and energy projects to deploy existing technology at infrastructure scale.

- **Business model innovation.** Deploying existing technology with a novel business model that enables faster scaling. The other types of ventures can all use business model innovation, but it is worth calling out specifically because it is a critical pathway for scaling climate and energy solutions.

This book will be relevant for all these ventures, but we wrote it with deep tech in mind in particular. There are already many books about how to start software companies. There are fewer books about how to start hardware companies but still a lot. There are hardly any entrepreneurship books with a focus on deep tech. That is a critical gap in the entrepreneurship literature. We need deep tech to solve the climate and energy problems of the 21st century (and probably subsequent centuries, too).

How Do I Use This Book?

The best time to read this book is before you even get started. Then, you should keep it around as a reference book to help you along the journey. If you are already working on a venture, we still recommend starting from Step 1. We hope this book will push you to productively reevaluate your path. It is never too late!

We also recommend reading through the steps in the order presented. Later, you may need to skip steps or circle back, which is part of the process. We have presented the steps in a way that enables and encourages iteration.

We have adopted many concepts (and even some direct language) from *Disciplined Entrepreneurship* and *Disciplined Entrepreneurship: Startup Tactics*, but we have consolidated this material. If this is your first foray into the *Disciplined Entrepreneurship* series, read on! We'll tell you everything you need to know. But keep in mind that if you want to explore certain concepts in further depth (or if you are already familiar and need a refresher), we strongly recommend referring to the previous DE books. We've added call-outs throughout the book like the ones shown here, which will refer you to the specific sections of prior DE books where you can learn more about the concepts being discussed.

We also want to keep adapting and supporting more climate and energy entrepreneurs, so as you read the physical book, we recommend that you also visit our website climateandenergyventures.com for a wide array of other resources, including information on how to access our custom artificial intelligence (AI) tools.

You can think of the AI tools as helpful agents shedding light on the key themes of this book, trained with extensive data from the MIT CEV class and real-world insights from previous generations of climate and energy entrepreneurs.

The world of climate and energy ventures is dynamic and will continue to evolve as the broader landscape shifts. Given that constant motion, this framework is a starting point that will continue to evolve and grow over time.

As that happens, let us know how we can improve upon the information that you are reading in this book. Our website de4cev.com has a form for you to get in touch with us. We would love your feedback and additional resource recommendations!

Think of both the steps in this book and the AI tools as helpful agents shedding light on the key themes of climate and energy entrepreneurship.

Notes

1. The "Dual Challenge" framing is something we borrowed from the nonpartisan group Open-Minds, founded by David Baldwin and Jeff Katz. They educated us on how to use the term, and we ask their forgiveness for taking liberties with how we describe it. OpenMinds has great resources and analysis on solutions that can address the Dual Challenge, which you can find here: https://openminds203x.org/.
2. For many years, this course was known as New Enterprises. The title changed to Entrepreneurship 101 in 2024.

Explore the Problem Landscape

In This Step, You Will

- Get a primer on the climate and energy challenges facing the world today.
- Develop a tool kit to dig deeper into these problems.
- Ultimately narrow this down to a problem that can be concretely solved through entrepreneurship.

Why This Step, and Why Now?

The first step of your journey as an entrepreneur in climate and energy is to find your place in the universe of potential problems. We could write books and books about the problem of climate change and its drivers, but for now, we will simply give you a high-level overview of these issues as a jumping-off point for your own exploration process. We will also share a structured process of breaking down big global problems into smaller individual problems that you can potentially address through your climate and energy venture.

Climate Change 101

The basic mechanics of climate change are well known at this point. Greenhouse gases enter the atmosphere, largely due to people burning fossil fuels, and they warm the planet, which leads to a wide variety of changes to our climate (see Figure 1.1).

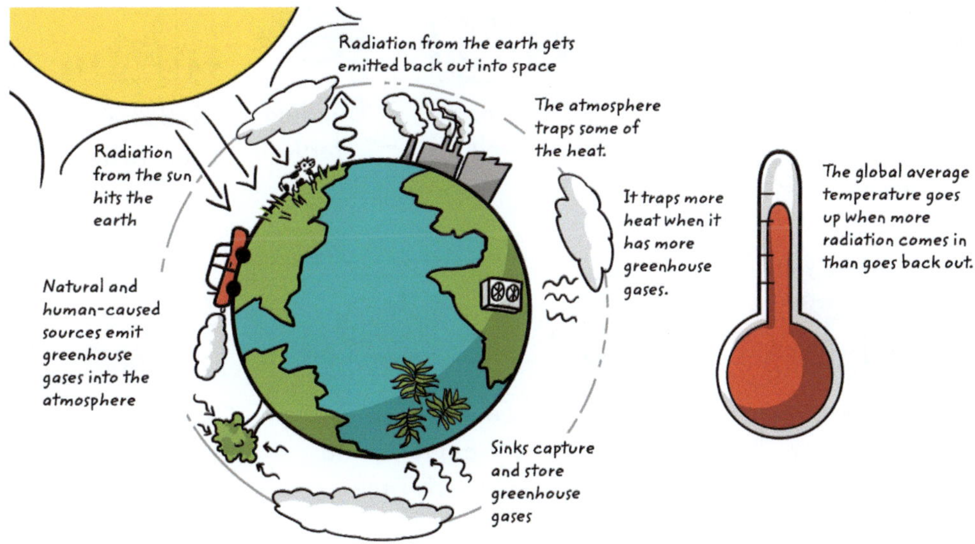

Figure 1.1: An overview of the greenhouse effect.

Earth's systems are dynamic, so some years are a bit warmer and others a bit cooler, but by looking at the trend, it's clear that we have now raised Earth's atmospheric temperature by well over 1°C since preindustrial times. Twelve thousand years ago, Earth's climate stabilized and entered a geological era called the Holocene. This led to humans settling, establishing communities, and creating governments and our current economy. Now, that stable climate is gone, so we need to build a new economy based on our new reality. This is a multi-trillion-dollar transition and a tremendous opportunity for entrepreneurs.

Climate and Energy Verticals

The scale of climate and energy problems is so massive that they can be overwhelming. It is helpful to break them down into smaller categories or verticals to narrow the potential universe of problems you could choose to solve. Here, we lay out 13 verticals that encompass most but certainly not all the problems you might consider in this space (see Figure 1.2). Note that some verticals might overlap—they're not mutually exclusive!

Figure 1.2: Climate and energy verticals.

- **Electricity generation.** Expanding the production of clean, low-emissions power.
- **Batteries and energy storage.** Finding ways to store energy for later use, enabling grid stability, integration of clean energy and electrification of transportation and industry.
- **Mobility.** Decarbonizing transportation by road, rail, air, or sea.
- **Sustainable fuels.** Introducing low-carbon alternatives to fossil fuels.
- **Building tech.** Reducing emissions from heating, cooling, and powering buildings.
- **Industrial innovation.** Seeking breakthroughs in manufacturing and heavy industry to reduce emissions, especially low-carbon cement, steel, and chemical production.
- **Circular economy.** Minimizing waste and maximizing resource efficiency by reusing, recycling, and redesigning materials and products across industries.
- **Agriculture and food systems.** Advancing practices and technologies that reduce emissions from farming, improve soil health, and create sustainable food production.

These verticals focus on reducing greenhouse gas emissions. This is currently the most common area of climate and energy innovation. Emissions from fossil fuels have been the primary driver climate change, so it makes sense that the world has focused on this problem. However, reducing emissions is no longer sufficient to avoid the worst climate impacts, so entrepreneurs must consider additional verticals as well:

- **Nature-based solutions.** Leveraging ecosystems to address climate challenges, including both mitigation of emissions and adaptation to climate impacts.

- **Water.** Ensuring reliable access to clean water for agricultural, industrial, and domestic use.

- **Emissions removal, capture, and storage.** Removing greenhouse gases from the atmosphere or capturing them at the source, and then either storing them permanently or repurposing them.

- **Global heat management.** Adjusting the earth's energy imbalance (put simply, this is the energy the earth receives from the sun minus the energy that it radiates back). We should not have to do this. It is and should be controversial, but highly credible organizations have been assessing options like releasing reflective particles into the atmosphere, adjusting global cloud cover, putting solar shades in space, and other ideas. We think this vertical will become more mainstream, just like emissions removal, which used to be a fringe concept.

- **Adaptation and resilience.** Helping people, economies, and ecosystems to withstand the impacts of climate change. The assumption of a stable climate is embedded in almost every aspect of civilization. As local climates shift, every community faces new risks, some acute (e.g., wildfires, storms) and some chronic (e.g., drought, changes in seasonal patterns). Climate adaptation is the process of responding to current hazards as well as preparing for future risks.

See Figure 1.3 for a visual representation of the role each of these verticals can play in addressing climate impacts.

Problem Segmentation

As you explore problems within climate and energy, we recommend a process called *Problem Segmentation*. This process can be used to explore problems in many other areas as well. The goal is to start with a public problem experienced at a high level across large swaths of society and break it down into a private problem faced by individuals or businesses who would be willing to pay to solve it. This framework comes from Jason Jay, director of the MIT Sloan Sustainability Initiative. Figure 1.4 shows in more detail what constitutes a public problem and what constitutes a private problem.

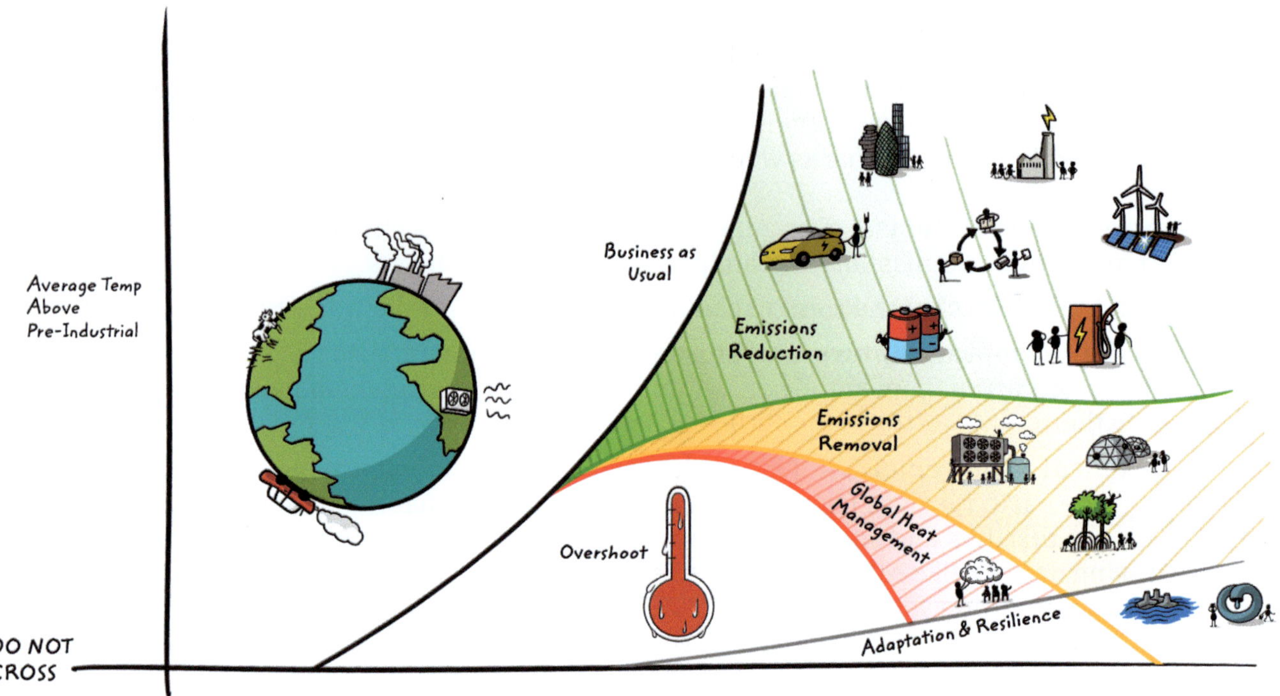

Figure 1.3: The big picture of climate and energy verticals. Adapted from the book After Geoengineering by Holly Jean Buck..

Public Problems	Private Problems
Concerned with properties of the whole "system" (economy, society, environment)	Concerned with issues as experienced by specific individuals and organizations
Considered among other public policy objectives and directions	Affected individuals and groups seek direct solutions
Debated in public conversations, mass media	Expressed relationally or in social media
Can scope down to private problems with specific beneficiaries	Can reveal infrastructure needs that are lurking public problems

Figure 1.4: Public problems and private problems, based on a framework developed by Jason Jay of the MIT Sloan Sustainability Initiative, who teaches it in his class "Innovating for Impact."

To do a Problem Segmentation, start by picking one of the climate verticals we mentioned. Then, articulate a public problem within that category. For climate and energy ventures, that problem will most likely be in terms of emissions or climate impacts. Other aspects might include social and financial considerations.

Once you have stated the public problem, list the relevant stakeholders:

- Who experiences the problem?
- Who does not experience the problem?
- Who contributes to the problem?
- Who has been excluded?

For each stakeholder, begin brainstorming subproblems. These are more specific questions about their relationship with the problem:

- How do they experience the problem?
- How do they contribute?

Keep drilling down into subproblems as much as you can. A great question to ask here is why? As you examine a problem's deeper layers, keep asking why? to get to its root cause.

When you complete this exercise, it should look something like Figure 1.5.

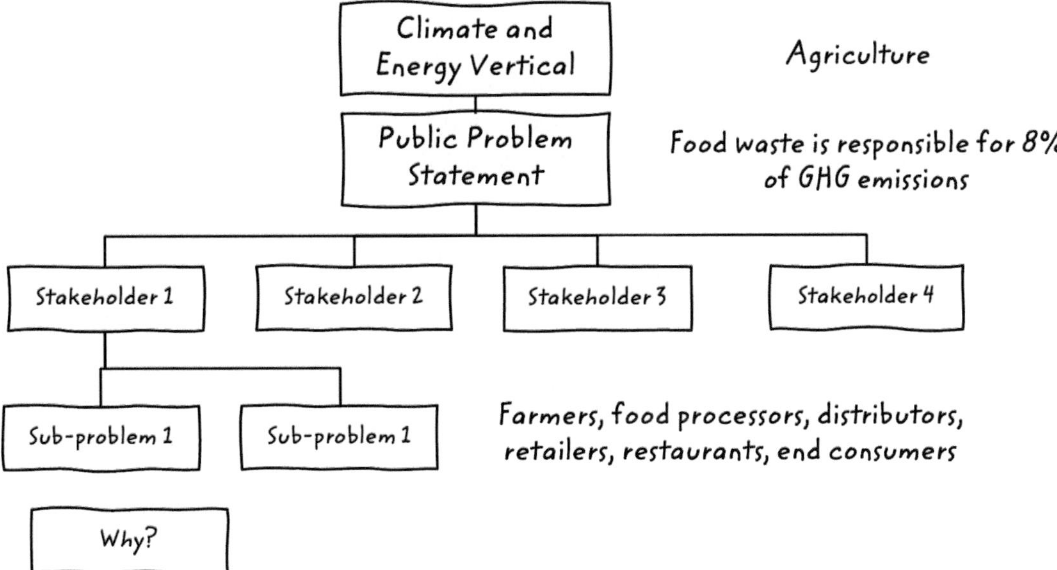

Figure 1.5: An example Problem Segmentation Tree.

At this point, we are brainstorming and learning. You can do this using only secondary market research (e.g., sources like market reports and articles). Generative AI can also be a useful tool to supercharge your process. However, directly interacting with people involved in your area of interest will be essential to fully understand the situation and possibilities. (We will discuss primary market research in Step 3.)

Estimate the Climate TAM for Each Segment

A key metric for each of your problem segments is what we have dubbed the Climate Total Addressable Market (Climate TAM). Whereas a traditional TAM analysis focuses on the private problem and its financial opportunity (see Step 10), your Climate TAM focuses on the public problem—what is the largest possible impact you could have on the climate?

A Climate TAM is a rough estimate of the opportunity before you have a specific solution in mind. If you are working on emissions reduction, a simple estimate is the relative share of emissions attributed to the problem you are trying to solve. You could also estimate your Climate TAM in terms of other metrics, such as emissions removed, warming avoided, lives saved, or economic losses prevented.

Your Climate TAM is not the only factor you should consider when deciding which opportunity to pursue, but it is an important one to think about early. It's not about getting precision; it's about understanding the order of magnitude of potential impact so you can feel confident that you are spending your time and effort in the right place. Before you build a climate and energy venture, you should ask yourself, "If I create this solution, and it becomes as big and successful as it could possibly be, would it have a meaningful impact on both people and the planet?" If the answer to that question is no, or in the more likely case, if you are unsure, then your Climate TAM is probably not big enough, and you should revisit your Problem Segmentation.

Output for This Step

After you have spent some time exploring the Problem Landscape, compile 5–10 of the most interesting and meaningful problems you've identified into a matrix like the one in Table 1.1.

Table 1.1: *Problem Landscape Matrix.*

Subproblem	Briefly describe a specific problem within the larger Problem Landscape you are exploring.
Stakeholders	Who experiences the problem?
	Who does not experience the problem?
	Who contributes to the problem?
	Who has been excluded?
Why?	Why does this problem exist? What contributing factors can you identify?
Climate TAM	What is the largest possible climate impact of solving this problem in terms of emissions reduced, emissions removed, warming avoided, lives saved, or economic losses prevented?

EXAMPLES

Spoiler Alert

Ricky Ashenfelter and Emily Malina began their entrepreneurial journey with a single statistic: up to 40% of food in the United States gets wasted.[1] Food waste is a major contributor to climate change. It is also a missed opportunity to feed people and for businesses to improve their bottom lines.

They knew that waste in the food industry was an important public problem, but they wanted to find a more specific private problem that they could tackle. Farms seemed too far away from the end consumer, and grocery stores and restaurants seemed too close. Eventually, they focused on food service distributors, who serve the restaurant industry and deal with some of the largest volumes of food and waste. What if those distributors had an easier way to donate excess food instead of throwing it away?

They launched a company called Spoiler Alert and landed the biggest food service distributor in the country as their first customer. However, there was not broad, replicable interest across the industry because most distributors are in the business of selling inventory, not giving it away. While they had found a pressing public problem, the private problem they had picked was not big enough to support a high-growth venture.

Ultimately, they pivoted and began working with large food brands to better manage excess and aging inventory. Their pivot reveals something important about exploring the Problem Landscape. While it may be the first step in the process, it never truly ends. Climate and energy entrepreneurs are constantly learning about problems, even many years into working on a solution.

MEER

As Ye Tao began researching problems in climate and energy, he realized that too little attention was being paid to the problem of heat. He left his former career running a lab at Harvard focused on high-resolution microscopes, and he founded a nonprofit called MEER (Mirrors for Earth's Energy Rebalancing). MEER applies reflective and infrared emissive materials to rooftops in areas at risk of extreme heat events, with initial projects in India, Sierra Leone, and California. This solution can reduce the internal temperature of a home by more than 6°C, which improves the quality of life in normal conditions and could be a literal lifesaver in a lethal heat wave.

In addition to the local cooling effect, there is also a global cooling effect. If people around the world adopt reflective rooftops, they will reflect enough energy back into space to meaningfully reduce Earth's temperature. For now, MEER's efforts are still small in scale, but they are researching and piloting solutions for freshwater reservoirs, coastal cooling, and agricultural water-saving that they or others can potentially implement at a larger scale in the future.

Ye's story highlights the importance of exploring the Problem Landscape as the first step in the journey of climate and energy entrepreneurship. By identifying an overlooked challenge like extreme heat, he was able to pivot his expertise toward a solution with both local and global impact.

Google

Many people within Google are looking to use the company's vast data and resources to make a dent in climate and energy problems. Juliet Rothenberg, product director of Google's Climate AI initiative, is one of those people. She aims to tackle big problems that are going to move the needle, so it might seem surprising that she worked on a partnership with American Airlines and Breakthrough Energy not to address the greenhouse gases emitted when planes burn fuel but rather to tackle contrails, the long skinny clouds that airplanes make during certain conditions.

Contrails trap heat in the atmosphere and surprisingly account for 35.3% of the airline industry's climate impact.[2] Lots of companies are working on the fuel problem—more efficient engines, sustainable aviation fuel, electrification, alternative transportation methods, and so on—but those solutions will take many years or decades, and new hardware and infrastructure, to bring to fruition. However, the team at Google realized that nobody was working to reduce contrails, and there was a relatively low-effort way to do so with software and procedure changes.

Google engineers spent thousands of hours poring over images to manually identify contrails, and they trained an AI model to do the same. The AI model could then determine parts of the atmosphere where contrails would likely form. Google shared that information with American

Airlines so their pilots could avoid those areas while in flight, reducing their impact at a very low cost. The changes are not even noticeable for passengers.

This example shows the importance of thinking beyond the climate and energy problems that we are aware of in our daily lives. Before you start developing a solution that may take decades to bring to market, you might just find a simpler solution lurking behind a different problem.

ADDITIONAL RESOURCES

There are additional resources for this step at www.de4cev.com/step1, including the following:

- Problem Segmentation Worksheet
- Spoiler Alert Case Study
- MEER Case Study
- Google Case Study
- Links to a multitude of informational resources on climate change, including Project Drawdown, Woodwell Climate Research Center, Probable Futures, the Intergovernmental Panel on Climate Change, and Open Minds.

Additional resources will be added as new and updated examples and information become available.

Notes

1. Dana Gunders, "Wasted: How America Is Losing Up to 40 Percent of Its Food from Farm to Fork to Landfill." *Natural Resources Defense Council,* August 16, 2017. https://www.nrdc.org/rcsources/wasted-how-america-losing-40-percent-its-food-farm-fork-landfill.
2. https://sites.research.google/contrails/.

Understand the Solutions Context

In This Step, You Will

- Gain a basic understanding of the dynamics of the energy industry.
- Appreciate the importance of timing for climate and energy solutions.
- Learn a structured approach for putting solutions into context.

Why This Step, and Why Now?

No problem exists in a vacuum, so it's important for you, as a climate and energy entrepreneur, to understand the context in which you will be building solutions.

Understanding the Energy Industry

Climate and energy ventures cover a wide range of industries, but many of them operate in or around the energy industry, so it is particularly important for you to understand that industry. For instance, electric utilities are often heavily regulated, and the metrics used to evaluate them are not obvious. This can lead to counterintuitive behavior that entrepreneurs must understand. If you ignore these factors, you will become frustrated and struggle to be effective.

Even if you are not directly working on energy, it's important to understand these dynamics, because energy is foundational to a wide range of other solutions. Many climate and energy solutions involve shifting systems in transportation, agriculture, buildings, and heavy industry to use less energy or less-polluting energy (see Figure 2.1).

Should I Be Disrupting the Big Players or Partnering with Them?

To some entrepreneurs, the incumbent energy industry may seem ripe for change, and that is true in many ways. However, even though the landscape is shifting, many startups can only succeed by collaborating with incumbents rather than competing with them head-to-head or "disrupting" them. In the consumer commerce industry, Amazon circumvented traditional retailers by identifying and leaning into the new capabilities unlocked by the internet. But high-volume commodities like electricity, fuels, and industrial chemicals have dramatically more sophisticated and capital-intensive supply chains and delivery infrastructure than consumer goods. The incumbents control much of the existing infrastructure, which cannot be easily duplicated or replaced. Often, the only way forward is through these companies, not around them. This means that large corporations in the energy industry can be both allies and rivals for climate tech startups.

The excellent and well-researched book *Entrepreneurship: Choice and Strategy* by Joshua Gans, Erin L. Scott, and Scott Stern dives deeper into how to navigate these relationships.[1]

Timing Is Everything

One of the most important things you need to understand as a climate and energy entrepreneur is the timing of your solution. Tesla would probably not have made it starting 10 years earlier, and it would have faced more competition if it started 10 years later. Tesla timed its launch very well with industry-wide advancements in battery technology, market demand, and government incentives.

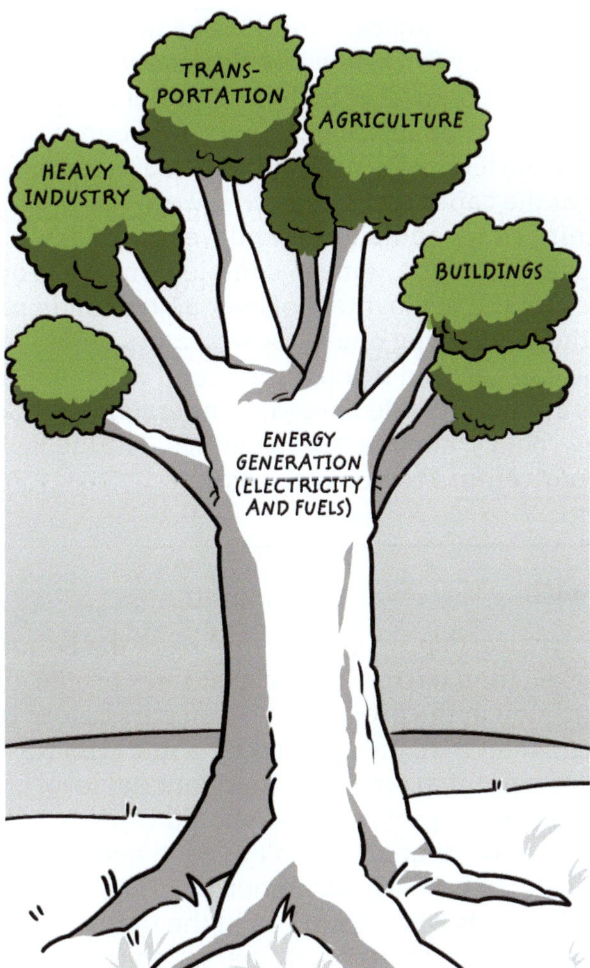

Figure 2.1: Energy is foundational to other categories of climate solutions.

There have been massive growth spurts in many sectors of the energy industry. For example, in the early 2000s, the United States saw a surge in natural gas plant construction, which drove up demand and prices for natural gas. This, in turn, drove up the price of electricity and made wind power more attractive. Policy drivers and advances in turbine technology further accelerated this growth, leading to wind power becoming a significant player in the energy mix. So much wind was deployed in areas like West Texas that the wholesale price of electricity regularly goes negative when it's windy!

The boom in wind energy benefited adjacent markets as well. There was massive transmission build-out in Texas, paving the way for many new electricity generation projects. Also, so much capital was attracted to wind development that turbine suppliers were sold out every year, and investors wanted access to more renewable projects that could benefit from tax credits and other incentives. Once solar photovoltaic technology advanced enough for the economics to make sense, that industry attracted many of the capital providers who were too late to the wind sector. Most recently, battery costs have come down sufficiently, and we have started to see mass deployment of electric vehicle and grid-scale battery systems to complement the growth in renewables. All together, these markets represent the deployment of over $1 trillion in capital.

Your solution may be further advancing one of these sectors or you might be working on the next big thing. Either way, you can succeed if you understand what truly drives scale in the climate and energy space. The trends are predictable once you understand the Solutions Context, including the interplay of technology, policy, and market dynamics. Timing isn't just luck. You need to recognize when to position your venture to ride the wave.

How to Structure Your Approach

In the original *Disciplined Entrepreneurship*, an understanding of the Solutions Context is developed by selecting a Beachhead Market, then narrowing the customer profile and Persona. Here, the Solutions Context is a separate step in the process, and it occurs before there is any specific idea or solution on the table. The original method has worked for some climate and energy entrepreneurs, but others will find it extremely helpful to develop a foundational level of understanding of the Solutions Context before deciding what problem they should work on.

Your understanding will grow over time. You don't need to become the world's foremost expert on a given industry, but it is useful to have a basic understanding before you begin to work on a solution. If possible, talk to individuals who've worked in the industry or founded other startups, even if you do not think they could be potential customers. These conversations will be part of your primary market research (Step 3).

It is helpful for someone on the Initial Team to have prior experience in the industry so you understand the status quo. However, you should not draw on experience exclusively from one industry, so that you're not *locked into* the status quo. Fresh perspectives are valuable for your team. Look to industries outside of climate and energy; it can be powerful to borrow and apply successful business models from other sectors. This is called *lateral innovation*.

Output from This Step

Use the template in Table 2.1 to define the Solutions Context. Do this for all subproblems from Step 1 that are interesting to you.

Table 2.1: *Solutions Context Matrix with Definitions.*

Subproblem	Pick an interesting problem or subproblem from the last step, drilling down to something as specific as possible.
Existing players— incumbents	What industries are most relevant to solving this problem? Who are some of the big existing players in those industries?
Existing players— startups	Who are the other startups currently or previously working in this space?
Previous efforts	What has already been tried in this space? Why has it succeeded or failed?
Adjacent efforts	What models have been successful in other industries that could be applied to your selected problem?
Barriers	What barriers can you identify? Why hasn't the problem been solved?
Market timing	What is happening in the industry right now? How might these dynamics unlock new opportunity? How might they constrain opportunity?
Policy timing	What is happening in the political environment right now? How might these dynamics unlock new opportunity? How might they constrain opportunity? (We will cover more on policy in Step 8)
Biases	What assumptions and biases surround this problem?
Innovation gaps	Do you have an innovative idea or technology that hasn't been tried before?
Next steps	Where can you learn more? Whom can you talk to? What hypotheses can you come up with? How would you test them?

EXAMPLES

Fervo Energy

Tim Latimer's experience in the traditional oil and gas industry helped him to see a huge opportunity for generating low-emissions electricity. His first job was working on natural gas rigs to develop solutions for high-temperature drilling. Much of the literature on that subject comes from the world of geothermal energy, which Tim had never heard of. Geothermal energy means using the heat of the earth to turn water into steam and generate electricity.

Historically, cost-effective geothermal has been limited to a small number of locations with unique geology—places like Iceland with a lot of hot molten rock not too far from the surface.

Many of these locations had already maxed out their geothermal capacity, but if there were a low-cost way to drill productive wells, that would vastly expand the locations where geothermal power could make economic sense.

Tim could see that the cost of drilling was going down rapidly. He realized that eventually it would make sense to leverage this technology and know-how for geothermal. It was just a matter of when. Initially, he tried to join existing geothermal startups, but nobody was hiring, and nobody wanted to talk about capital for new ideas.

He realized he'd have to become an entrepreneur. He went to Stanford, met his co-founder Jack Norbeck, and the two of them launched Fervo Energy, which would become the first company to commercialize enhanced geothermal systems.

A key aspect of Fervo's success is timing. They launched their company at a time when drilling costs were drastically reduced, and they also benefited from an increasing trend of customer interest in clean, firm power (over intermittent renewable energy like solar and wind). Additionally, Tim's experience in the oil and gas industry was a tremendous asset, since he had firsthand experience with the latest innovations in drilling.

MacroCycle

Like Tim Latimer, Stwart Peña Feliz cut his teeth in the oil and gas industry. As a process engineer at ExxonMobil, he got up close and personal with developing and operating massive infrastructure, like a $1 billion chemical project. He was just one small cog in a very large machine, yet being one small cog can give you tremendous insight into how the machine works.

One of Stwart's biggest assignments was at ExxonMobil's first unit that recycled plastic waste. The facility took in discarded plastic and used it as part of the feedstock for raw materials that could be made into new plastic or used for fuel and other purposes. By observing the plant operations, Stwart could see that there were still many steps to go toward a fully circular, sustainable system.

A few years later, Stwart pursued his MBA at MIT's Sloan School of Management. There, he met Jan-Georg Rosenboom (whom we'll feature in Step 4) and co-founded MacroCycle, a company that chemically upcycles plastic and textile waste into new plastic material to be used as a drop-in solution with potentially zero greenhouse gas emissions and no additional premium.

By immersing himself in the Solutions Context, Stwart was able to clearly identify the gaps where a better recycling solution was needed. He also learned that scaling up breakthroughs in the energy industry is extremely difficult and that the path to a full-scale solution is not straightforward.

ADDITIONAL RESOURCES

There are additional resources for this step at www.de4cev.com/step2. These materials include the following:

- Solutions Context Worksheet
- Fervo Energy Case Study
- MacroCycle Case Study
- Link to Bill Aulet's articles on "What's Wrong with Energy Investing? (Parts I and II)"

Additional resources will be added as new and updated examples and information become available.

Note

1. Joshua Gans, Erin L. Scott, and Scott Stern, *Entrepreneurship: Choice and Strategy*. First edition. New York: W. W. Norton & Company, 2024. The book can be purchased here: https://seagull.wwnorton.com/entrepreneurship.

Begin Primary Market Research (PMR)

In This Step, You Will

- Understand the importance of primary market research (PMR).
- Learn how PMR differs at different stages of the journey.
- Learn practical strategies for effective PMR specifically for climate and energy ventures.

Why This Step, and Why Now?

Primary market research (PMR) drives the process of new venture creation. It is the practice of observing and engaging with customers and learning from them about their world and the problems and opportunities they face. Others call this *customer discovery* or *ethnographic research*, but we call it *primary market research* to emphasize the key role of primary sources: direct interaction with customers and other relevant market participants. PMR continues throughout all the subsequent steps, but it is important to start early. *Disciplined Entrepreneurship: Expanded and Updated* calls PMR the fuel for traversing the 24 Steps, which is accurate, but instead of fuel, let's call it the electricity that powers the journey.

PMR helps validate your choice of overall problem or technology before you consider a specific market application. It is essential to use PMR to validate the initial hypotheses you developed in the first steps. You can start with secondary market research, though you need to get to PMR quickly.

Many climate and energy entrepreneurs start by working on a technology before considering starting a company based on it, so they often have a solution in search of a problem! In a linear approach, an entrepreneur would choose a problem, then do PMR, and then go on to develop the solution. However, if you already have a technology, PMR is a critical tool to assess whether you have the right application for that technology. You just need to be extra careful about any preconceived notions you might bring to the process. The best application is often entirely different from what you might originally think!

The PMR Family

There are multiple types of PMR, which serve different objectives and involve different methods. We can break them down into a set of groupings called the PMR Family, originally developed by our colleague Macauley Kenney, who is a lecturer and entrepreneur-in-residence at MIT.

PMR 0.0: Problem Space Investigation

This is the earliest phase of PMR, and it happens before you have settled on a specific problem, idea, or technology. The objective is to figure out what problem you want to solve or what opportunity you want to pursue. Right now, this type of PMR will likely be most important for you. It enhances your exploration of the Problem Landscape from Step 1, and your understanding of the Solution Context from Step 2. It will also directly inform your Founder-Problem Fit, which we will cover in Step 4.

- Example insight: Food waste is a major contributor to climate change.

PMR 1.0: Solution Investigation

This is the phase when you narrow your focus from a public problem to a private problem and then ultimately to a specific customer. The objective is to find a pain point to address and to understand in detail who experiences it. This phase will be particularly important once we get to Market Segmentation (Step 7), Market Stepping Stones (Step 10), and Profiling Personas across your Decision-Making Unit (Step 11).

- Example insight: Large food distributors lose money by failing to sell inventory before it reaches its expiration date.

PMR 2.0: Product Investigation

The objective of this stage is to develop product specifications and build your solution. You need to continue doing PMR to account for the customer perspective as the details of your solution come into focus. This type of PMR will be important when you begin to define your solution (Step 10), build a Proof of Concept (Step 19), demonstrate Initial Market Traction (Step 20), build a First-of-a-Kind project (Step 23), and Scale Up (Step 24).

- Example insight: Vendors could save money and throw out less food if they had a platform to sell soon-to-expire inventory in secondary markets. They would use and buy this platform with XYZ features.

Remember that PMR is not done when you move onto the next step! It will continue throughout all the steps of the Disciplined Entrepreneurship process.

Best Practices for PMR

PMR is covered in Step 1A of *Disciplined Entrepreneurship* and in great detail in Tactic 3 of *Startup Tactics*. Initial PMR should be qualitative, in-depth, and structured. Later, you can do more quantitative research (like surveys), but you should start by going out and speaking with people directly, so you can follow the thread of the conversation if it goes in an unexpected direction.

Here, we will give just a short summary of the key elements of good PMR.

Hypotheses

Define an explicit set of hypotheses to test, and be explicit about what information might prove or disprove them.

Target List

Create a target list of people you want to speak with. Stay focused by setting criteria for whom you should interview. When a person meets these criteria, they are considered qualified. At the beginning, you can be fairly open in your approach, but eventually you will want to focus only on qualified subjects.

Question Guide

Draft questions in advance, but don't stick too rigidly to the script. Be flexible and follow the conversation in any unexpected directions that spark your curiosity. Remember that you should be having a conversation, not filling out a survey. Follow up when an answer has gaps or if you want to learn more about anything. Consider these issues:

- What questions do you need to ask to test your hypotheses?
- Are the questions as broad and open-ended as possible at the beginning?
- Are you as happy to prove your hypotheses wrong as you are to prove them right?

At the end of every interview, open new doors by asking some variation of these questions:

- What should I be asking that I have not asked you already?
- Do you honestly think I am headed in the right direction?
- Who else should I talk to?

Bias

Avoid the various forms of bias that can skew your findings:

- Confirmation bias means only seeking information that confirms your views.
- Selection bias is when you only seek out certain types of people and leave out others with potentially useful feedback.
- Social acceptability bias is when people say positive or flattering things, even when they don't represent the truth. This type of bias is especially prevalent for climate and energy ventures, because interviewees may feel an implicit social pressure to say they care more about climate than they actually do.

Record Insights

Use an insights grid to keep track of what you learn. Table 3.1 provides a template, which we have adapted from *Startup Tactics*.

Table 3.1.: *PMR Insights Grid.*

INSIGHTS GRID	Name	Qualified	How Important Is the Problem or Theme? (Scale of 1–5, 1 is highest)			Follow Up?	Notes
			Problem or Theme 1	Problem or Theme 2	And so on		
Example	Tod Hynes	Y	1	3	2	Y	
1		Y/N				Y/N	
2		Y/N				Y/N	

Should I Ask About Climate?

The unfortunate truth is that potential customers will probably care less about climate than you might think, especially when it comes to spending money. Climate can be part of your PMR, and one of your goals may be to gauge how much interviewees care about climate impact. However, your interviews should not assume an interest in climate, and they should certainly not just be about climate. A big goal of your early PMR will be to figure out what your interviewees care most about and what drives their decision-making. A safe hypothesis is that the main drivers will not be climate related.

Here are some things that most customers do (or should) care about that you may also address:

- Do they want a lower cost option?
- Do they want a more secure supply?
- Do they care about price stability?
- Do they care about the risk of loss or degradation of their own assets or that of their supply chain?
- Do they have to meet new regulations?
- Are they at risk of losing business due to customer or government pressure?

They will frequently be interested in all these issues, so you need to get them to prioritize by forcing them to weigh the importance of each. One way to do that is to ask them if they had 100 points to allocate, how many points they would give to each priority?

How Do I Talk to Big Companies?

Many climate and energy ventures will need to do PMR with large companies and other large institutions. When reaching out to individuals at these institutions, you do not have to start at the top. Usually, emailing the CEO is not a wise first step. Focus on people within the organization who directly deal with the problems you are interested in exploring. This could include the board or C-suite, but it is most often better to start lower in the organization to understand the problem, opportunity, and context with employees. Then you can go back to higher-level people if it makes sense. The sustainability team can be a great entry point for PMR—they will likely be interested in talking to you—but their priorities will be very different than those of others within the company who may have more of a direct impact on the buying process.

The key is that you engage with the people who will understand the problem and how your solution can help the customer solve this problem. Do not treat these large organizations as a monolith; you can easily talk to 10 people within the same company and get 10 different perspectives, and getting those different perspectives is crucial. If you feel you are talking to the wrong people within the company, ask them to connect you with the right people—but don't phrase it that way, of course!

What If I'm Selling a Commodity? Why Should I Care About Customers?

Many companies in the climate and energy space end up selling commodities like a kilowatt-hour of electricity or a liter of fuel. In that case, it may seem like the customer paying for the product does not care about anything other than price, but do not assume this. They could also care about a wide variety of other factors, like the source of energy, which relates to the security of supply.

You also need to realize that the buyer of the commodity may not be your only customer. While they are paying for your product, there is often some kind of project that is producing the commodity, and you need to raise project financing to develop the project. In that case, the bank or investor financing the project is also a customer. They are paying you up front for the return your project will provide them, and you need to understand what they require. Understanding their needs should be part of your PMR. We get into more detail on this in Steps 23 and 24.

Quality over Quantity

As you go about your PMR, make sure to get data across multiple dimensions: rational, economic, political, personal, and emotional. Remember that it is not simply the number of interviews but how you balance quantity with quality. It is good to try and talk to as many people as possible, especially while you are in the exploratory phase, but once you begin to home in on your problem and solution, you need to focus.

Remember that PMR is much more than interviews. For instance, if you can visit an industrial plant and see it in action, you will learn far more than you would from talking to dozens of plant operators.

Output from This Step

Create a PMR plan that includes the following:

- A set of hypotheses to test (this should be dynamic and constantly evolving—remove the hypotheses that you disprove, and refine or add hypotheses as you collect more information)
- A thorough target list of the people you want to interview
- A detailed question guide, which you can adapt for different roles and industries
- An insights grid, ideally with a ranked set of priorities for each interview subject

Remember that for now, you are focusing on PMR 0.0 (Problem Space Investigation), and you will need to repeat this exercise for PMR 1.0 (Solution Investigation) and PMR 2.0 (Product Investigation). In fact, your PMR plan should be a living document that you revisit constantly.

EXAMPLES

Via Separations

Shreya Dave often compared her technology to cookware. After making pasta, you use a strainer to separate pasta from water. However, the standard for separating materials in many industrial situations is to use heat. This is equivalent to boiling off the water to get the pasta, and it is just as inefficient. Mechanical filtration (like a strainer) can reduce the energy needed for separation by 90%.

Shreya's strainer was a nanoporous membrane made of graphene oxide. She started Via Separations to commercialize the technology, along with her advisor Jeffrey Grossman and her labmate Brent Keller.

To figure out the best application, Shreya and her co-founders dove into PMR. It did not take many conversations for them to choose to focus on industrial separation. The question was, which industry?

Over six weeks, they did 106 interviews across 15 different industries. They took every meeting, even the ones that did not seem immediately relevant. At the end of every interview, they asked, "Who else should we talk to?" And they followed up with those people.

Shreya in particular became obsessed with PMR. At her friend's wedding, she heard that one of the groomsmen was an engineer at an ammonia plant, so she went up to him and peppered him with questions for as long as was socially acceptable.

After thorough PMR, the team could see that there was a promising opportunity in the pulp and paper industry, which was mainly using thermal separation. Those customers had a lot to gain from switching to mechanical separation, but only if Via could reconcile the technology and the economics. To cover what happened next, we will need to get into the subject of Techno-Economic Analysis, so we will come back to Via's story in Step 6!

EQORE

Donald Groh noticed that his family real estate business was paying through the nose for electricity. This inspired him to dive deep into commercial and industrial billing structures. He told his friends Jorge Nin and Valeriia Tyshchenko about the problem. They both had experience with battery engineering projects. The three of them teamed up to work on the problem and developed a working hypothesis: they could lower energy bills by using batteries to reduce peak demands.

It seemed like they had found a promising opportunity, but so far, they only had a sample size of one. They didn't want to build a venture just to solve a problem for Donald's family business. They needed to talk to other energy users. The team initially emailed thousands of big energy users for interviews, with little response. So they developed qualifications for interviewees based on their location and the size of their facilities, until they eventually had a very specific picture of whom they wanted to talk to. They then did more personalized outreach directly to the folks on this narrower list. Their response rate went up. As they had more conversations, they became more certain that they were working on an important pain point for manufacturers in particular.

Thanks to their extensive PMR, they were able to deeply understand their problem, their solution, and their potential customers before spending any time or money on building a product.

ADDITIONAL RESOURCES

There are additional resources for this step at www.de4cev.com/step3. These materials include the following:

- PMR Planning Worksheet
- Via Separations Case Study
- EQORE Case Study

Additional resources will be added as new and updated examples and information become available.

Find Founder-Problem Fit

In This Step, You Will

- Apply a personal filter to the landscape overview in the previous steps to decide what sort of problems within climate and energy you would like to tackle.

Why This Step, and Why Now?

Starting a company is deeply personal. It requires the founder to put in their blood, sweat, and tears. It is not enough to be motivated by a desire to make money or even a desire to save the planet. Entrepreneurial thought leader Brad Feld says that a successful venture requires more than passion; it requires "obsession." *Disciplined Entrepreneurship: Expanded and Updated* refers to this motivation as raison d'être (French for "reason for existence"). The book includes the following warning: "Please don't try to start a company because you simply have an idea or technology. That is choosing to run in a marathon because you thought it was a nice idea to go for a run on a sunny day. You won't last."

Due to long timelines and high capital needs, starting a climate and energy venture is more like an ultra-marathon. It can sometimes take well over a decade to go from initial exploration to commercial deployment at scale. Thus, founders need to be especially intentional about what they spend their time and energy building.

Finding Your Ikigai

A good starting point for Founder-Problem Fit is the Ikigai framework, a Japanese concept that means "reason for living." It was popularized outside of Japan in the book *Ikigai: The Japanese Secret to a Long and Happy Life* by Héctor García and Francesc Miralles.

According to this framework, people should seek purpose in life at the intersection of the following four categories:

- What does the world need?
- What can you be paid for?
- What are you good at?
- What do you love doing?

For climate, what the world needs ties back to Step 1 (Problem Landscape). You need to realize that even if you know a lot about climate and energy, you only know a little compared to the whole. Nobody has the full picture, and you need to talk to lots of different people to help guide you to the right path.

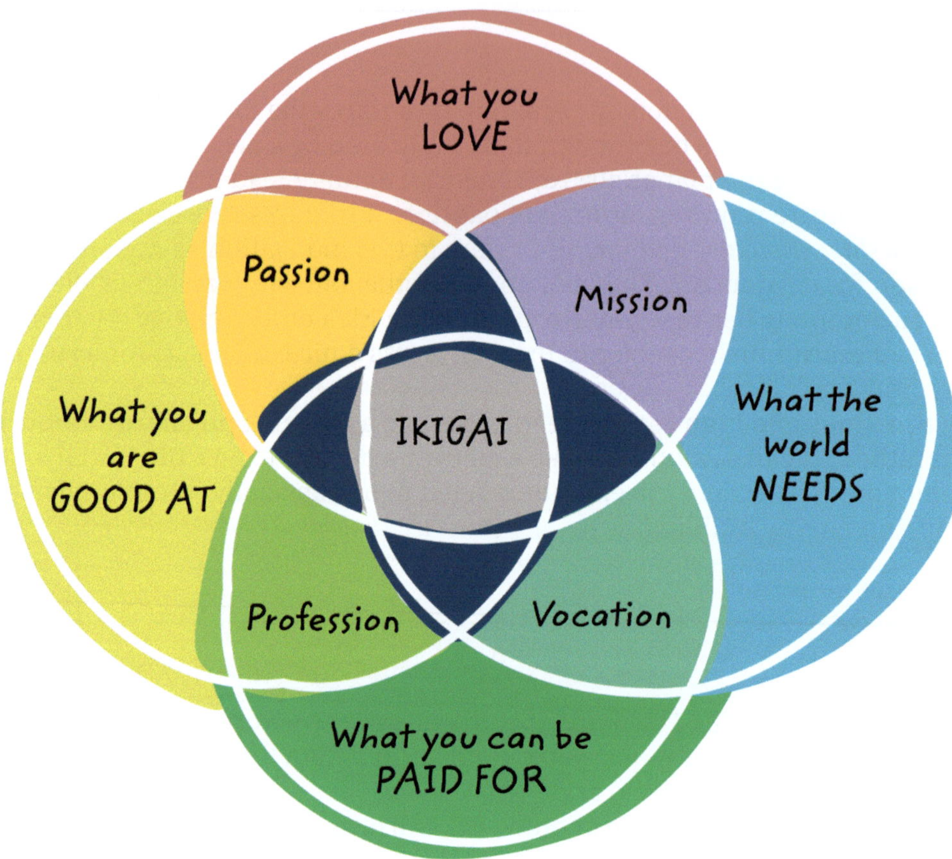

Figure 4.1: The Ikigai framework

Source: Adapted from Héctor García and Francesc Miralles.

What you can be paid for corresponds with the Solutions Context as well as the customer theme (Who pays? For what? Why and how?), which will continue to arise throughout this book.

It is mainly up to you to figure out the other two categories (what you are good at and what you love) through self-reflection. There are tools that can help you learn about your strengths from others who know you well. You can potentially make up for what you're not good at by teaming up with others who have complementary skill sets (covered in Step 5). However, if you don't love the problem you're solving, you won't be able to fix that down the road, so it's better to figure this out earlier rather than later.

A Passion for Climate Is Not Enough

Many climate and energy entrepreneurs might want to reflect their passion for climate in the personal bubbles of the Ikigai framework (e.g., under "What do you love?" they might say, "I love taking action to address the climate crisis!"). This sense of purpose is absolutely essential, and we have talked to many founders who have said that the potentially planet-saving nature of their work keeps them going during the tough times.

However, be careful of leaning into this too much. A sense of purpose alone is rarely enough to drive the hard work of starting a company. The advice from Brad Feld that we mentioned at the start of this step is especially relevant for climate and energy entrepreneurs. You need to be more than passionate; you need to be obsessed. That means being obsessed with not only the mission but also the unglamorous tasks and problems necessary to achieve that mission. You do not need to enjoy all those tasks—few people do—but you need to be motivated to get them done day after day and skilled at doing so. Maybe you enjoy solving complex engineering challenges, or maybe you enjoy talking to people and figuring out productive channels for collaboration. These are very important skills in climate and energy that are not directly related to solving planetary problems. As you complete your Ikigai framework, make sure to reflect on the full set of skills and obsessions that drive you as a person, not just your climate passion.

Output from This Step

Use the following questions based on the Ikigai framework to guide your exploration of Founder-Problem Fit:

- What does the world need?
  - What did you identify as a key unsolved problem? (Draw this from Step 1.)
  - What is the Climate TAM of your problem? (We mentioned this in Step 1 as well—if someone solves this problem and the world adopts it, will it make a big difference?) Does that order of magnitude get you excited?
  - How might solving this problem benefit the world in ways beyond climate?
- What can you get paid for?
  - Is the timing right for your potential solution to the problem?

- Are there specific individuals who would be willing to pay for solutions? (Draw this from Step 2, and we will explore it further starting in Step 7.)
- What are you good at?
  - What are your top strengths and skills?
  - Where are you confident that you know what you're doing?
  - What sorts of tasks or projects do others often ask you to help them with?
  - What do you contribute that you know is a different perspective from others?
  - Where do you have extensive experience and personal insight? (As we mentioned in Step 2, it is often very helpful to have direct knowledge of your industry or technology—not necessarily 20 years of work in your field, but some reason that you can bring particular value to the problem.)
- What do you love doing?
  - What activities and hobbies bring you joy?
  - What gives you energy?
  - What rabbit holes do you find yourself going down over and over again?
  - What gets you in a state where you're so focused you don't stop to eat?
  - What projects have brought you the greatest sense of fulfillment? What projects do you find yourself continuing to talk about or think about years down the line?

EXAMPLES

Ayar Labs

Alex Wright-Gladstein knew she wanted to be a serial entrepreneur commercializing solutions to reverse climate change. She went to MIT for an MBA so that she could meet people across campus who were inventing high-impact technologies. Over the summer, she volunteered to help recruit projects for the Climate & Energy Ventures course so that she could learn about as many technologies as possible.

One project stuck out more than any of the others. MIT Professor Rajeev Ram had helped to invent the first processor chip to communicate using light rather than electricity. This capacity could potentially enable 1,000× improvements, unlocking a new era of computing efficiency and speed.

When Alex walked out of her meeting with Professor Ram, she was "blown away," but she knew she needed to make her choice with more than gut instinct. She came up with three criteria. The first was Climate TAM—would the venture make a serious dent in addressing climate change? The second was personal fit—could she see herself working with the inventors super closely? The third was the technological readiness—was the technology developed enough to leave the lab?

Alex's case is a classic example of Founder-Technology Fit. Initially, she was more motivated by impact than by industry. She was not necessarily looking to solve the problem of energy use in computing, but it was meaty enough for her to sink her teeth into, and she found a technology that had potential to make a real difference. Alex was uniquely prepared to see that she had come across the right technology at the right time, and she was willing to put in the hard work to build a company around it.

MacroCycle

Jan-Georg Rosenboom started his career as a rock star, literally, before he decided to pursue a PhD in chemical engineering. For most people, a PhD is by no means an obvious offshoot of heavy metal music, but for him, the connection was a "no brainer." His process of composing music bore many similarities to the scientific method. Start with an initial idea, iterate through cycles of testing and validation to find the optimal conditions, and then share it with the public.

When the time came to pick what to study, Jan-Georg drew from his experiences as a musician. He remembered the festivals where he used to perform. At the end, the ground was a wasteland, littered with plastic bottles and cups. With those conditions in mind, Jan-Georg chose to study sustainable plastics.

Jan did his PhD at ETH-Zurich and then went on to do a postdoc at MIT, where his mentor was the legendary Professor Bob Langer. Professor Langer frequently told Jan-Georg to "focus on big problems," so Jan-Georg kept working on the problem of plastics recycling, constantly considering whether technologies had potential to get adopted in the market. He developed a new method to chemically upcycle and rebuild polyethylene terephthalate (PET), and this became the basis of the company MacroCycle.

Jan-Georg had found a problem to solve that was a fit for both his skills and his interests, and potentially the world and the market as well. He ended up partnering with Stwart Peña Feliz, whom we featured in Step 2. In the next step, we will tell you more about their path to working together as a team.

Tom Atkinson (EnerNOC)

After working as a software developer for the investment giant Goldman Sachs, Tom Atkinson became interested in climate change. He tried working on several different problems, but none really resonated with him. Then, he met Tod Hynes at MIT in 2006. When Tod heard about Tom's background, he asked, "Have you ever heard of EnerNOC?" EnerNOC was a leading company in demand response and distributed generation management, which essentially means paying big electricity users to use less or turn on distributed generation during peak demand periods, reducing the need for expensive peak power plants.

One of EnerNOC's main objectives at that point was to build out a Network Operations Center (NOC), the digital command hub where they would monitor and manage energy usage and distributed generation across their network of participating facilities. This opportunity aligned with Tom's passion for climate and energy, and it was also a match for one of his greatest skills: building high-performing technical teams. The world badly needed demand response, since the technical and regulatory enabling factors had just aligned to make it feasible, and the EnerNOC team had raised millions in venture capital funding, which they were eager to put to use.

By aligning his passion for sustainability with his technical skills, Tom found his Ikigai, illustrating the power of purposeful career transitions. "When those four factors meet in the middle and you find yourself sitting there in the center of that Ikigai diagram, it is just a beautiful feeling," he reflected. "Some of the most fulfilling years of my life were working with that phenomenal team to put the NOC in EnerNOC."

ADDITIONAL RESOURCES

There are additional resources for this step at www.de4cev.com/step4. These materials include the following:

- Founder-Problem Fit Worksheet
- Ayar Labs Case Study
- MacroCycle Case Study
- Tom Atkinson Case Study
- Links to personal strength identification exercises such as VIA Character Strengths and Reflected Best Self

Additional resources will be added as new and updated examples and information become available.

Build the Right Initial Team

In This Step, You Will

- Learn why it is important for a venture to have multiple founders.
- Analyze the composition of a strong founding team.
- Figure out how to find potential co-founders and formalize co-founder relationships when the timing is right, including how to split equity.

Why This Step, and Why Now?

Research shows that ventures perform better when they have multiple co-founders. This is especially true for climate and energy ventures because they often need to address a wide range of disciplines to be successful, including technology, policy, business, and finance.

After going through the previous steps, you should have some idea of what problem you are trying to solve. Now, you should make a clear and conscious choice about whom you will work with to solve it.

Can AI Be My Co-Founder?

We are crossing a threshold into a world of artificial intelligence (AI)-first or AI-native startups. There will be a lot of solopreneurs who can manage to leverage AI to amplify their strengths and compensate for their weaknesses, but that is still a dangerous path, especially in this field.

There is something very difficult to replace about a human co-founder. AI is a great advisor, not a great final decision-maker or doer. Another person allows for a gut check on important decisions and can hold you accountable to prioritize tasks that are important but difficult and not necessarily urgent. Importantly, a co-founder can help carry the load for you when important life events occur (like births, deaths, or illnesses).

Working with a team allows for a balance of responsibilities. There are tasks that can only be done by humans, especially when it comes to interacting with other humans, and it helps to distribute these tasks. Being able to have at least one other person to start with is a huge stress reliever in a pressure-packed endeavor.

The Secret Sauce from MIT

Part of the recipe for success of the Climate & Energy Ventures (CEV) course at MIT is the process of forming interdisciplinary teams with complementary skill sets. The course has an application process and requires a mix of backgrounds including science ("researchers"), engineering ("hackers"), business ("hustlers"), and policy ("wonks").

Overall, the course maintains a ratio of roughly 40% technical students, 40% business students, and 20% policy students, with some students fitting into multiple categories. The course is project based and enables students to simulate the process of developing a robust plan for a new venture over one semester. Five- to six-person teams form over the first few weeks, with teams keeping that same 40-40-20 ratio. This forced makeup of the teams is a crucial part of the course to combat the human tendency toward homophily—that is, we like to work with people like us. In general, salespeople are most comfortable working with salespeople, engineers with engineers, and so on. But comfort does not make for high-performing teams.

You can use the same principles to build your Initial Team. Your team will need most, if not all, the following perspectives, and one individual cannot cover them all:

- **Industry expert** who has deep experience in the Solutions Context from Step 2 and can speak the language of potential customers and partners

- **Technical lead** who can understand the business priorities at a high level and translate them into a clear and achievable set of research and engineering tasks; also can explain the technical aspects clearly to a nontechnical audience inside and outside of the team
- **Deep technical talent** who can build something new and troubleshoot where there is no manual or playbook
- **Customer-facing sales lead** who is familiar with missionary sales and can convince early customers, especially large yet slow-moving institutions, to buy a potentially new solution from a new company and work closely with those customers through the early stages of implementation
- **Finance lead** who can plan and manage the process of getting money from investors in increasingly large amounts, selling them on the overall vision, the numbers, and the pathway to financial viability
- **Operations lead** who can manage the team as it grows, including the logistics of business administration, like paying people, finding lab and office space, and buying equipment
- **Policy expert** who can navigate the legal and political considerations of your solution and may need to influence policy (more on this in Step 8)
- **Expert advisors** who can help anticipate and navigate roadblocks

At the beginning, the co-founders will each have to take on several of these roles at once and then delegate as the team grows. Eventually, you may have whole teams responsible for some of these functions (we will get into team expansion in Step 22).

Team members must work together closely, respect what one another does, and have a level of interest in their colleagues' roles. The strength of the connection between the team members is more important than the individual strength of each team member. Make sure you all can work together and bring out the best in each other.

It Takes a Village

Your Initial Team does not just include co-founders. Part-time advisors or even part-time team members (sometimes called *fractional hires*) can fill any gaps, especially the technology, industry, and policy experts. Even though these are not full-time co-founders, they still need to be vetted carefully, especially if you are going to give them a stake in the company (known as equity)—and don't do that until they have proved their value.

You will also encounter many mentors and supporters who are eager to help you, and they usually do not require equity—if they do, that can be a red flag. The good supporters will want to get to know you a lot better, build a relationship, and see how things develop before they are willing to invest their time. You need people who believe in the cause and will play the long game with you.

Hackathons, competitions, accelerators, incubators, and fellowship programs are a great way to connect with potential supporters in the ecosystem and test them out.

The Co-Founder Dating Game

Many people compare the process of recruiting co-founders to dating, and they are not wrong. The goal is to get to know someone deeply to assess whether there is a potential for long-term partnership, and you may have to go through a few or even many different people before finding your entrepreneurial soulmate.

Start by finding ways to meet as many people as possible, including in-person events and online communities. Refer to Step 0 in the expanded and updated version of *Disciplined Entrepreneurship* for more ways to meet potential co-founders.

Once you have identified some good candidates, try them out on short-term tasks or projects before committing to starting a company with them. It is totally acceptable for someone to contribute to your venture in the early stages and not be a co-founder. Just be clear and upfront about expectations. You might even want to have some simple legal documents in place before they do any work so that all their work belongs to the company, and they cannot later make claims of company ownership.

How Many Co-Founders Should I Have?

In the MIT CEV course, the project teams have five or six people, but not all of them continue after the class, which is good because a team that large is difficult to sustain in the longer term. We have generally seen the most success in teams with two to three co-founders. Beyond that, the ownership of the venture begins to get spread too thin, and decision-making gets muddled.

However, it is far more important to build a team with the right people than with the right number of people. You may have identified more than two people with whom you want to start a company. If that group is rock-solid and battle-tested, it could be the right size of team for your venture.

Figure Out Everyone's Fair Share

Once you are confident in your Initial Team, you and your co-founders will need to settle the equity arrangements. Do not do this too early. You should start thinking about it now, but you want to establish a fit with your co-founders before going through the specifics of formalizing the relationship.

You should have a series of conversations with your co-founders about your strengths, weaknesses, values, motivations, expectations, and commitment. You could choose to use a defined list of questions or to develop a general set of topics for a more freewheeling discussion. Either way, you need to carve out time to have big conversations, because these topics are unlikely to come up organically as you get deep into hustle and bustle of starting your venture. There are no hard and fast rules for splitting equity. It is up to your team to figure out the split that best reflects everyone's past contributions and, much more importantly, their future commitment.

One best practice is to use a vesting schedule. Usually, nothing is earned until someone has been at the company for a year. At that point, the person has demonstrated commitment and gets the full year's vesting amount. After that, the stock invests on a monthly pro-rata basis. The vesting is conditional on continued employment and commitment to the company as spelled out in the options agreement your lawyers put together. You may want to consider a longer-than-typical vesting arrangement given the long timelines required to build climate and energy companies, and accelerated vesting in case you find early success. You can issue more stock later to correct imbalances, so these equity splits do not have to, and generally will not, live forever.

Remember that equity is basically worthless at the outset of the company. If the venture is successful, then the shares could become valuable, but the distribution of equity needs to properly incentivize the team to actually go out and create that value. That being said, do not underestimate the emotional value of equity in the company. It makes people feel ownership and gives them a chance to share in the upside of success, so treat it very seriously.

MIT Sloan Professor Jared Curhan's research shows that in negotiations, the final numbers generally matter less than how the people feel at the end of the process.[1] Make sure everyone feels heard and is comfortable with the outcome. If you cannot reach an agreement, you may have bigger problems with team dynamics, which need to be dealt with sooner rather than later.

When Your University Is Part of the Initial Team

If you are developing technology developed at a university, it is likely that your institution will have rights to any intellectual property (IP) related to your technology. If you are commercializing university IP, you will almost always need a license from its tech transfer office. Every university is different in how it approaches tech transfer, but the university will generally want to take a cut of equity as well as a royalty agreement. Many climate and energy entrepreneurs hire a lawyer to help them negotiate these terms.

Just like your equity split with your co-founders, your shared goal in the process should be to allow for the long-term success of the venture so that all parties get as much value as possible. One of your key priorities should be to remove or adjust any terms that might limit future success and growth.

Output from This Step

Use Table 5.1 as a guide in assessing potential co-founders during the search process.

Table 5.1: *Co-Founder Evaluation Matrix.*

Personal chemistry	Do you enjoy working with this person? Do you have a good rapport?
Complementarity of skills	Do you complement one another's skills and experiences?
Role on the team	Which of the key roles for a climate and energy venture could you see this person filling? (You will likely need to select multiple roles for members of the initial founding team: industry expert, technical lead, deep technical talent, customer-facing sales lead, finance lead, operations lead, policy expert, expert advisor, and so on)
Reliability	Can you rely on this person to complete hard tasks well and on time?
Energizing effects	Are they "energy amplifiers" and not "energy drainers"? Do they give you and others more energy when you work with them?
Psychological safety	Can you and your potential co-founder develop a sense of psychological safety that will enable you to constructively handle conflict, such as external obstacles and internal disagreement?
Personal priorities	What are each of your personal priorities for the next 5–10 years in terms of family, finances, and so on? Your co-founders' priorities should be compatible with yours, but they will not be identical.
Geography	What are your potential co-founder's geographical preferences and constraints? How do they compare to yours?
Raison d'être	What is their why? Why do they want to start a climate and energy venture? Are you aligned with them on the raison d'être for the new venture?
Equity considerations	You should not allocate equity right off the bat, but you should keep track of some of the factors that will go into this decision. How have they contributed to the venture so far? What future commitment do you expect from them? What incentives might they need for maximum motivation?

EXAMPLES

MacroCycle

Stwart Peña Feliz and Jan-Georg Rosenboom came from vastly different worlds but shared a common vision for tackling the global plastic waste crisis. Together, they co-founded MacroCycle, a company that makes plastic using a novel chemical recycling technology.

Stwart started as a chemical engineer at ExxonMobil and eventually moved over to the business side of the energy industry (see Step 2). Jan-Georg started as a heavy metal rocker and eventually went into the research side of chemical engineering (see Step 4). They first crossed paths in MIT's CEV course.

Jan-Georg saw the course as a venue where techies like him could find business and policy students to help them with their "crazy science ideas." Stwart happened to be a business student on the hunt for techies with crazy science ideas. Despite being trained as an engineer, Stwart recognized that he did not have the technical skills to develop a breakthrough on his own.

After the course, they spent another semester testing one another out as co-founders before formalizing anything. During this time, they dove further into exploring MacroCycle's potential as a venture.

The early days of MacroCycle involved many late nights working on grant and prize applications and tough conversations about topics like splitting equity. Both founders were involved in almost everything at that point, but they needed to specialize more and more as the venture gained momentum. Jan-Georg focused on the technology development, intellectual property, and early customer validation, while Stwart focused on investor relations, pitching, and sales partnerships.

They also had complementary decision-making approaches, with Stwart relying more on intuition, and Jan-Georg weighing all the options thoroughly. They resolved conflicts by talking them out and hearing one another's perspectives, supported by data. They often found that they were so effective in convincing each other of their respective views that they would flip-flop on their positions and still end up disagreeing.

Stwart and Jan-Georg had many ups and downs, but they were far stronger as a team than either would have been independently.

AeroShield

At first, Elise Strobach was surprised and a little bit annoyed when Kyle Wilke signed up to join her team in the CEV course. She and Kyle had both been PhD students in Professor Evelyn Wang's lab at MIT, but they were working on entirely different projects.

Elise Strobach had spent the last several years studying aerogels—ultralight, porous materials that are very powerful insulators. She and her fellow researchers had a breakthrough in creating silica-based aerogels that were completely transparent, unlocking their potential use in windows. Meanwhile, Kyle Wilke was working on coatings and had no direct experience with aerogels.

As soon as they started working together, Elise realized she was wrong. Kyle's technical background was an asset because he understood materials science as well as the research and development process, so they could quickly get into the weeds on technology.

After a few months, they were enthusiastic about continuing as a team, a decision reinforced by winning MIT's Climate & Energy Prize. They legally incorporated AeroShield Materials to accept the $100,000 prize.

Eventually, a former classmate and MBA student, Aaron Baskerville-Bridges, began helping part-time with customer interviews and developing their business plan. Elise had a conversation with Aaron about his expected compensation. Aaron said equity was most important, not cash, because he wanted to be invested in the company's long-term success. This signaled to Elise that she and Kyle should consider making him a third co-founder.

She and Kyle had already distributed equity when they incorporated the company. They had set aside just over 10% of the shares for the employee option pool and then split the rest 60:40, reflecting that Elise had been the originator of the technology and had worked on it for longer. The vesting schedule also reflected these contributions. To bring Aaron into the company, Elise and Kyle offered him the full option pool. He accepted, and they all agreed to take an equal salary. Eventually, they realized Aaron's stake was too low to reflect his contributions to the company, and they took measures to correct it. Equity conversations can be thorny, but they are essential, and they work best when everyone is clear about their values and expectations.

Thiozen

As a PhD student, Ryan Gillis developed a new pathway for making hydrogen out of water and hydrogen sulfide (a common waste product in several industrial processes). This technology formed the basis of what would become Thiozen. His PhD supervisor Bill Green was already on board as a co-founder, but they had established that he would be a technical advisor, not involved in the venture's day-to-day operations. This arrangement is relatively common for faculty members involved in entrepreneurial ventures.

Ryan decided to look for a full-time co-founder who could provide an alternative perspective, pick up the slack on the many uncomfortable but important tasks of building a venture, and balance out some of his self-identified weaknesses (mainly sales and networking). When he pitched his idea in the CEV course, he connected with Ajay Bawa, an MBA student with experience running his family's defense manufacturing plant.

After working together for a semester, Ryan decided to formally bring Ajay onto the team, which required allocating equity across the three co-founders. Before discussing anything with Ajay and Bill, Ryan did what came naturally to him: calculations (see Figure 5.1). He recognized that Bill had limited time, so he allocated a healthy equity portion to him to ensure that he cared enough about their success to take time away from other important responsibilities. To Ajay, who was still a student, Ryan allotted a smaller, longer-vesting equity share. He also arranged an upgrade to Ajay's equity share upon completion of his degree to incentivize him to become a Thiozen founder. Ryan protected himself from equity loss through both the vesting and the initial allotment.

Nervously, he called the team into Bill's office and wrote everything out on a whiteboard, complete with the math and full written justification. The first 5 minutes of the meeting were quiet as everyone read through his proposal. After another 25 minutes of discussion, everyone accepted the terms with no amendments, and they walked out of the room as an Initial Team.

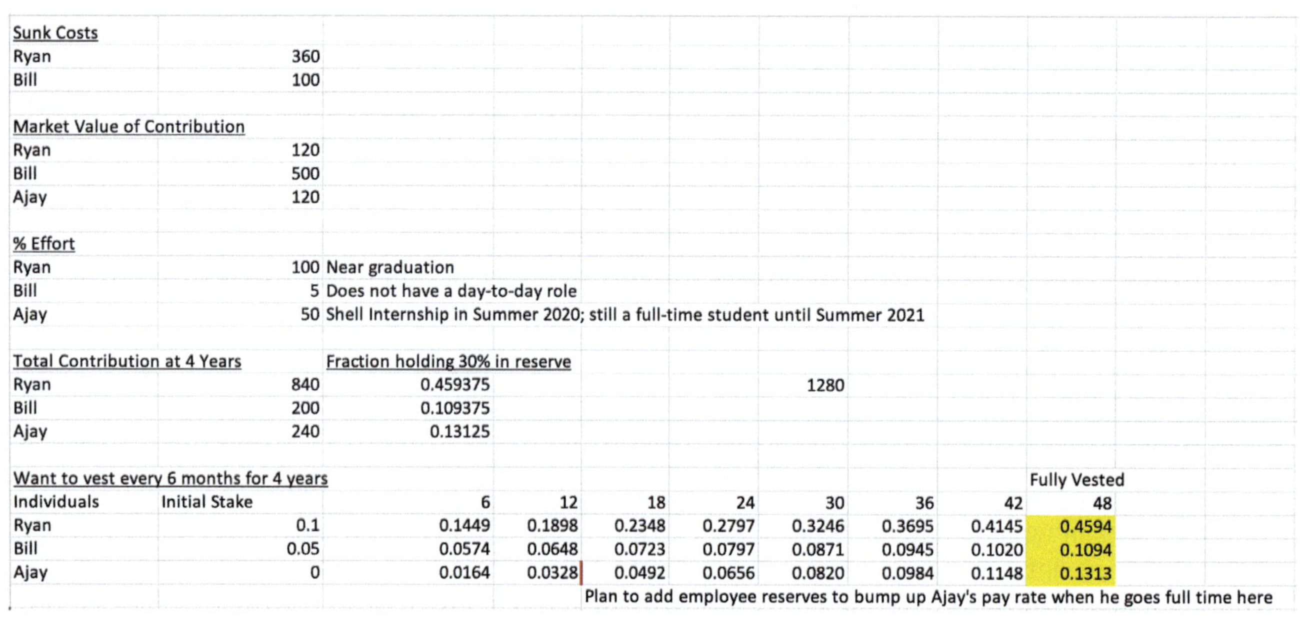

Sunk Costs									
Ryan	360								
Bill	100								
Market Value of Contribution									
Ryan	120								
Bill	500								
Ajay	120								
% Effort									
Ryan	100	Near graduation							
Bill	5	Does not have a day-to-day role							
Ajay	50	Shell Internship in Summer 2020; still a full-time student until Summer 2021							

Total Contribution at 4 Years		Fraction holding 30% in reserve			
Ryan	840	0.459375		1280	
Bill	200	0.109375			
Ajay	240	0.13125			

Want to vest every 6 months for 4 years

Individuals	Initial Stake	6	12	18	24	30	36	42	Fully Vested 48
Ryan	0.1	0.1449	0.1898	0.2348	0.2797	0.3246	0.3695	0.4145	0.4594
Bill	0.05	0.0574	0.0648	0.0723	0.0797	0.0871	0.0945	0.1020	0.1094
Ajay	0	0.0164	0.0328	0.0492	0.0656	0.0820	0.0984	0.1148	0.1313

Plan to add employee reserves to bump up Ajay's pay rate when he goes full time here

Figure 5.1: Ryan's proposed equity allotments for the would-be co-founders of Thiozen

ADDITIONAL RESOURCES

There are additional resources for this step at www.de4cev.com/step5. These materials include the following:

- Co-Founder Evaluation Worksheet
- MacroCycle Case Study
- AeroShield Case Study
- Thiozen Case Study
- Link to Gloria Lin's "50 Questions to Explore with a Potential Co-Founder" as published by First Round Capital
- Link to a benchmarking guide to equity splits for university spinouts originally created by Manny Stockman of Osage University Partners

Additional resources will be added as new and updated examples and information become available.

Note

1. Jared R. Curhan, Hillary Anger Elfenbein, and Noah Eisenkraft, "The Objective Value of Subjective Value: A Multi-Round Negotiation Study," *Journal of Applied Social Psychology* 40, no. 3 (March 2010): 690–709, https://doi.org/10.1111/j.1559-1816.2010.00593.x.

Start Brewing the TEA (Techno-Economic Analysis)

In This Step, You Will

- Learn how to match a particular technology to a particular problem.
- Set up a detailed quantitative analysis of a potential solution that flows smoothly from a technological model into a financial model and translates between the two.
- Derive useful insights about the long-term profitability of your solution.

Why This Step, and Why Now?

Climate and energy entrepreneurs often work with complex technologies, which means they need to assess whether a solution works at all before they can begin exploring potential for it. The solution must be both technologically viable and economically feasible. If a given technology works perfectly but is vastly more expensive than other reasonable alternatives, even at scale, then it is highly unlikely to succeed in the market.

The process of determining how the technological and economic possibilities overlap is called Techno-Economic Analysis (TEA, pronounced "T-E-A").

A TEA is a quantitative model that connects a solution's technical and economic aspects. It ensures that a process or product can be delivered according to desired factors (including cost, price, margin, rate of return, or other metrics).

There are several reasons to do a TEA:

- It helps you assess if your solution is cost competitive in the market.
- It enables you to perform a sensitivity analysis to better understand your priorities.
- It facilitates feedback to technical teams about how to spend limited resources.
- Further down the line, it can provide insight to investors on potential returns.

Like primary market research (PMR), TEA provides a structured process to make decisions about what your solution will be and how to make money from it. Another similarity to PMR is that TEA continues to evolve across the rest of the steps. These two tools reinforce each other. The insights derived from PMR determine the desired factors for the TEA, and the capabilities revealed through TEA open questions to explore through PMR.

TEA is a complex topic. It is deeply technical, and there are many ways of structuring the analysis as well as many methods of calculating some of the important numbers. We will provide you with an overview in this step, but you will inevitably need to dig deeper and seek other sources as you do your own analysis.

What If I Don't Have a Technology?

TEA is important for both technology-led entrepreneurs (i.e., a tech-push pathway) and problem-led entrepreneurs (i.e., a market-pull pathway). Technology-led entrepreneurs need to be in constant conversation with their technology, so TEA is essential. Problem-led entrepreneurs need to do a version of TEA as well, where they identify the possible technologies and solutions that could potentially address their problem and evaluate which ones make economic and practical sense. The matrix in Table 6.1 can help support this analysis.

By the time you do an initial TEA, you need to have some concept of what technology you'll be using, but you should not be designing a fully fleshed-out product at this point. You will continue to refine your TEA as you design your product and even after it is on the market.

Table 6.1: *Technology-Problem Matching Matrix.*

Problem	Existing Solution A	Existing Solution B	New Tech C	New Tech D
Technology readiness. How soon can the technology be deployed?				
Cost. How does the cost compare with other solutions, and is it on track to get cheaper over time?				
Performance. How well does the solution perform relative to other solutions?				
Finance. Do the financial mechanisms exist to support this solution at scale? (More on this in later steps.)				
Other factors. Are there other factors that will support or hinder this solution?				

Structuring Your TEA

A unique aspect of a TEA is that it feeds a technological model into a financial model. These two modes of analysis are very different. A technological model is not standardized. The structure and variables depend entirely on the technology. By contrast, a financial model often follows a highly standardized and well-known structure, though the specifics can still vary greatly. Building a TEA requires creative translation between the two models. There's no set template, but your goal should be to keep it clear and readable.

Start by defining the scope for which you are completing the analysis. For example, are you trying to determine the cost of a new electrolyzer technology, or the cost of hydrogen produced through the new electrolyzer? Or maybe the overall profitability of the plant? You will likely need all these estimates for different purposes. Make sure to consider the scope most relevant for your eventual customer, not just the one that looks best for you.

Next, do a process flow diagram. The idea is to understand the component pieces of the solution, and the process by which they are created or manufactured. Pick the right level of abstraction for the model to remain understandable to an audience who does not understand the technology.

Figure 6.1: Your TEA brings together a technological model and a financial model

For each step, document the following (if relevant):

- Inputs (feedstock, utilities)
- Conversion process (what's turning into what)
- Outputs (including byproducts)
- Labor
- Time
- Costs associated with the inputs, labor, and time
- Revenue from the output (if any)
- Incentives (more on this in later steps)

Define the relationships and equations that govern the product or process and combine everything into a single model. This will usually take the form of a spreadsheet. Each line of the model will be a specific measurable unit (kilogram of material, kilowatt-hour of electricity, etc.), and ultimately, everything will lead to a set of costs and revenues.

Document the assumptions behind each part of the model. Eventually, you can add different scenarios to account for uncertainty. Start with an upside (your best-case scenario), a downside (your worst-case scenario), and the base case (a reasonable point in between the other two).

Your TEA will be full of information and assumptions. You might be wondering how to gather all the data you will need. Here are some possible sources:

- For internal assumptions (information related directly to your solution), use your own measurements from the lab or the field.

- For external assumptions (information outside of your solution, like the price of electricity), primary market research is ideal (see Step 3), but sometimes you can get satisfactory information from secondary market research.

- You can look for comparable technologies and build parts of your model based on their info, adding assumptions as necessary. If you use this strategy, keep in mind that existing studies or comparables are likely using old information. Has something changed? Have the costs of your technology come down? Do you have a breakthrough that further reduces costs? Timing is extremely important, and you should have a good understanding of the major economic drivers for your solution and how the broader field of solutions is evolving. If you decide to look for comparable examples, the Department of Energy's Joint BioEnergy Institute maintains a library of techno-economic models that may be useful.

Regardless of where you get your information, make sure to gut check each assumption with experts or your own judgment. Quickly assess each input and output. If something seems off (e.g., if a number varies greatly from what you might expect), then it deserves further scrutiny.

The North Star of Climate and Energy Solutions: IRR > WACC

The key metric for TEA is not efficiency or even cost—it is profitability. A successful solution needs to sustain itself financially over time. While cost is a key intermediate output, you should aim to determine your internal rate of return (IRR)[1] for a given application of the technology and eventually assess how it compares to the weighted average cost of capital (WACC).[2] In other words, will the technology generate enough profit to pay back the money needed to get it off the ground? If IRR is greater than WACC, then the technology can be financed at scale. If not, then the solution will be difficult, if not impossible, to finance. Your model is built on a set of assumptions—it is not an objective truth—so the question to ask here is not simply "Is IRR greater than WACC?" but rather "What needs to happen for IRR to be greater than WACC?"

IRR and WACC are complicated financial numbers that you will probably not be able to calculate right off the bat. But it is extremely important that you understand these concepts and work toward quantifying them, because this is the language major capital providers speak. If you can provide an attractive IRR, then you (or your customers) will have plenty of capital available to finance your technology or solution. If not, then financing will be extremely difficult. Keep in mind that earlier-stage technologies are riskier and typically require a higher IRR to attract capital. As markets mature, their cost of capital typically goes down. It is also important to understand the market context. Higher interest rates can increase the costs of capital for even the most proven solutions. This has caused challenges for renewables, which have high up-front costs relative to their operating costs, compared to fossil fuel solutions, where the situation is the opposite.

Many people like to focus on the efficiency or cost of their technology because those things are relatively easy to calculate. However, a highly efficient technology is not necessarily more profitable (e.g., when it's much more expensive than other options). Similarly, cost can help you to compare products within similar categories, but a low-cost technology is not necessarily more profitable than other options (e.g., when the selling price is also lower). This is why it's important to focus on IRR.

A major challenge of focusing on IRR is that it is highly influenced by how a technology is used in the field. Where is the technology located? How is it being used? What are the incentives available? What are the other costs associated with using or deploying the technology? It all depends, and most people, especially engineers, don't like that answer.

While IRR is important, keep in mind that several solutions have scaled without requiring their customers to have a positive IRR. For example, Tesla went to market and went public selling luxury electric cars that people drove a few thousand miles per year. Their customers were definitely not concerned with the economics, but Tesla competed by having the best high-end electric car. They were also clear about their intentions to get costs down and launch lower-cost vehicles, which could provide nice returns to the consumer in the right applications.

Another vehicle example is how Toyota was much more successful than other car manufacturers in launching hybrids. Toyota was not the first to market, but they found the right blend of efficiency and function with the Prius. Most importantly, they didn't have a non-hybrid version of the Prius, making it hard (if not impossible) for customers to calculate the relative economics. Other car manufacturers made a hybrid version of one of their popular cars, like the Ford Escape or Honda Civic. The problem with that approach was that customers could easily figure out the additional cost compared to the fuel savings, which wasn't worth it in most cases.

Note that both these examples are primarily business-to-consumer solutions, where customers may be more emotional than business-driven.

OTHER USEFUL METRICS

While the ultimate metric for TEA is profitability, your analysis may yield other useful metrics as well. Here are a few examples:

- **Minimum selling price (MSP)**, measured in dollars: This is the lowest cost at which a product can be sold without losing money. It is also known as the break-even price. It reflects all the variable costs that go into making the product. If the MSP is higher than the market price, then the product will need to be sold at a premium to make any profit.
- **Levelized cost of energy (LCOE)**, measured in dollars/kWh: The sum of all costs during the lifetime of an electricity source (construction, operation, end-of-life) divided by the sum of all the electricity generated. Theoretically, this metric allows for a consistent apples-to-apples comparison of different electricity sources, but in practice, there are many different ways to calculate it.
- **Total cost of ownership (TCO)**, measured in dollars: The cost of owning or using a product, such as an electric vehicle or a more energy-efficient appliance, throughout its life cycle. This cost can be compared to that of the conventional alternative to ensure that the product makes a profit while generating savings for the customer.

Deriving Insights from the Analysis

Once you have your TEA, the next step is to use it to produce actionable insights. The following are some of the questions you could potentially answer through your TEA:

- What is the IRR of a project or facility using our technology? Is this number attractive for customers and investors?
- Will our process or product compete with incumbent technology?
- How will our process or product compete with other new technologies being developed?
- What are our unit costs of producing this technology? What will the margin be if we sell at market prices? Alternatively, what price do we need to set to reach a target margin?
- What are the most significant contributors to cost?
- What needs to evolve from the first unit sold to the nth unit sold for the product to scale?
- Are we focusing our research and development efforts on the right variables? For example, what will our customers care about more? Efficiency? Cost? Longevity?

We're Not in Kansas Anymore

One of the most effective ways of getting useful insights out of your TEA is to perform a sensitivity analysis, where you rank a set of variables based on how much a change in each will affect a certain outcome. When the variables are stacked from most to least sensitive, the result resembles the funnel of a tornado, so the diagram is often called a tornado chart.

The tornado chart in Figure 6.2 analyzes the IRR for a hybrid powertrain for commercial vans. We can see that policy incentives have a huge impact on the IRR for this solution, so it's worth

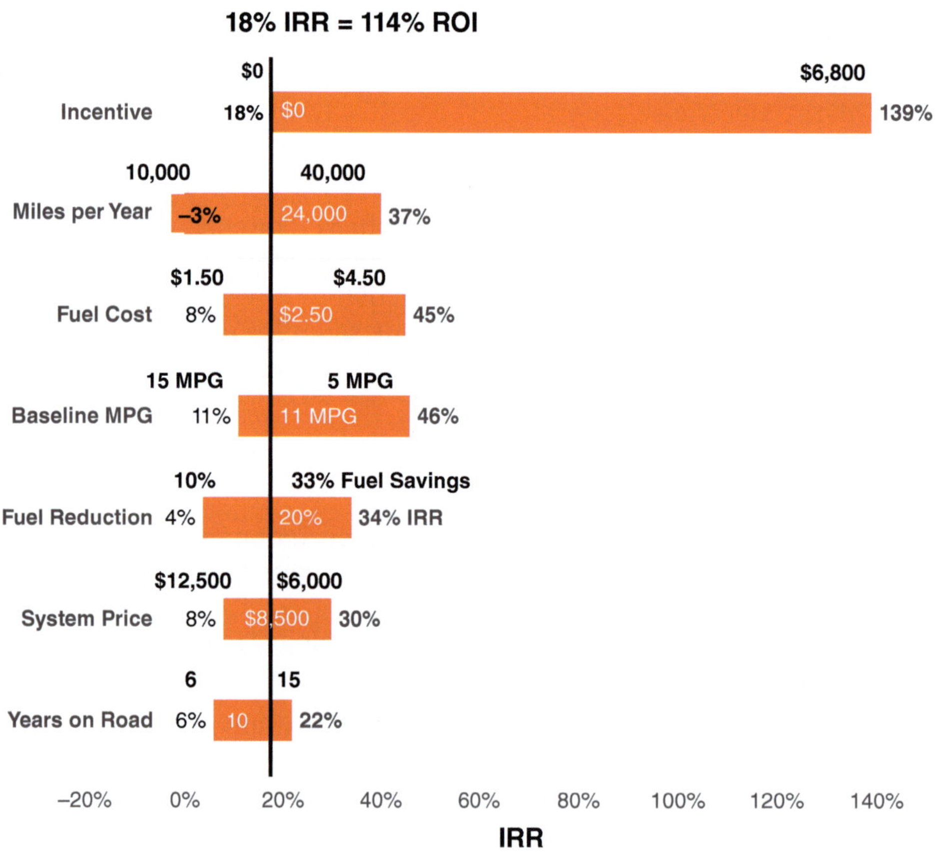

Figure 6.2: A tornado chart showing the IRR for a hybrid powertrain and its sensitivity to a set of relevant variables. Base case assumptions for the IRR calculation are in white letters on the orange bars and result in an 18% IRR. The orange bars represent the range of IRR while adjusting each variable based on the downside and upside assumptions, and they are stacked according to size.

spending effort and resources to lobby the government for these incentives (see Step 8). The next three most important variables (miles per year, fuel cost, and baseline miles per gallon) are not directly associated with the hybrid technology. They are external variables driven by how and where the customer is using the vehicle. This means it's important to engage the right customers and ensure they are using the technology in the right applications.

Spilling the Tea on Common TEA Mistakes

We will close with a few final pieces of wisdom about your TEA based on mistakes that entrepreneurs commonly make:[3]

- **Model for initial and commercial scale.** While it's your economics at scale that really matter, you also have to start somewhere. Define and evaluate your solution both for your early scale and at commercial scale. It will be important to understand how you can make money at small scale, then how you grow to full scale.

- **Keep assumptions reasonable.** Use real-world ranges and be conservative. Don't assume you will get the best possible rates right away.

- **Consider price dynamically.** If you compare your price to the market price, remember that competitors can undercut you in the short term or prices can decline in the long term.

- **Beware of false precision.** Ultimately the TEA is just a model and an approximation. Allow for a significant margin for error.

- **Focus on customer priorities.** Your output should align with what customers care about based on your PMR. Refine it in later steps as you get a more specific understanding of your customers.

- **Don't get stuck in analysis paralysis.** Start with an initial version that you understand. You can later return to your TEA to iterate and improve it.

THE TROUBLE WITH TECHNOLOGY READINESS LEVELS (TRLs)

TEA is complementary to another metric that is commonly used to evaluate the state of emerging technology: Technology Readiness Levels (TRLs). This nine-level framework was originally developed by NASA to assess whether technical breakthroughs were ready for application in outer space, and it is now commonly used for the practical application of any complex technology. By contrast, the point of TEA is not to assess the readiness of a given technology but rather to project how a technology performs once it's mature.

The Department of Energy's Office of Technology Transitions has created an alternative to TRLs called *Adoption Readiness Levels (ARLs)*. This framework accounts for factors beyond the state of the technology, such as "product-market fit, demand pull, supply chain, regulatory risks, and workforce availability." All these factors map fairly well to topics that we will cover in later steps of this book, so you could potentially use ARLs as an alternative assessment of your progress. But unlike this book, the ARL framework does not tell you how to address these important factors. It only gives you a snapshot of where you stand.

Output from This Step

If you don't yet have a technology in mind, use the Technology-Problem Matching Matrix in Table 6.1 to figure out which technology might be the best fit for your problem.

Once you have a technology (especially if it is a newly developed technology), complete at least a rudimentary TEA that includes the following:

- A clearly defined scope (component level, product level, the plant level, etc.)

- A process flow diagram or another summary (depending on the type of technology) that roughly outlines all the necessary technical components

- A set of assumptions on how the system will operate:
  - Internal assumptions from your own research and measurements
  - External assumptions derived from primary or secondary research
  - Comparables from similar technologies

- A key metric that assesses the performance of your technology in economic terms (e.g., IRR, MSP, LCOE, TCO). This metric will be the ultimate output of your TEA, and it is what you will subject to additional scrutiny, such as sensitivity analysis. You might identify a few different metrics that matter—but be careful about tracking too many things! There should ideally be one key metric and at most two or three.

EXAMPLES

Via Separations

As part of the papermaking process, the world's pulp mills were concentrating a billion gallons per day of a by-product called black liquor, and they were doing that using heat to evaporate excess liquids. The Via team was not sure their filtering technology would work as an alternative, but they knew they could access a big market opportunity if it did. To figure out whether their technology was fit for purpose, they leaned heavily on their TEA, which was based on both internal and external assumptions. The internal assumptions related to Via's membrane technology, and they could be validated directly in the lab. The external assumptions were related to the process where the membrane would be used, including factors like volume and rate of chemicals moving through the system and energy consumption at each step.

The output of the model was dollars per year of value generated for a given customer. That value came from three different categories: less money spent on energy for separations (this usually meant burning less natural gas on-site), less money spent on extra chemicals to relieve bottlenecks, and more revenue from increased production (because the process moved faster).

The highest of these three value drivers depended on the specific customer and the market conditions (like the cost of natural gas). For any customer, once the team figured the yearly value generation, they could compare that to the cost of the solution and calculate the IRR.

Eventually, the TEA evolved from a technical assessment to an indispensable sales tool. The Via team could go to any customer and quickly calculate exactly how much value they could create for them.

Teasha Feldman-Fitzthum (EverVest, XL Fleet, and Commonwealth Fusion Systems)

Teasha Feldman-Fitzthum used TEA for three distinct purposes: as a product, for selling a product, and for building a company.

First, Teasha aimed to start a company that would offer improved wind resource predictions to lower financing costs for wind farms. However, through primary market research, she and her team realized the real need in the industry wasn't just better predictions—it was translating technical data into financial projections for investors.

This insight led to a pivot. The company, EverVest, developed a platform that could take broad project datasets—covering everything from feedstocks to financing structures—and generate financial outputs. The platform became a tool for project developers and investors to assess financial viability of infrastructure projects, effectively making TEA the product itself.

After a few years, Teasha joined XL Fleet, where TEA played a critical role in selling hybrid vehicles and hybrid retrofit kits. Unlike EverVest, where TEA was the product, XL Fleet used TEA to demonstrate the value of its offerings to customers. The focus was on total cost of ownership, specifically analyzing fuel savings that customers could achieve by adopting XL Fleet's technology.

After that, Teasha worked at Commonwealth Fusion Systems (CFS), a company aiming to commercialize fusion energy. At CFS, TEA wasn't just a tool for evaluating projects or selling products—it was deeply embedded in the company's DNA. TEA was integral to the company's strategy, product design, and development. The driving metric was cost per kilowatt-hour, a critical benchmark for the commercial viability of fusion power plants.

ADDITIONAL RESOURCES

There are additional resources for this step at www.de4cev.com/step6. These materials include the following:

- Technology-Problem Matching Worksheet
- TEA Foundations Worksheet
- Via Separations Case Study
- Teasha Feldman-Fitzthum Case Study
- Links to useful TEA tools from Conductor Labs, the US Department of Energy, ChemCatBio, the Joint BioEnergy Institute, and more

Additional resources will be added as new and updated examples and information become available.

Notes

1. Internal rate of return (IRR) is the annualized percentage return an investment is expected to generate. It helps compare investment opportunities—higher IRR generally means a more profitable investment.
2. Weighted average cost of capital (WACC) is the average rate a company must pay to finance its operations, considering both debt (like loans) and equity (like investor funding).
3. Many of these tips come from Shayle Kann, Greg Thiel, and Melissa Ball of Energy Impact Partners, as recorded on the Catalyst podcast. "Climate-Tech Startups Need Strong Techno-Economic Analysis," *Catalyst with Shayle Kann*, Canary Media podcast, October 5, 2023. https://www.canarymedia.com/podcasts/catalyst-with-shayle-kann/climatetech-startups-need-strong-techno-economic-analysis.

Segment the Market

In This Step, You Will

- Brainstorm a wide array of potential customers and markets for your business.
- Narrow down your list to your top four to six markets.
- Compare those markets to one another in a structured and rigorous way.

Why This Step, and Why Now?

By this point, you should have an idea of the problem you're solving and the technology that you will use to solve it, and you should already have talked to some of the people who experience this problem. Market Segmentation is a critical next step to turn your idea into a business.

The Initial Brainstorm

Start by brainstorming all the potential customers you could target. You should already have some idea of the possible universe of customers based on Steps 1 and 2, but you have not yet made a comprehensive list of everyone who might be a customer. Keep an open mind and try to think of potential applications or audiences that didn't initially seem obvious.

What defines a *single* market segment? If you are considering selling to industrial manufacturing plants, you may wonder, do all these plants constitute one segment? Do I need to segment them by what they are manufacturing? By how big they are? By what type of machinery they use?

You can think of a market segment as a group of potential customers who share three fundamental characteristics:

- They buy the same product.

- They buy it in the same way (i.e., same use case, value proposition, channel, price range).

- There is word-of-mouth between them; they significantly influence each other.

Your initial market segments will almost surely need to be broken down further, so start with what feels right and look more closely at segments that seem promising. When you think you've segmented as far as you can, you're probably getting close. Do at least one more iteration. The more specifically you define your first market, the easier all the subsequent steps will be. Poor Market Segmentation is the root cause of most failures in starting new ventures.

Narrowing Down

It's not possible to analyze every potential customer segment, so you will have to narrow down the field to what you believe are the best four to six candidates so you can do a deeper dive to compare them and determine your potential first market.

How do you narrow the field down? Look at your ideas with a critical eye to eliminate the ones you feel are not a good fit. Here are some potential filters you could use:

- **Solution viability filter.** This is where your TEA comes into play. Rule out markets for which your solution is not economically or functionally viable.

- **Personal filter.** Rule out any markets that are not consistent with the values, passions, and goals of the founding team (Steps 4 and 5). It is also worth mentioning that many climate entrepreneurs may hesitate to work with energy incumbents (i.e., the fossil fuel industry). That is understandable, but do not rule them out too quickly, because these incumbents can sometimes be large, well-resourced partners that unlock pathways to scale further down the line. However, they can also have vested interests in preserving their major business lines, which will cause them to move more slowly than you might like.

- **Market size filter.** Rule out any markets not large enough to be worth pursuing. Don't be too picky here. There are lots of really good niches in the climate and energy space. If you find a promising segment that may be too small, you can still pursue it if it naturally leads to larger markets. We will cover this further in Step 10.
- **Market attainability filter.** Rule out any markets that will not be readily accessible to your sales force. For example, it's exceedingly difficult to sell to customers who don't buy from early-stage ventures.
- **Competition filter.** Rule out markets with entrenched competition that could block you. Some competition is good because it proves there is a market. Be careful not to let the existence of competition scare you away. Only rule out markets if there are a few powerful and dominant players.

Output from This Step

Now that you have narrowed your market opportunities, build a matrix to analyze the top market segments to organize your research. You can use the criteria in Table 7.1 as a template, but you do not need to include all of them. Choose the ones that will be most valuable in helping you to evaluate potential markets. Balance comprehensiveness with simplicity.

Table 7.1: *Market Segmentation Matrix with Definitions.*

Market segment name	Carefully name the market segment so it appropriately captures precisely the group you want and no more.
End user	This is the person who actually uses the product, not the economic buyer or the champion (more in Step 12)—it is not a company or a general organization but a real person.
Task	What exactly is it that the end user does that you will significantly affect or allow them to do that they could not do before?
Benefit	What is the benefit that you believe the end user will get?
Urgency of need	What is the level of urgency to solve the problem or capture the new opportunity for the end user?
Example end users	Who are example users that you can, have, or will talk to so as to validate your perceptions on this market segment?

Lead customers	Who are the influential customers (i.e., lighthouse customers) that if they buy, others will take note and likely follow?
Willingness to change	How conservative is this market segment? How open are they to change? Is there something to force change (i.e., impending crisis)?
Frequency of buying	How often do they buy new products? What does their buying cycle look like at a high level?
Concentration of buyers	How many different buyers are there in this market segment? Is it a monopoly? Oligopoly (a small number of buyers)? Or many competitive buyers?
Size of market (no. of end users)	Roughly how many end users exist (10s, 100s, 1Ks, 10Ks, 100Ks, 1 million, etc.)?
Estimated value of end user ($1, $10, $100, $1K, $1 million, $1 billion)	Do a first-pass estimate of the value of each end user, again to a relevant order of magnitude so we can make some relative decisions now, but then we will dive much deeper into this and other numbers later.
Competition/alternatives	What will be your competition from the end users' perspective? Of course, there is the "do nothing" option, but who else would be competitors if the user fully analyzed their options?
Other components needed for a full solution	Since most customers will only buy a full solution and not components, what are the other elements needed to construct a full solution to achieve the benefits? These are the complementary assets that you do not currently have but would need to build or acquire to give the end user a total solution.
Important partners	Who are the partners or distributors you will have to work with to build and scale your solution for this market?
Climate TAM	You estimated this for the problem segment in Step 1. Now estimate it for the market segment. Will serving this market have a positive benefit for the planet? Your solution does not need to have a big impact right away, but does going after this market open up a pathway to transformative impact further down the line?
Other relevant market considerations	This allows for customization of your segment for any market-related factor not covered in the previous categories.
Other relevant personal considerations	This category includes where the market segment is geographically centered, the founding team's values, existing knowledge and contacts in the market, and so on.

In *Disciplined Entrepreneurship*, the steps go directly from segmenting the market to selecting an initial market known as a Beachhead Market. In this book, we first add two dimensions to your analysis: policy (Step 8) and business model (Step 9). These are hugely important concepts for climate and energy ventures, affecting much more than Market Segmentation, and they will come up many times throughout the venture creation process. Thus, each one merits its own step.

A NOTE ON USING ARTIFICIAL INTELLIGENCE (AI) TOOLS (ESPECIALLY FOR THIS STEP)

It is important to understand the underlying logic of this step, and it is good to start the process manually with your team to generate great discussion.

That being said, if you only use manual research methods, you will be at an enormous and potentially fatal disadvantage. The Market Segmentation Matrix can, at least initially, be filled in with secondary market research, which is exactly the type of task that a well-prompted large language model will do dramatically faster and better than humans. The AI tool will almost instantaneously come up with a set of potential market segments and then compare and contrast them.[1] This is invaluable.

That being said, AI by itself is not enough, as you need to understand the first principles to guide the AI systems and adjust them appropriately based on your situation, values, and primary market research. AI tools will save you time, but you must think critically about everything that comes out, including what *isn't* there. Don't use the tools to replace human interaction; use them so you can spend your time engaging potential customers (and others) more wisely. And reading and understanding the AI tools' output needs to involve your team so that when you complete this step, the whole team is on board with the resulting decision.

EXAMPLES

AeroShield

AeroShield's aerogels may have been clear, but the market for them was not.

Finding the right application required several different layers of Market Segmentation. The first market they considered was solar thermal energy, in which systems trap heat from the sun to warm water. However, when the team realized their aerogels were clear enough to use as insulation inside of windows, they went for that larger opportunity and impact.

Deciding to focus on windows was an important step, but it was nowhere near the level of specificity that they needed. From there, they had to decide whether to apply their solution to new windows or to retrofit existing ones, whether to tackle the commercial or residential markets, and whether to target traditional windowpanes or door windows.

Ultimately, AeroShield chose to start with new-build residential door windows, with their customers being door manufacturers. There were many reasons for this choice, but a big one was that in the United States, there is a product efficiency rating system called Energy Star, and most residential windows are Energy Star rated. In 2023, Energy Star expanded ratings to include doors as well. Suddenly, door manufacturers began to care a lot more about insulation. That regulatory change created a Window of Opportunity for AeroShield, ironically one that shifted them away from traditional windowpanes. This shows the importance of policy in Market Segmentation, which we will cover further in Step 8.

Many years elapsed between their initial consideration of solar thermal energy and their ultimate focus on door windows. In the interim, they were often considering multiple levels of sub-segmentation at once, but the thoroughness of the segmentation was critical. If the team had stopped once they decided on windows or new windows or residential windows, then they may have missed the promising opportunity they ended up finding in residential doors.

A123 Systems

In 2001, Yet-Ming Chiang and his team at MIT developed a groundbreaking lithium battery technology. Batteries can be used in many different end-use applications, so they had a large set of potential market segments to choose from. Based on the unique characteristics of the technology, the team identified several top contenders:

- Power tools
- Grid-level energy storage
- Local energy storage
- Medical devices
- Consumer electronics
- Electric vehicles
- Plug-in hybrid vehicles

They used many factors to evaluate these segments, but they placed the highest weight on ease of entry, market size, and technology fit.

Ease of entry was critical, since they were an early-stage venture without many resources. The team prioritized markets where they could overcome initial hurdles, such as regulatory challenges, customer acquisition, and competition from entrenched players.

Technology fit was also important. The team assessed how well their battery's unique attributes matched the performance requirements of each market.

Finally, the team considered market size. They sought a segment large enough to sustain the company's growth in the short term while providing a clear path to scale in the long term.

ADDITIONAL RESOURCES

There are additional resources for this step at www.de4cev.com/step7. These materials include the following:

- Market Segmentation Worksheet
- AeroShield Case Study
- A123 Systems Case Study

Additional resources will be added as new and updated examples and information become available.

Note

1. An example of this can be seen with the MIT tool for general Disciplined Entrepreneurship called JetPack through a demonstration by Shari Van Cleave. https://www.youtube.com/watch?v=ULuptPyECUA.

Plan for Policy Sticks and Carrots

In This Step, You Will

- Analyze how the levers of policy affect you and your customer, as well as how policy might change in the future.
- Apply this analysis as an additional layer to your Market Segmentation.

Why This Step, and Why Now?

Most climate and energy ventures cannot survive for long without considering policy, and this
needs to happen early in the process. All organizations need to consider policy, but there has
been a trend among Silicon Valley tech startups to ask for forgiveness rather than permission.
For instance, Uber launched its platform to drivers and riders before asking permission from city
governments. By the time cities caught wind of what was happening, Uber had already built up a
solid customer base, and the company cemented itself as a major player in urban transportation,
whether cities wanted them there or not.

Subverting government laws and procedures obviously brings up concerns from an ethical
standpoint, but for climate and energy ventures, it is often a moot point, because circumvent-
ing the government is simply impossible. In stark contrast to the Uber example, let's say you are
hoping to generate electricity with a new form of nuclear technology. You can't simply hook up
your reactor to the grid and ask for forgiveness later. You need to work with governments, and you
should do so from the very beginning.

Think of policy as an additional lens for your market analysis. Policy might make some market segments more or less favorable. It could even change where in the world it makes the most sense for your venture to operate. This is why we encourage founding teams to have someone who is policy savvy or at least interested in becoming so.

Policy Often Comes Down to Sticks and Carrots

Broadly, we can split policy into Sticks and Carrots. Sticks are regulations that specify how things should be done and penalize noncompliance (for instance, permitting laws, environmental protection standards, and energy market access). Carrots encourage and reward desirable outcome (for instance, subsidies, grants, and tax incentives).

In the United States, incentives are the predominant form of climate-specific policy passed through Congress. There are many complex reasons for this, but the short version is that it's easier for a politician concerned about reelection to tout something positive to their constituents (i.e., an incentive) rather than something negative (i.e., a tax or restriction). While the general idea of climate policy can be highly polarizing in the United States, the specific incentives tend to be popular across party lines. Regulations are also highly relevant to climate and energy ventures, especially those dealing with electricity markets. Siting, permitting, and interconnection are some of the largest barriers to the growth of renewable energy across the United States.

In industries related to climate and energy, there are also often large externalities, which are costs (or benefits) of an activity affecting third parties who are not directly involved in that activity. Greenhouse gas emissions are negative externalities of the highest order. Policy can help to price in some of these externalities. An example of this is California's cap-and-trade policy. It restricts companies to a certain limit (or cap) on emissions, and they need to pay if they exceed that limit. If companies are below their cap, they can sell the right to emit (known as an allowance) to other companies. This is called trading, and it provides a financial incentive for companies to reduce their emissions even further below the limit.

Governments can also incentivize individual actions to benefit the whole that people or companies would not otherwise take. For example, utilities often run energy efficiency programs with rebates. This is a form of incentive that is supported by state-run energy agencies (usually called *public utilities commissions*) because offering a rebate for more energy-efficient appliances can reduce the need for adding more electricity generation, and it can thus reduce costs at the system level.

So far, we've mainly discussed state and federal policy, but climate and energy ventures need to understand relevant Sticks and Carrots at all levels: local, state, national, and sometimes even international.

While policies differ across countries and jurisdictions, the same principles apply. Climate and energy ventures need to analyze the policy landscape, and they need to do so early, usually before selecting a market pathway.

In this step, we will discuss three categories of policy considerations:

- Policy and you
- Policy and your customer
- Future policy changes

Policy and You

The first level of policy analysis is understanding how policy directly affects your venture. Research all the Sticks and Carrots that might affect you, building on anything you uncovered in Step 2. AI can be an incredibly useful tool to accelerate this research. You can use the template in Table 8.1 to structure your analysis, or to develop your prompts for an AI large language model.

Table 8.1: *Policy Matrix—Level 1: Policy and You.*

Questions	Sticks (create a column in your matrix for each Stick that's relevant)	Carrots (create a column in your matrix for each Carrot that's relevant)
What potential impacts could this policy have on your venture (positive or negative)?		
If those impacts are realized, to what degree will this policy contribute to the success or failure of your venture (high, medium, low)?		
Who are the key decision-makers and gatekeepers?		
Do you need to complete any applications or proposals? How long do these processes typically take? (The answer should be a range.)		
What data or other evidence do you need to show that you've complied with the Sticks or qualified for the Carrots?		

Policy and Your Customer

The second level of policy analysis is understanding how policy Sticks and Carrots directly affect your customer. This can be a major driver for your sales. If you understand what your customers are most concerned about, then you can potentially unlock new value for them, especially when the policy landscape is changing (for instance, if your solution could help them comply with regulations that would otherwise be much more complicated or costly to deal with, or if your solution could enable them to qualify for an incentive).

Your customers (if they are buying on behalf of businesses) might already have staff in place to help them navigate the policy landscape. In some cases, policy is less of a barrier for large incumbents because they have larger teams, established relationships with government, and more overall experience navigating policy. However, the ball is still in your court to make their job easy and help them help you. They may know many of the policy players and can help you navigate the system.

If your solution depends on an incentive, consider that the process to receive incentives can be cumbersome, especially when multiple parties are involved. For instance, let's say your solution is only profitable with an incentive, and receiving that incentive requires your customer to complete detailed paperwork. If it takes a year for your customer to go through the bureaucracy (which can happen—we've seen it!), then you are on the hook for the money in the interim. That sort of timing issue can really affect your cash flow, which can be dire for startups.

To avoid this risk, you need to proactively engage with your customers and get the best terms possible. A big customer's cost of capital is much less than a startup's cost of capital, so they have a much greater capacity to eat the cost in the short term as they wait for the incentive to come in. As an entrepreneur, you should also engage with policymakers so they understand the implications of lengthy administrative processes. At a minimum, you need to know the impact of incentives on your cash flow and plan accordingly. There are firms that will lend against these types of revenues so spend the time and effort to come up with a solution that works for your business.

Use Table 8.2 to analyze how policy affects your potential customers as well as how this creates risks and opportunities for your venture.

Future Policy Changes

The third and final level of policy analysis is considering potential changes in the near future. Policy is a shifting landscape, and you have the potential to influence it! Yes, even if you are a small company with limited funds, you can influence policy. You can reach out to your representatives and meet with them or their team to share what you are doing and why you should get special

Table **8.2:** *Policy Matrix—Level 2: Policy and Your Customer.*

Questions	Sticks (create a column in your matrix for each Stick that's relevant)	Carrots (create a column in your matrix for each Carrot that's relevant)
For which market segments is this policy applicable?		
What potential impacts could this policy have on your potential customers (positive or negative)?		
To what extent can your solution help your customers realize the positive impacts and/or avoid the negative ones (high, medium, low)?		

attention. It is their job to represent you. You need to understand this, and when the cogs of government start to turn, you should proactively ensure your solution is in the mix.

The incumbents and your competitors are most likely pushing for specific legislative language that will benefit them, and it may not benefit you, even if you are in the same market. Policy is typically written by young staffers, and companies will feed them very specific language, which gets placed into bills. You can do this, too; you don't need an expensive lobbyist. Just find the right people to engage with. Many staffers enjoy engaging directly with companies and entrepreneurs, and politicians love new and growing companies in their districts.

Major bills get passed because politicians want to benefit their districts. If you really know your sector, you should be able to go through relevant legislation and match the various paragraphs and incentives with the companies that wrote the language. This is true at the state and local levels, too. This is the way things work, and you are at a disadvantage if you don't engage. It takes time and attention to forge these relationships, and you need to engage well before the bills go to a vote. At the right time, it can be worth engaging professional service providers and lobbyists, and you may even hire your own experts. Consider it another key aspect of running your company and assign the responsibility to someone on your leadership team from the start. You can adjust your strategy and resource allocation as your company evolves.

It can help to have someone on the team with policy expertise who manages government relationships. This role will likely fall to the founders in the early days of the venture. Calling up local elected officials may seem like a waste of time when there is so much other work to be done, but a small investment in government relationships can pay off in spades further down the line.

There are also many aspects of policy you will not be able to shape, so you will need to be reactive rather than proactive. It's up to you to figure out when that's the case. Either way, you need to get a sense of which way the political wind is blowing. Use Table 8.3 to get started.

Table 8.3: *Policy Matrix—Level 3: Future Policy Changes.*

Questions	Sticks (create a column in your matrix for each Stick that's relevant)	Carrots (create a column in your matrix for each Carrot that's relevant)
What is the realistic wiggle room on this policy? (In political science, this concept is called the Overton window.)		
How feasible would it be to have an impact on this policy?		
If you were to make an impact on this policy, how long would it take to come into effect?		
What impact would changing this policy have on your venture?		
How might other factors shape policy in this area?		
What impact would those externally driven changes have on your venture?		

Output from This Step

Complete the Policy Matrix for each of the three levels of policy consideration (using Tables 8.1, 8.2, and 8.3).

Based on this analysis, go back to your Market Segmentation and add an additional row, "Policy Headwinds/Tailwinds" (these terms are borrowed from nautical terminology: tailwinds are factors that accelerate your success; headwinds are factors that inhibit it). Summarize your key findings from the analysis for each market segment. Are any market segments relatively less attractive than they were before? Are any of them more attractive?

EXAMPLES

EnerNOC[1]

Tim Healy and David Brewster co-founded EnerNOC to harness the transformative potential of demand response—a system where electricity consumers could get paid to adjust their usage during peak demand periods. At the end of the 20th century, US utilities underwent a process called deregulation, which meant opening the industry to competition by separating generation from transmission and distribution. Deregulation allowed independent companies to compete in electricity generation and other services (like demand response), and it opened the door for companies like EnerNOC to try out new solutions. In a deregulated system, the electricity grid is managed by a set of organizations called independent system operators that balance supply and demand in real time, coordinating the operation of power plants and overseeing competitive electricity markets where generators and utilities buy and sell electricity.

During this time, the State of Connecticut faced growing electricity demand, and new power plants or transmission lines couldn't be built quickly enough to meet it. The EnerNOC team made the case to the state regulators that their demand response model was a faster, cheaper, and more flexible alternative. As a result, they secured a pivotal contract in Connecticut that validated their business model and set the stage for rapid growth.

Federal policies like the Energy Policy Acts of 2005 and 2007 further emphasized demand response as a key solution to grid reliability and efficiency challenges. These policies created a favorable environment for EnerNOC to secure additional contracts, attract customers, and scale operations across the United States.

Talus

About half of the world's population depends on food grown with ammonia-based fertilizer.[2] Hiro Iwanaga founded Talus to help feed the world by producing "green ammonia" locally, reliably, and without any GHG emissions. He and his team developed a modular ammonia production system that could run on electricity, air, and water.

Given the minimal inputs needed, they could theoretically make their product for any farmers anywhere, so who would be their first customers? Policy played a big role in that decision.

In the long term, Hiro and his team wanted to target places like the US Midwest, where farmers could buy and use large quantities of ammonia. However, US farmers were only paying about $500 per ton for ammonia, and the cost for Talus's green ammonia was $800 per ton at a minimum. Their product was chemically identical to what farmers were already using, and they knew there was no way those farmers would pay a $300 premium based on climate benefits alone.

Talus needed to find a different market where they could compete on price. Sub-Saharan Africa seemed promising, because there was not much existing infrastructure to make or transport ammonia. In many areas, farmers regularly paid over 3× what farmers in the United States paid for fertilizers. With their sights set on this market, Talus got a grant from the Gates Foundation and built their first systems in Kenya.

Then, policy turned the whole economic calculation on its head. In 2022, the United States passed the Inflation Reduction Act (IRA), which included an incentive for producing green hydrogen. Talus qualified for this incentive since they made green hydrogen as part of their green ammonia process, and it was enough to make their green ammonia cost competitive for US farmers. Talus responded by switching their focus to building several systems in Iowa. They still planned to build more systems in sub-Saharan Africa, but that would be easier to do once they reached scale in the United States and could access better financing.

At the time of writing this book, the future of the IRA incentives is uncertain due to the change in presidential administration. Fortunately, Talus can switch back to international markets if needed. This is the advantage of a modular system that you can ship anywhere in the world (relative to a massive project that is tied to a specific location and takes many years to develop and build).

Talus is a great example of a company that took advantage of incentives when they appeared, but they are not 100% reliant on those incentives. They can adapt to a changing policy landscape.

ADDITIONAL RESOURCES

There are additional resources for this step at www.de4cev.com/step8. These materials include the following:

- Policy Analysis Worksheet
- EnerNOC Case Study
- Talus Case Study

Additional resources will be added as new and updated examples and information become available.

Notes

1. William Aulet and Gaëtan Bonhomme, *EnerNOC - 2008*. Cambridge, MA: MIT Sloan School of Management, August 24, 2008.
2. Jan Willem Erisman, Mark A. Sutton, James Galloway, Zbigniew Klimont, and Wilfried Winiwarter, "How a Century of Ammonia Synthesis Changed the World." *Nature Geoscience* 1, no. 10 (2008): 636–39. https://doi.org/10.1038/ngeo325.

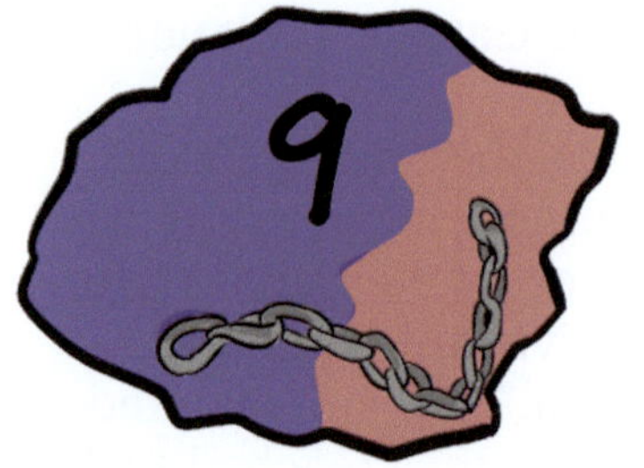

Get a Grip on Your Business Model

In This Step, You Will

- Work out where you should operate in the Value Chain.
- Develop an early concept of how your solution will make money, especially if you are pursuing an opportunity driven by business model innovation.
- Apply this analysis as an additional layer to your Market Segmentation.

Why This Step, and Why Now?

A business model describes how a venture makes money. The concept of a business model does not come up until Step 15 of the original Disciplined Entrepreneurship framework; however, this step comes much earlier in the process for climate and energy ventures, especially those commercializing new technology. Why do these ventures need to think about making money so much sooner? It seems awfully greedy for entrepreneurs who are largely driven by their desire to save the planet. The reason is not so much about capturing as much value as possible but rather figuring out your place the Value Chain.

Like energy in the food chain, value moves through different levels of customers, taking different forms for each.[1] Think of a grain of sand. That simple grain of sand could be an input to something far more complex, like a solar panel, but it takes many steps to get there. First, the grain gets collected with many other grains and sold to a refiner. Then, the purified silicon crystals get bought and sold through a series of manufacturers who make increasingly more valuable products: a polysilicon ingot, a wafer, a solar cell, and full solar module. Ultimately, the solar module gets installed as part of a project where it can generate electricity. Possibly, the material gets recycled when it reaches the end of its life. That whole process is called the Value Chain.

Now, let's say you have invented an alternative to silicon, an improvement to that initial grain of sand. Where do you sell it on that Value Chain? There is no easy answer. You could conceivably enter the Value Chain at multiple places. You could do as much as possible yourself and capture all the value, but then you would need to figure out all the extra steps and possibly do them poorly. Or you could sell your product early in the Value Chain and risk another player further along the Value Chain capturing the value you have created. It is a difficult trade-off. The right choice depends on the properties of your particular solution and your potential markets, and it is one of the most important decisions that you will make about your venture. It determines what product you build and whom you sell it to, so you must get a grip on your business model before you select your initial market.

Find Your Place in the Value Chain

Begin this step by mapping out your Value Chain. List all the various links of the chain. Draw on your Solutions Context from Step 2. Then, assess where you might choose to focus along that chain. You can use Table 9.1 as a guide.

Table 9.1: *Value Chain Matrix.*

Name of Value Chain link	In a few words, summarize each link in your Value Chain.
Technology fit	How well suited is your technology for this link in the Value Chain? What additional capabilities would you need to develop to operate here?
Customers	Who are the major customers that you would be selling to? Provide specific examples.
Competitors	What other players exist at this link of the chain? How satisfied are customers with their solutions?
Suppliers	What key inputs or components do you need to operate at this link in the chain? Where might you source them from? How easy or difficult would this be?
Business models	Based on the previous answers, which business models would make sense at this link of the chain? What are competitors doing? What do customers expect? What limitations might you face based on the capacity of your technology or the earlier links in the chain?

Common Business Models for Climate and Energy Ventures

To complete this step, you'll need to understand a few common business models in the climate and energy space. Remember that we are working at a very high level right now. You are not coming up with a detailed value-capture strategy or a go-to-market plan—you haven't even selected a market yet! For now, you are just wrapping your head around where and how your solution will operate so that you can find the right customers. Also keep in mind that the business models described here are not mutually exclusive, and they are not set in stone. Many ventures evolve their approach over time.

- **Direct sales of the final product.** This is the most straightforward model. You develop a novel technology or product and sell it directly to your customer. Companies using this model can build, own, and operate their own manufacturing or outsource production to third-party contract manufacturers.

- **Licensing.** You license your intellectual property (IP) to another company, which uses its own resources to build and own the solution. This approach enables you to avoid the complexity and cost of scaling production yourself. The downside is that the licensee captures the upside from selling the output, and there's always a risk they may attempt to replicate your technology, so strong IP protection is critical. Licensing can be particularly challenging for startups because it's difficult to find large companies willing to take a risk on unfamiliar technologies without clear benefits or established demand.

- **Equipment sales.** You develop a proprietary product and sell the equipment needed to produce it to manufacturers who then sell the end product to customers. This model enables you to focus on your core innovation while leveraging others to handle production and distribution. It works well when your equipment is a critical enabler of the final product.

- **Distributors.** In this model, you do not produce anything novel but you bundle other products together and possibly tie in additional services, such as data insights.

- **Developers.** Developers focus on creating infrastructure projects, such as solar farms or wind projects, and selling them to long-term owners once they're operational or near completion. This model lets you capture the high-value development phase without tying up capital in long-term ownership. It's a proven approach in renewable energy but requires expertise in project development, permitting, and financing.

- **Own and operate for a fee.** In this model, you retain ownership of the solution or asset and charge customers a fee for its use or the service it provides. For example, companies that build and operate renewable energy projects often sell electricity through power purchase agreements. This model provides long-term revenue streams but requires significant up-front capital and operational expertise.

- **Shared savings.** This model involves sharing the financial benefits of cost savings with your customer. For instance, energy service companies might install efficiency upgrades at no up-front cost to the customer and then split the energy bill savings over time. While this aligns incentives, it's notoriously difficult to implement due to disagreements over baselines and changing conditions. Success requires clear contracts and robust measurement systems.

- **Asset management.** Here, you manage assets owned by others, such as renewable energy projects or energy storage systems, in exchange for a management fee or a share of the revenue. This model leverages your expertise in optimizing performance and reducing costs without requiring you to own the assets outright. It's a lower-risk way to generate steady income but depends on your ability to demonstrate value through operational excellence.

- **Joint venture.** A joint venture combines elements of licensing and ownership. You partner with a customer or another company to co-develop and co-own a solution, sharing both risks and rewards. For example, you might co-develop a carbon capture facility with an industrial partner, where they provide financing and you bring the technology. This model enables you to gain operational experience and share in the upside, but it requires strong alignment with your partner and can be complex to structure.

- **Move higher up the Value Chain.** In this model, you sell a critical component or technology that integrates into a larger system. For instance, you might develop a breakthrough battery material and sell it to battery manufacturers rather than producing full batteries yourself. This approach enables you to focus on your core innovation while leveraging existing players in the Value Chain to scale. The trade-off is that your customers may capture more of the downstream value your innovation creates.

The Importance of Business Model Innovation

As you consider the business models we just described, keep in mind that "none of the above" remains a completely valid option, and you can create value by pioneering a model that has not already been tried or that has only been tried in a different industry.

In many cases, business model innovation is the main driver of opportunity for climate and energy ventures. As described by former US Secretary of Energy Ernie Moniz, the energy industry involves many "exquisite supply chains." It is a vast and intricate system, and this complexity creates opportunities for you to find shortcuts and disruptions.

What Does the Value Chain Look Like for Software and Services?

The early focus on the Value Chain is most relevant for deep tech ventures that are developing hardware products. For other types of ventures, it's a little more straightforward. Software ventures often sell directly to the user or the user's organization. Project developers bring many organizations together to create value at the project level.

Even if you are building a solution in one of those categories, you still have important decisions to make about your value capture strategy, especially if you are aiming to commercialize a newly developed business model. Business model innovation requires you to be extremely intentional about your market selection. You should seek customers who have the most to gain from a more direct or efficient way of doing business.

What If My Product Is a Commodity?

For many climate and energy ventures, the technology is highly novel and complex, but the output is essentially a commodity (e.g., a kilowatt-hour of electricity, a kilogram of hydrogen, or a liter of clean water). The business model is easy in those cases, right? Just sell the commodity to someone who's already buying it, at the same price or lower than what's already on the market.

Producing a commodity and selling it on the open market makes sense in theory, but it is not always an available option. There are some key questions to answer first: at what scale do you need to build your technology to compete on price with the existing commodity market, if you can compete on price at all? Roughly what would it cost to build the technology at that scale? Are there smaller functional versions of your technology you can build along the pathway to scale? What are the economics for those versions? Do you need to charge a premium for the sustainability benefits?

Fortunately, you have a tool at your disposal to answer some of those questions: your Techno-Economic Analysis (TEA)! Go back to your TEA to figure out what a pathway to technical feasibility might look like. Then you can start to plan out what your business model might look like at each stage of that pathway.

Output from This Step

It may be daunting to identify a business model before you have a clear idea of your customer or your solution, but you do not need to have everything figured out just yet. Right now, you only need to get a grip on the options and how they might affect your market selection.

If you are considering where to enter in a complex Value Chain, start by completing the Value Chain Matrix in Table 9.1.

Next, add another row to your Market Segmentation Matrix called "Business Model Compatibility." If you don't need to navigate a complex Value Chain, you might be able to jump right to this part. Summarize your key findings for each market segment. Which market segments are compatible with your initial business model? Which ones are more compatible with business models that you can adopt later? Are there any segments that you can rule out entirely?

In some cases, you may find it useful to create an entirely separate Market Segmentation Matrix for each link of the Value Chain because each involves a different set of customers.

EXAMPLES

Ayar Labs

Alex Wright-Gladstein and the Ayar Labs team were commercializing a computer chip that could communicate with light instead of electricity, unlocking massive improvements in speed and energy efficiency. Early on, they faced a key decision—where in the Value Chain to introduce the technology. Should they build a whole new breed of computer chip? Or should they license the IP to other players with more experience in building chips?

What about vertically integrating and building entire data centers? Then, they could sell superfast and efficient cloud services. That would be the most lucrative opportunity, but it would mean going head-to-head with some of the major behemoths of the tech industry.

Before deciding, they did extensive primary market research and learned that a shift was underway in the semiconductor industry. In the past, chipmakers had included many different functionalities on huge single chips. More recently, they had begun to split that functionality into separate smaller chips called *chiplets* that got bundled together into what was called a *chip package*. This new development opened a Window of Opportunity for Ayar Labs. They could sell chiplets to established chipmakers, striking a balance between building the simplest possible version of the product and capturing as much value as possible.

Choosing to build their light-based capabilities into a chiplet gave them some idea of where to focus the technology development process and narrowed the field of potential customer segments.

Helix Carbon

Helix Carbon had a better way to turn carbon dioxide into useful products, but the challenge was figuring out who would pay for it.

They did a TEA and calculated that, under the right conditions, they could produce syngas, a mixture commonly used in industrial applications, below the market price. The economics worked best when they did everything on-site at an industrial facility, and their technology was well suited for that. They could use flue gas directly from a waste stream, without needing additional purification. They also had a long-lasting catalyst, so the system wouldn't need much maintenance. These technical considerations helped them narrow their Market Segmentation. They focused on markets where customers both produced carbon dioxide as a waste product and used syngas as an input.

They also needed to think about their business model. Two potential markets seemed most appealing: plastic polymers and steel. Both were a good fit for the technology. However, Helix Carbon's system would be extremely expensive to build at scale, to the tune of tens of millions of dollars, and they needed a customer who could finance a project of that size. Eventually, they wanted to own and operate their own facilities and make money from selling syngas, but they knew that would be hard to do at the beginning. Instead, they planned to start making money by selling the entire system, which meant they needed a customer with a low cost of capital who was accustomed to financing and owning large infrastructure projects. That would have been a hard sell for the plastic polymers industry, but it was fairly run-of-the-mill for steel.

Once they factored in their business model considerations, the choice was an easy one. They would focus on steel.

ADDITIONAL RESOURCES

There are additional resources for this step at www.de4cev.com/step9. These materials include the following:

- Value Chain Worksheet
- Business Model Worksheet
- Ayar Labs Case Study
- Helix Carbon Case Study

Additional resources will be added as new and updated examples and information become available.

Note

1. Some savvy readers might criticize this analogy because energy is lost at each level of the food chain, while value is gained at each level of the Value Chain. This is valid. Kudos to you for your ecological knowledge.

Select Market Stepping Stones

In This Step, You Will

- Determine a decently sized Beachhead Market that is reachable and winnable with the simplest and fastest-to-build version of your solution.
- Set your sights on the Big Prize, which is a massive global market that would enable you to have a transformative impact on people and the planet.
- Identify reasonable Market Stepping Stones that enable you to move incrementally from the Beachhead Market to the Big Prize.

Why This Step, and Why Now?

Alright, we're finally here. It's time for you to choose a market! And not just one market but a series of them. The original *Disciplined Entrepreneurship* advocates for initially staying laser-focused on the Beachhead Market, using a classic land-and-expand strategy. We are not contradicting that wisdom but adding nuance to it.

Climate and energy ventures very much need to start by focusing on a Beachhead Market. However, this is almost always a stepping stone to other markets, leading toward a very large long-term market opportunity that we call the Big Prize. The Big Prize is a massive global market with the potential to keep growing, and capturing a significant share of that market would have a transformative impact for people and the planet.

This is not entirely unusual. Using the beachhead as a stepping stone toward bigger opportunities is an explicit part of the original 24 Steps. As part of choosing a Beachhead Market, you need to see a path to significant additional markets in order to scale your venture to a level where it has meaningful impact. The difference for climate and energy ventures is that you need to set your sights on the Big Prize early, at the same time as selecting a beachhead. You might even identify the Big Prize first and work backwards to figure out the right beachhead.

It can take many years and millions of dollars to build a successful venture. For that to be worthwhile for you (and for your investors, if or when you have them), there needs to be a big potential payoff down the line. You need to have a clear vision of the Big Prize and a plausible pathway to get there.

The Beachhead Market: Your First Stepping Stone on the Path to Scale

It is important to be strategic with your choice of a Beachhead Market. Your initial focus should be on customers who highly value what you offer, are willing and able to buy a product at your stage or from an early-stage company within a reasonable time frame, and who can enable you to grow the business.

A strong beachhead sets you on a course to the Big Prize, while also bringing some critical early revenue in the door. The revenue from the product should be higher than your costs, but you should not necessarily expect your venture to be profitable based on your beachhead alone—although it's much better and a huge advantage if it can be!

In some cases, you can start by selling a product at a loss. This can help you shorten the path to market when dealing with long sales cycles, but it is risky. Be careful if you go down this route. You need to have the funds to do it, and you need to have a tight plan (ideally based on firm quotes) on how you get your costs down, as jokes about making up for it in volume get tiresome rather quickly. You also need to be sure that your original offering is sufficiently impressive that it gives your company a positive reputation, not a negative one. It does not have to be perfect or the full product, but it still needs to create meaningful value for the customer and show the potential for more in the future.

A critical aspect of the Beachhead Market is that it enables you to start developing the technology behind your solution without needing to build it at full scale. Ideally, a beachhead should be reachable with the simplest and fastest-to-build version of your solution. This enables you to prove out some of the assumptions behind your Techno-Economic Analysis (TEA) in a relatively short period of time. Critically, it starts the customer feedback loop to keep you focused on building the right product that the customer will pay for.

The beachhead should also generally be a market that exists today at full maturity (or something close to it). This point may seem painfully obvious, but climate and energy ventures often deal with systems in a state of flux. The world is undergoing a massive energy transition and unprecedented geophysical shifts. These changes are bound to upend existing markets and create new ones. Entrepreneurs in this space need not only to understand the current state of affairs but also to anticipate a potential future that looks very different. The hockey player Wayne Gretzky put it more concisely: skate to where the puck is going to be, not where it has been. This is all well and good for some of the later Market Stepping Stones, but not for the early ones. Your beachhead customers should be ready to buy as soon as you have a product ready. When you are working with a complex technology, there is already a risk that your solution may not work at all, so there should be little to no risk that your customers will buy it once it does.

Expanding Beyond Your Beachhead

Once you have selected your Beachhead Market, the original Disciplined Entrepreneurship framework presents two directions for expansion. You can sell your existing product to a new market, or you can sell a new product to your existing market. Selling a new product to a new market is almost always a recipe for failure. This remains true for climate and energy ventures, but they have to think about it slightly differently. The stepping stones should be driven by the evolution of the solution, both the technology and the business model. Each subsequent stepping stone should give you a chance to build a bigger and better version of the solution, or possibly to implement an improved business model.

DISCIPLINED ENTREPRENEURSHIP

REFER TO STEP

24

PRODUCT PLAN

For any solution driven primarily by technological innovation (tech push), you are more likely to expand by selling the next version of your solution to new markets than by selling new solutions to the same market. That being said, if you can sell an improved solution to the same market, that is ideal, because you already know the market well, but it's likely you have already met their needs. That means you will often need to move onto a different market at this stage. Remember, you should not be trying to sell a totally new product to a new market. You should be selling an evolution of your existing product to a new market. Unfortunately, this strategy brings some of the same challenges as selling a new product to a new market, because you need to learn how to sell to the new market while also adapting your solution. This is a key difficulty for tech-push ventures.

To address this challenge, climate and energy entrepreneurs sometimes work on multiple versions of their solution simultaneously. They build a version of their solution for their Beachhead Market, while also developing the technology to apply it to subsequent stepping stones. Is this split focus a distraction? Absolutely. Does this make them undisciplined? Maybe. It depends on whether or not they are doing so with a clear plan in mind, coupled with their confidence in their company's ability to access additional capital. Given the long timelines for many climate and energy solutions, splitting time and attention across multiple stepping stones can often be a necessity. That is why we recommend planning out Market Stepping Stones. The disciplined approach is to be strategic about managing limited resources and to focus as much as possible on the beachhead.

Eyes on the Prize

Your Beachhead Market and your subsequent Market Stepping Stones should all lead to a clear destination: the Big Prize. This is the ultimate goal of your venture: a large market with a large climate impact. The Big Prize is a solution that benefits both people and planet. It should effectively solve the global problem that you identified in the earlier steps of this book. As such, in many cases, it may make the most sense for you to start by identifying the Big Prize and then work backwards to identify the appropriate Market Stepping Stones to get there. However, in other cases, the stepping stones may help you to set your sights on a Big Prize that is both meaningful and attainable.

How to Choose Your Stepping Stones

We have put together a set of questions that will help guide you in selecting your Market Stepping Stones (Table 10.1). Ultimately, the right Market Stepping Stones depend on the specific aspects of your technology and the state of the market landscape. Decide carefully and strive for alignment across your team because this path is one of the most important elements of your strategy as an early-stage venture. You are building a whole organization on selling to your customer. It may be very difficult to adjust that organization toward a different set of markets as you progress.

Total Addressable Market (TAM) Calculation

For each of your stepping stones, you should calculate a Total Addressable Market (TAM). The TAM will be helpful in determining whether the market is too big or too small, but remember that it is a general estimate. You should not present it as a precise number. It is important to always show your assumptions so that others can understand your logic. You should be most precise about your Beachhead TAM. You can be looser in approximating your subsequent stepping stones, which are more likely to be ballpark estimates.

Table 10.1: *Guiding Questions for Selecting Your Market Stepping Stones.*

	Beachhead Market	**Middle Stepping Stones**	**Big Prize**
Market size	Is it big enough to sustain the company to the next phase of growth? But small enough that you are not trying to take on too much?	Is it larger than the Beachhead Market? Is it big enough to sustain the company in the next phase of growth?	Is the target market large enough to create a satisfying payoff for investors, potentially arriving many years down the line?
Solution compatibility	Can you reach this market with the simplest and quickest-to-build version of your solution?	Does it enable a productive evolution of your technology—a big enough jump that you're learning new things but a small enough jump that it will not take too long to get there?	Does your solution give you a competitive value proposition in this market?
Time and path to market	How soon can you start making revenue? What barriers exist to get to that point? Can you reasonably access these customers as a new venture? Will they buy from you?	How soon can you expand to this market? Is this market a step closer to your long-term goal, rather than a distraction? Is the target market one you will be able to access directly or through realistic partners?	Do you have a reasonable path to access this market in the long term? How long will it take to reach to this market? Will investors be patient enough for you to get to this point?
Innovation	Are customers willing to try brand-new technology?	Are customers willing to try still-evolving technology?	Are the customers willing to switch from their status quo?
Willingness to pay	Will customers pay a premium for the initial solution?	Will customers pay a premium for an evolving solution?	Can you charge a competitive price at scale? Do customers have a compelling reason to buy?
Policy	Does the target market have relevant Sticks and Carrots? Are these likely to change in the short term?	Does the target market have relevant Sticks and Carrots? Are these likely to change in the medium term?	Does the target market have relevant Sticks and Carrots? Are these likely to change in the long term?
Climate	Do customers care enough about climate to pay a high premium?	Do customers care enough about climate to pay a moderate premium?	Is the target market large enough that success at scale would have a substantial positive impact on the planet?
Personal filter	Is the market consistent with the values, passions, and goals of your team?		

When discussing TAM, remember to clarify the scope. There is the Beachhead TAM, which will be small enough for you to address and get your arms around and win, but then there will be the TAM for each Market Stepping Stone and the Big Prize. These follow-on TAMs will be much larger, and they represent the dream of the new venture in the long term.

Beachhead TAM

Start by estimating the number of end users in the Beachhead Market. You will use a combination of top-down analysis (based on secondary market research) and bottom-up analysis, what is called *counting noses* (i.e., counting the number of end users one by one).

In a top-down analysis, you will use what you know about your customers (more on this in Step 11) to locate secondary research that helps you demonstrate how many of them exist.

Once you have determined the number of end users in your market, determine how much revenue each end user is worth to you each year. This part is tougher. Remember, you're not determining the price of your product (that starts in later steps); you're making a first-pass estimate on the customer's willingness and ability to pay for a solution. Don't indicate precision that you clearly do not have, but instead focus on getting the right order of magnitude.

Here are three good ways to start an estimate on the annualized revenue per end user:

- **Customer's current spend.** Identify how much customers already spend on existing solutions or products to address the same pain point, and use those expenditures as a benchmark.

- **Customer's available budget.** Figure out the customer's overall income or revenue and estimate what portion of that could be allocated to your solution.

- **Comparables:** Look to similar products or solutions in a different market, and use those as a benchmark. Finding accurate parallels between markets might require some creative thinking on your part.

Generally, in the United States, a Beachhead TAM that is between $20 million per year and $100 million per year is a good target. Anything above that, and especially if it is over $1 billion, will suggest that the Beachhead TAM is too big for a startup to reasonably conquer, and further segmentation will be beneficial. Some climate and energy ventures might veer toward a very large TAM, especially if they are selling electricity or other widely used commodities, but remember we are focusing only on the Beachhead TAM, not the entire market opportunity. It is even possible that an initial TAM of $5 million per year could be a successful business, if you can capture that first market quickly and convincingly.

Subsequent Stepping Stones

Use the same general methodology to calculate the TAM for each follow-on market, but for this step you really only need ballpark estimates. You should not spend much time on follow-on TAMs right now—probably one-tenth or less of the effort and analysis you did for your Beachhead Market. You probably collected much of the information you need for this step during your initial Market Segmentation (Step 7).

If you want to attract venture capital and build a big business, the general rule is that the broader TAM (for 10 or fewer follow-on markets), plus your Beachhead TAM, should add up to over $1 billion. Some investors might even want to see market opportunities greater than $10 billion. Bigger is generally better for the TAM of the later Market Stepping Stones and the Big Prize, but not for the Beachhead TAM.

Output from This Step

Use the guide in Table 10.1 to help you select a reasonable set of Market Stepping Stones, including your Beachhead Market and your Big Prize. Not all of the market segments that you identified in Step 7 need to be included as Market Stepping Stones. In fact, most of them should not be. Your stepping stones should be the markets that you actually plan to tackle, in the order that you plan to tackle them. Your team should make these selections rigorously and strategically.

Calculate a TAM for each of your Market Stepping Stones using the methods described earlier in this step, and add them up to get an overall TAM for your venture.

EXAMPLES

Solugen

We have previously mentioned the high price of poker for climate and energy ventures. Few founders understand that concept better than Sean Hunt and Gaurab Chakrabarti, who met over a poker game!

Sean was an expert in metal catalysts, and Gaurab was an expert in biological catalysts (also known as enzymes). Both thought that their respective technologies were underused in chemical production. Eventually, they realized that by combining these catalysts, they could get the best of both worlds.

They developed an initial reaction to turn sugar into a mix of hydrogen peroxide and organic acids. Their Big Prize was to turn Solugen into a major chemicals company, producing chemicals with sugar and starch rather than fossil fuels. They knew they would not be able to go toe-to-toe with large-scale chemical manufacturers right away. They could only compete on price when they reached economies of scale.

They started with a Beachhead Market that may not be intuitive: float spas (also called *sensory deprivation tanks*). The float spas had one thing Solugen was very good at dealing with: dirty water. Solugen's initial product was an excellent cleaning agent. Also, critically, the float spa owners were willing to buy small quantities of chemicals for a high average selling price.

For their next Stepping Stone, they aimed to sell higher volumes at a higher price, so they launched a line of cleaning wipes called Ode to Clean, which they sold directly to consumers online.

After that, they needed an even bigger stepping stone. They learned that upstream oil and gas companies were dealing with a water chemistry that was not too different from float spas, but in much larger volumes. This market would support a full-scale plant and propel Solugen closer their Big Prize.

Carbon-to-Fuel Technology

After finishing his PhD at Yale University, Staff Sheehan developed a new way to turn carbon dioxide into hydrocarbons and alcohols, including ethanol. His TEA revealed that he could achieve relatively low-cost ethanol, giving him confidence the technology had commercial potential. Staff knew making fuel would be the most exciting Big Prize because global demand for low-carbon fuels was set to grow as industries and governments sought to decarbonize.

Staff also knew that he couldn't get to low-cost fuels right away. It was a huge market to tackle, and he wouldn't be able to produce fuels at a high enough volume or a low enough cost in the early days. Instead, he needed Market Stepping Stones.

Staff decided to start with a completely different Beachhead Market: alcoholic spirits. He and his team set up a small facility in Brooklyn and began selling air-based vodka to the hottest bars in New York City. Spirits are basically just ethanol and water, so they were not too difficult to produce with Staff's technology, and by focusing heavily on the branding and storytelling, the team could charge a high premium.

Then, when COVID hit, they began making hand sanitizer, and then a couple years later, they started making perfume. It helped immensely that they were selling consumer products, which they could sell at a premium with strong marketing, rather than trying to start by selling a commodity like fuel.

These early Market Stepping Stones provided enough technical progress that Staff and his team could start to focus on the fuel market. They began producing fuel for test flights and launched partnerships with major airlines as well as the US government. They were still a long way away from fully capturing the Big Prize, but their earlier Stepping Stones got them close enough to give it a shot.

A123 Systems

After a thorough Market Segmentation (which we covered in Step 7), the team at A123 Systems selected power tools as their Beachhead Market. One of the technology's core strengths was high power, so tools with A123 batteries had more power than what you plug into the wall!

They did well in this market, which enabled them to raise substantial funds from government and private investors, but investors pressured them to go right for the Big Prize. This led them to pursue General Motors' flagship plug-in hybrid product, the Volt, as an entry point into the electric vehicle (EV) market, which was quite nascent at the time.

A123 took massive steps to pursue this market, but unfortunately GM selected a large and established supplier with higher energy density for their Volt battery supply. A123 also ran into other issues when a different customer recalled many cars that were already on the road. This led to the company entering bankruptcy in 2012.

Chinese conglomerate Wanxiang then bought up A123's assets after a bidding war. The twist of the story is that Wanxiang ended up using A123's technology to sell car batteries. Not powertrain batteries like A123 had been trying to do, but rather the smaller 12-volt batteries that are used to start the engine and power electrical components in gas-powered cars. This is not a sexy market for investors, but it's a much better Market Stepping Stone than trying to jump to the hybrid or EV market right away. Advances in A123's technology meant that Wanxiang could eventually compete in the EV market a full decade later.

Hypotheticals are tricky, but it is possible that if A123 had more cautiously selected their Market Stepping Stones, then they could have eventually captured their Big Prize in the EV market.

ADDITIONAL RESOURCES

There are additional resources for this step at www.de4cev.com/step10. These materials include the following:

- Market Stepping Stones Worksheet
- Solugen Case Study
- Carbon Conversion Technology Case Study
- A123 Systems Case Study

Additional resources will be added as new and updated examples and information become available.

Profile Personas Across the Decision-Making Unit (DMU)

In This Step, You Will

- Build a systematic understanding of the people who use your solution and who make or influence the decision to acquire it.

- Use primary market research (PMR) to create detailed demographic and psychographic profiles of these individuals.

- Identify real people as Personas who will embody the different perspectives and create thorough fact sheets about them to further enhance your understanding.

Why This Step, and Why Now?

Now that you know which markets you're targeting, you need to understand the customers within those markets, starting with your beachhead.

You may hear the terms *customers* and *market* used interchangeably, but they are very different. A market is an abstraction representing a group of people and organizations with similar characteristics, but customers are always specific people. Even when a startup is selling business to business (B2B), which is the case for many climate and energy ventures, they're still selling to people because businesses are just organizations of people. In this step, you will identify the specific people who use your product, as well as everyone involved with the decision to buy it.

At this stage, focus on customers within your Beachhead Market. It is important to maintain focus on the tangible next steps to keep the company going. If you don't nail the beachhead, it will be much harder to reach the Big Prize.

The process of profiling Personas makes your target customer tangible so that all members of the founding team (and all employees) have absolute clarity and focus on the same goal of making your target customer successful and happy. Rather than guessing about what your potential customers might want, you can answer these questions definitively.

Mapping out the Decision-Making Unit (DMU)

If you are selling to a business, you will need to identify all the people who will be involved in the decision to acquire your solution. We call this the *Decision-Making Unit (DMU).* Some people will actively approve or block the acquisition, while others will present opinions that can sway the acquisition process.

There are three primary roles in the DMU:

- **End user.** This is the person who will actually use the product.

  - For climate and energy ventures, the end user is often someone in an industrial facility whose primary concerns are keeping things running without disruption and not spending too much money. Climate is usually low on their list of priorities, if it shows up at all.

  - Your end user could also be an individual consumer. For instance, this could be someone who is putting solar panels on their roof, replacing their heating system, buying plant-based food or an electric vehicle, or seeking out products with a low carbon footprint. Even when climate is a motivator, these consumers will not want to make many trade-offs, and they will want options that provide them with a better overall experience.

- **Primary economic buyer.** This is who will pay you when the end user uses the product. This person controls the budget. Sometimes, the primary economic buyer is also the end user. There may also be multiple economic buyers in some cases. For climate and energy ventures selling to businesses, the economic buyer is often a more senior person in the company who cares more about cost and performance than climate.

- **Champion.** The champion is the trusted internal person who advocates for the purchase of the product. This may or may not be the end user or economic buyer. The champion may also be referred to as the *advocate.* Many climate and energy entrepreneurs will spend a lot of time engaging with a company's sustainability lead. This person can be a valuable champion since they are the most likely stakeholder within the organization to prioritize the climate benefits.

However, they are not your user or economic buyer. The sustainability lead can be a fantastic entry point to the rest of the organization and a key advocate for your cause, but they rarely hold decision-making power.

There are also three additional roles within the DMU to consider:

- **Primary and secondary influencers.** These individuals often have a depth of experience in the subject matter and can influence the rest of the DMU, including the champion and end user.
- **Person with veto power.** These individuals can reject a purchase for any reason. In climate and energy, regulatory compliance is a common reason that solutions are vetoed. The person with veto power is usually either a regulator or a compliance officer within the organization. Review your policy analysis (Step 8) to make sure you understand relevant policy considerations!
- **Purchasing department.** This department handles the logistics of the purchase. Individuals in this department can be another obstacle because they primarily look to drive prices down, even after the decision to purchase has been made by the primary economic buyer. In general, you should neutralize them but not sell to them directly.

Once you know some of the people in your DMU, they can help you fill in the gaps across the rest of the DMU. Usually, your first point of contact will be the sustainability champion or the end user. Ask them questions like these:

- Who else would be involved in the decision to pilot or purchase this solution?
- Who has the most influence on the decision?
- Who could stop this from happening?
- Whose budget will the money come from to pay for it?
- Who else needs to sign off?
- Who will feel threatened by this, and how do you think they will react?

Getting this information will help you start to understand the DMU, but it's not necessary to ask these questions all at once. In a B2B setting, make sure to talk with a number of different end users in the organization because they may have different pieces of the information you need. Remember: organizations don't buy products, people buy products.

Understanding your customer's DMU is integral to how you sell your product. It will give you insight into your odds of success and, importantly, the resources, skill, and time it will take for a new customer to acquire your product. The DMU exercise is especially important for climate and energy ventures because of the broader and more powerful set of players, like regulators.

Customer Profiles and Personas

You should develop detailed customer profiles and Personas for each person within the DMU.

A profile is a narrowly defined set of qualities that describes the people you most commonly find within a particular role of your DMU. It includes demographics (statistical qualities, like age and gender) and psychographics (psychological qualities, like fears and motivations). A Persona is a specific person (ideally a real person) with a name who represents a particular role within your DMU. Another way to describe these concepts is that a profile is a set of characteristics, while the Persona is a fully realized character.

The best way to find the Persona for your end user is by building a profile and then selecting someone who best fits that profile. Another approach starts by selecting a Persona and working backwards to build a profile with that person in mind.

This can be a useful shortcut for some of the secondary roles within your DMU. If you choose the second strategy, ensure that the Persona you select is truly representative of others you will encounter in that role, not an outlier. While some people are uncomfortable picking a real person, it is super helpful. It can also be difficult. If something is true in general, it must be true in specific, and you generate more credibility and confidence by using a real person as your Persona.

In either case, the most important way you can learn about the Personas in your DMU is through extensive PMR. You need to deeply understand each role, especially your end user and economic buyer, and you need to talk to many, many customers before you can determine which people and characteristics are truly representative of the larger group. Refer back to what you have already learned in Steps 2 and 3. If you have industry experience, that will be an asset for this part of the process.

The process of creating Personas is important, so you should involve all the key members of your team. Even if they do not think they have a lot to contribute, team members will end up enjoying, embracing, and getting a lot of value out of the process. They will feel ownership, understand the nuances that might not get written down, and gain appreciation for the other members of the team and their perspectives.

Output from This Step

Map out your customer's entire DMU and summarize your understanding by creating a series of fact sheets about the Persona for each role. Include an image of each individual and list their key characteristics. Once you have your fact sheets, summarize the key points somewhere visible to the whole team. You might start by taking large sheets of paper and posting them on the wall. Some ventures make a cardboard cutout of the end user Persona and keep it in the office. Other ventures refer to an electronic version to consider each Persona's perspective when making important decisions.

Include the following information in your fact sheets. You will not be able to find out everything right away, but the goal is to paint a picture that is rich and colorful.

- **Demographics.** Quantifiable traits like age, gender, income, and education. These characteristics will help you identify whom to target, but their usefulness depends on how well they reflect actual attitudes and behaviors.

- **Psychographics.** These are qualitative insights, like priorities, motivations, fears, and aspirations. They are harder to measure but critical for understanding your Persona's behavior and decision-making. In particular, make sure to identify the Persona's top priorities and rank them in order of importance.

- **Proxy products.** Analyze which similar products and solutions the Persona already buys. These purchases will reveal existing behaviors, complementary needs, and potential interest in your solution.

- **Watering holes.** These are physical or digital spaces (e.g., industry conferences, online forums) where your Persona gathers with other like-minded individuals. They are ideal channels for spreading information and validating user traits.

- **Day in the life.** Map the Persona's daily routine, priorities, and challenges. This provides a real-world context for how your solution fits into their workflow and improves their experience.

EXAMPLES

Mechanical Water Filtration Systems

A good example of profiling Personas across the DMU comes from a team with a water purification technology. Their Big Prize was drinking water, but for their Beachhead Market, they focused on data centers, which had fewer barriers to entry. They identified a strong value proposition: by reusing water for cooling, they could reduce environmental impact, electricity costs, and carbon emissions. As an added benefit, their solution improved uptime (the amount of time the data center could be in active operation).

Their PMR revealed that the end user was the facilities manager. After many interviews, the team started to get a clear picture of this end user by creating a Persona, Chuck. When the team first started, they believed their unique selling proposition was being environmentally friendly, but their PMR showed that Chuck cared very little about this.

Chuck's main priority was preventing data center downtime because both his higher-ups and customers expected data centers to be reliable. Business growth and budget constraints were priorities two and three. Environmental issues ranked only fourth in Chuck's priorities, but he had to be conversant in them. The team mapped out the rest of the DMU and explored the relationship among the facilities manager (Chuck), the data center manager (Steve), and the chief information officer or CIO (Sally). Steve, more ambitious and financially savvy, was the primary economic buyer, while Sally had veto power but little influence.

Other players you see on the map in Figure 11.1 had to be kept in mind as well, despite not being primary players in the process. Not understanding all these constituencies could lead

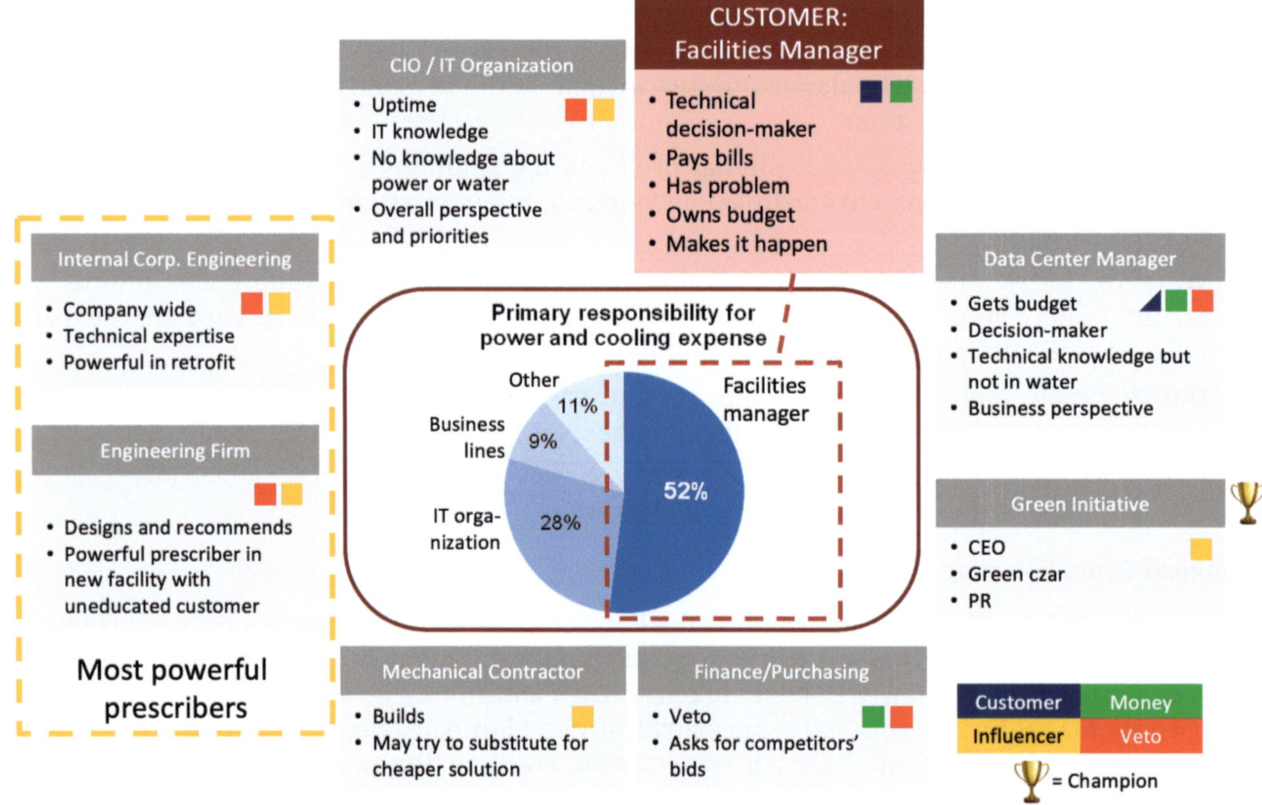

Figure 11.1: DMU for B2B Mechanical Water Filtration Systems example

to mystifying delays in the sales process; offending them or proposing something counter to their interests would likely kill the proposed sale.

Infinite Cooling

As MIT PhD students, Maher Damak and Karim Khalil developed Infinite Cooling to capture and reuse water from cooling towers. After talking with people at about a dozen power plants, they sketched out the DMU (see Figure 11.2).

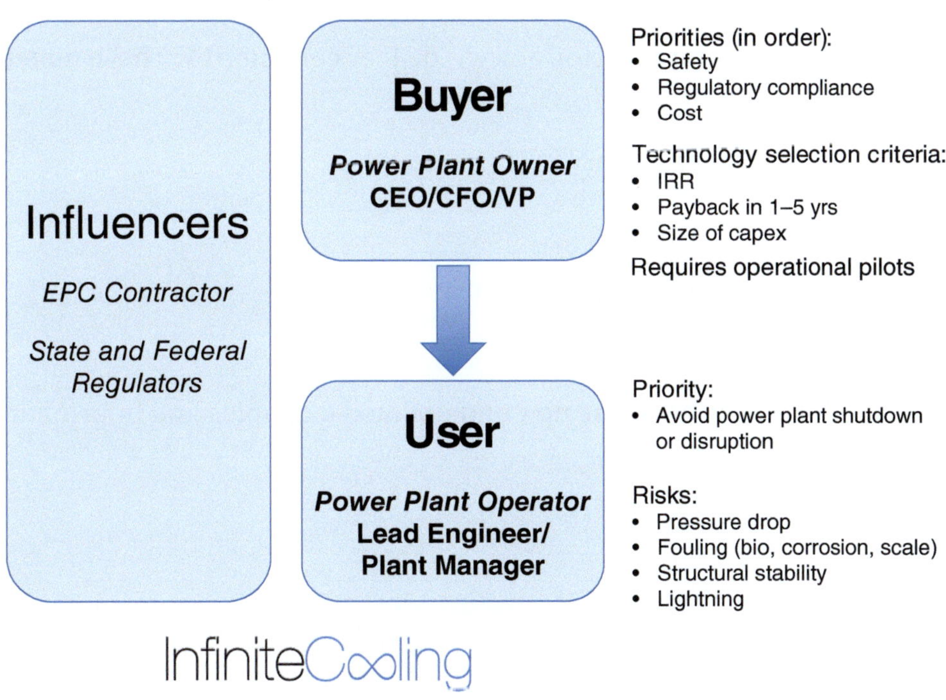

Figure 11.2: The DMU for Infinite Cooling, based on initial PMR.

The economic buyer was the power plant owner, who prioritized safety, regulatory compliance, and cost, in that order. Their decision-making hinged on financial metrics like internal rate of return and payback period. The end user was the operator, whose top priority was to avoid shutdowns or disruptions. To engage these users, Infinite Cooling needed to emphasize how their system would integrate seamlessly into existing operations without introducing risks like pressure drops, fouling, or structural instability. Influencers included government regulators, who could shut down projects for standards violations, as well as engineering contractors, who would evaluate and install new technologies.

ADDITIONAL RESOURCES

There are additional resources for this step at www.de4cev.com/step11. These materials include the following:

- End User Profile Worksheet
- Persona Worksheet
- DMU Worksheet
- Water Filtration Systems Case Study
- Infinite Cooling Case Study

Additional resources will be added as new and updated examples and information become available.

Define the Solution

In This Step, You Will

- Create concise verbal and visual representations of your solution for potential customers as well as your own team.

- Focus on the benefits of your solution and not just the features or the technology.

- Describe in detail how the Personas in your Decision-Making Unit (DMU) realize they have a problem/opportunity, find out about possible solutions, analyze those solutions, acquire a solution, use it, get value from it, pay for it, buy more, and tell others about it.

- Start to understand the full scope of the opportunity you are helping your customer to realize and the solution that you are building for them.

Why This Step, and Why Now?

Clearly defining your customer provides a consistent vision of whom you are serving. Everyone can then work toward that vision. It is just as important for your team to have a consistent vision of what you're offering to your customer. You may think that is obvious, but you would be surprised how individual team members can have totally different conceptions of what they're trying to build. In this step, your team needs agree on what it is that you're creating. Define the offering at a high level and map out how your customer will interact with it. An image of the solution is also important, even if it is just a simple diagram.

A clear and concise description of your offering will be helpful internally and externally as you communicate your venture to customers and various stakeholders who can help you in the journey. If you do this well, it will be a huge asset for startup prize competitions, where environmental impact often gives climate startups a leg up.

It is very important to *not* build your solution yet, as much as you might want to. Not only will you almost surely build the wrong thing, which will unnecessarily increase the already high costs of your entrepreneurial journey, but you could also stop listening to the customer and get attached to your solution.[1] In other words, you will move into advocacy mode when you should still be in inquiry mode with the customer at this point in the journey. Wait and be patient so that you build the right product.

Your Technology Is Not Your Solution

The traditional wisdom of *Disciplined Entrepreneurship* is that you should fall in love with your problem, not your product. But when you are commercializing deep tech, it can be true that your venture is somewhat married to your technology. It would be very hard to entirely abandon that technology and find a new one. At that point, you might as well start a whole new venture.

However, a technology is not a product or a solution. Just as there are many different problems you can solve with a given technology, there are also many ways that you can apply a given technology to solve a problem. In this step, we are not focusing on your technology's properties, but on the specific application of your technology to meet the needs of your customer. This definition of the solution differs from a technical explanation (though it may include one), and it can change over time, even with the same underlying technology.

It's easy to get deep in the weeds of the science, but usually your offering comes down to a set of inputs that gets turned into a set of useful outputs through some innovative process.

We can think of many climate and energy solutions as a box. Inside, there's some novel technology that functions better than the existing alternatives. The box is integrated into a process and improves it, usually by saving time, energy, or money. This whole system is the solution. A good Solution Definition needs to clearly explain what is happening inside the box, why it is unique, and how the box is integrated into a larger process.

Write a One-Line Summary of Your Solution

A good starting point for defining your solution is to summarize, in as few words as possible, what your venture does and for whom. This will give you a clear sense of the key elements to highlight. Work with your team to write a one-sentence description and come to a consensus. A good solution summary not only explains the solution but articulates why customers should want it.

One simple template you could use is the following:[2]

- For [xx people]—This comes from your market selection and Personas.
- Who have [yy problem]—This comes from your problem selection and Personas.
- We do [zz solution]—This is your solution summary and value proposition (Step 13).

Another format is even simpler.

- Our solution is _______.

Fill in the blank with something as specific and concrete as possible. It is maddening how many companies fill their websites and other material with generalities that don't explain what they actually do. Avoid writing something general like "Our solution is a novel technology that revolutionizes energy generation." In fact, avoid the terms *revolutionize*, *disrupt*, and "the future of _____." They are cliches that convey little meaningful information.

Here's a good one-line description from NONA Technologies, a company that we will discuss further as one of the examples for this step:

"We're making desalination effortless with cutting-edge electronic technology."

Create a High-Level Product Specification

At its core, a High-Level Product Specification is a drawing. It is a visual representation of what your product will be when it is finally developed, based on what you know at this point. You can draw it without understanding all the underlying details, coding, supply chain, manufacturing, and other elements to bring a real product to market. The goal is to have enough descriptive information for your target customer to give feedback and for you to gain consensus within your team on where you are going while maintaining flexibility.

To begin, take a blank piece of paper and make as simple a visual representation of your product as possible. Slowly increase the level of detail, but keep it simple. Only add what is essential. Key design considerations include the following:

- **Visual.** What does the solution look like? The important part here is that you have something concrete and specific enough that your team understands thoroughly.

- **Focus on benefits.** Focus on the benefits to the customer instead of the technology or the functionality. Think about the specific Personas you identified in Step 11. How does the solution address their top priorities?

- **High level.** Don't include too much detail! Offer just enough to show high-level functionality that will drive the benefits.

- **Hits the spot.** Make sure the product specification resonates deeply with the Personas across your DMU.
- **Flexible.** Make sure your product specification allows you to iterate with your various Personas across the DMU about key features, functions, and benefits.

It's amazing how much drawing a picture of what your product will be forces convergence on a team and removes misunderstandings. It sounds like it should be easy to do, but more often than not, entrepreneurs find it harder than expected because disagreements arise within the team. Now is the time to resolve any issues because later on the costs of doing so will be higher.

This simple visual representation of your product can now be shared with potential customers, immediately generating an unambiguous understanding of your product. You are not selling the product but rather interacting with customers to more thoroughly understand the strengths and weaknesses of your product spec. This is very important. There is still a lot to learn before you are sure you have the right product and know how you will make it, price it, and distribute it. Your product specification will change over time and be refined, like all of the other steps in this book.

Define the Customer Life Cycle Use Case

Once you have a clear definition of your solution, create a visual representation of how your customer will interact with it, from initially learning about the product all the way to encouraging others to buy it, too. This is called the *Customer Life Cycle Use Case*, and it enables you to see how the product will fit into the customer's Value Chain and what barriers to adoption might arise. We have flipped the order of the High-Level Product Specification and the Life Cycle Use Case from the original *Disciplined Entrepreneurship* because of the complexity of climate and energy solutions. Doing the product spec first makes it easier to understand the customer's life cycle.

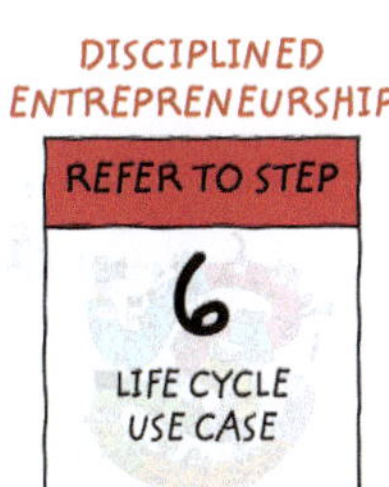

It is also helpful to outline your customer's current workflow because that makes it easier to integrate your product into their operation. Customers who are generally satisfied with their current process will rarely want to radically overhaul it, even if your product provides benefits over their current system.

The following factors are all essential parts of the Customer Life Cycle Use Case:

- How end users will determine they have a need and/or opportunity to do something different
- How they will find out about your solution
- How they will analyze your solution

- How they will acquire your solution

- How they will install your solution

- How they will use your solution

- How they will determine the value gained from your solution

- How they will pay for your solution

- How they will receive support for your solution

- How they will buy more product and/or spread awareness (hopefully positive) about your solution

The Customer Life Cycle Use Case should be visual, using diagrams, flow charts, or other methods that show sequence.

As a quick note of clarification, in the original *Disciplined Entrepreneurship*, the concept is called the *Full Life Cycle Use Case*. Here, we call it the *Customer Life Cycle Use Case* to clarify that we are only talking about the life cycle of the solution in relation to the end user. In sustainability science, the term *life cycle* refers to the full set of materials and processes that go into the solution as well as what happens to those materials when the solution is no longer in use. This is closely tied to the concept of the Value Chain (Step 9). At this stage, we are only concerned with the solution's life cycle as it pertains to the customer. We will discuss life cycle impacts beyond the customer in Step 15.

Output from This Step

Create a one-line description of your solution, a High-Level Product Specification, and a Customer Life Cycle Use Case. Come to agreement on these things as a team so that everyone has a common definition of the solution.

Then share this Solution Definition with potential customers through primary market research, and refine further based on their feedback

EXAMPLES

NONA Technologies

Bruce Crawford came to MIT to start or join a hardware company that added value to the world, and Junghyo Yoon's water desalination technology seemed to fit the bill. Traditional desalination happens either through distillation (boiling saltwater and then collecting the water vapor) or reverse osmosis (using a thin membrane to filter out the salt). Junghyo's technology separated salt and contaminants from water using an electric current, making the process simpler and cheaper for many potential applications. They decided to start by selling a portable desalination device to sailors to provide fresh drinking water at sea.

They began applying to various competitions, which gave them many chances to explain the technology to a broad audience. Bruce's nonexpert status proved to be an asset. Junghyo had what's called the *curse of knowledge*: he knew so much that it was hard to see things from the perspective of an outsider. Bruce was thinking about what a novice (like him) could easily understand and digest in just a few seconds.

We can look at some slides from their pitch decks to see the evolution of their Solution Definition. Their original explanation of the technology (Figure 12.1) is very much like what you might read in a scientific journal.

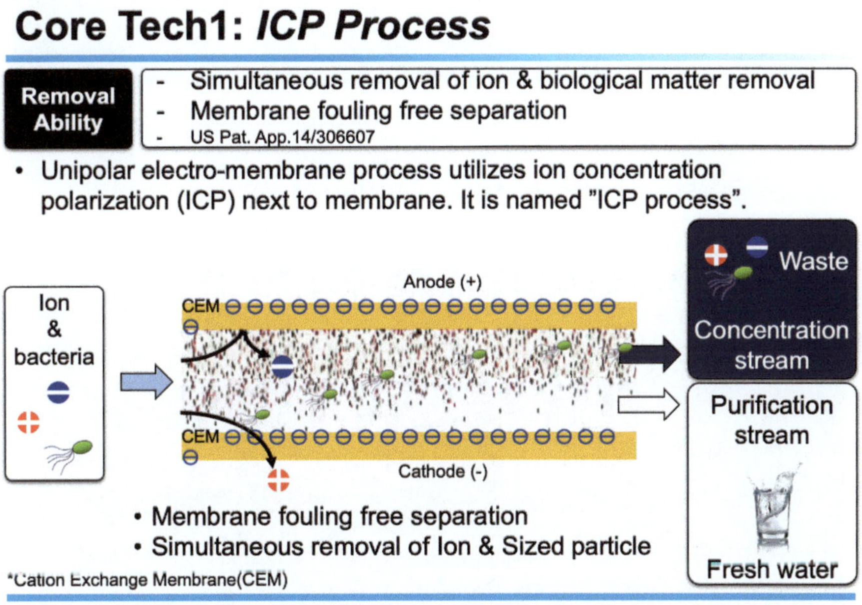

Core Tech1: *ICP Process*

Removal Ability
- Simultaneous removal of ion & biological matter removal
- Membrane fouling free separation
- US Pat. App.14/306607
• Unipolar electro-membrane process utilizes ion concentration polarization (ICP) next to membrane. It is named "ICP process".
Ion & bacteria
Anode (+)
CEM
CEM
Cathode (-)
Waste
Concentration stream
Purification stream
Fresh water
• Membrane fouling free separation
• Simultaneous removal of Ion & Sized particle
*Cation Exchange Membrane(CEM)

Figure 12.1: An early explanation of NONA's technology

Source: Adapted from Kwak, R., et al., (2016)
Markus Mainka / Adobe Stock Photos

The next iteration is more visually appealing with simpler text. It also focuses more on the benefits and less on the underlying science (see Figures 12.2 and 12.3).

They then made an even simpler version that got the point across in a matter of seconds.

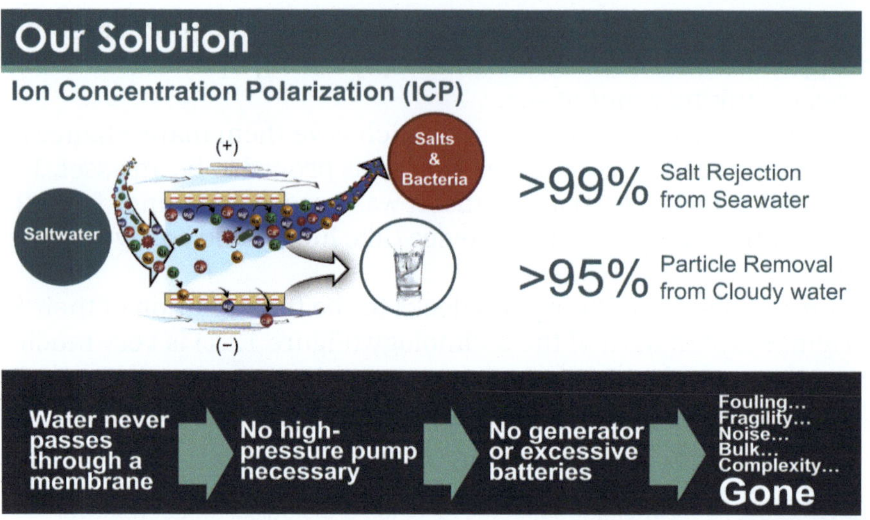

Figure 12.2: NONA adapted their explanation of the technology to make it more visually appealing, with clearer benefits to the end user.
Source: Markus Mainka / Adobe Stock Photos

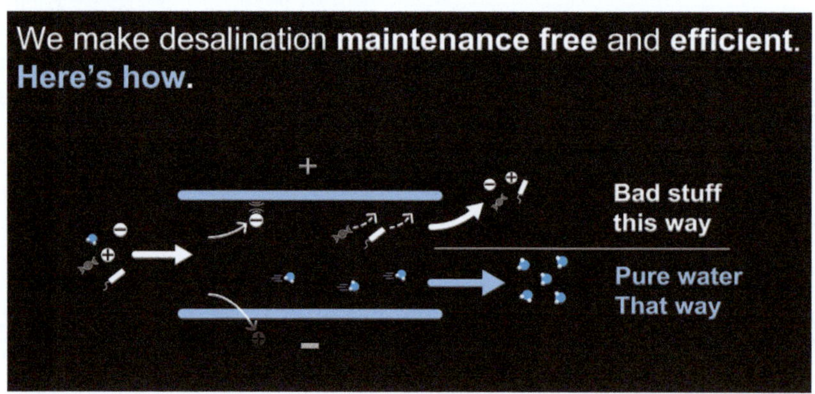

Figure 12.3: An even simpler explanation of NONA's technology.

So far, we have focused on their description of the technology, but as we mentioned before, a technology is not a product. They also created a rendering of what the product itself would look like (Figure 12.4).

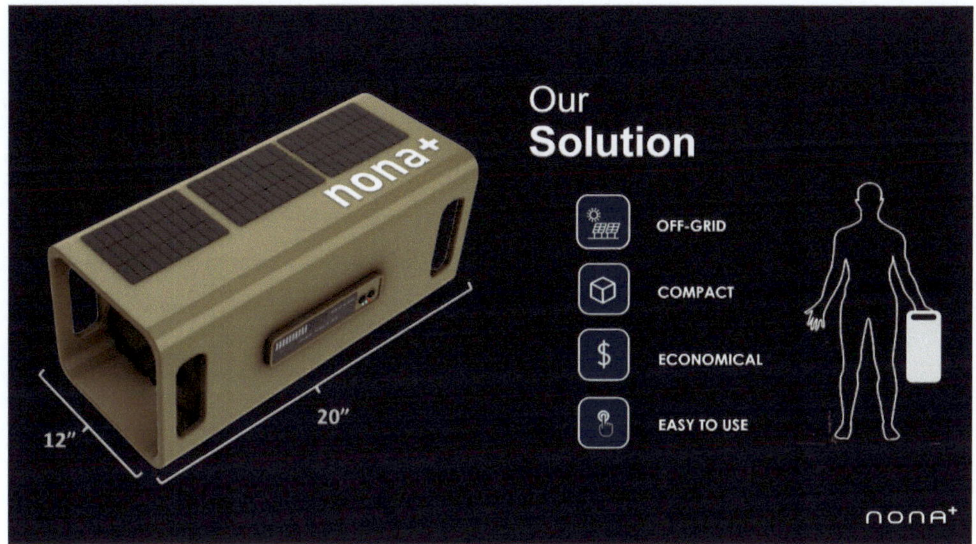

*Figure 12.4: A render of NONA's portable desalination product
Permission from Bruce Crawford of NONA Technologies.*

By translating complex science into clear, compelling narratives and visuals, Bruce and Junghyo were able to bridge the gap between technical innovation and market understanding. Their communication efforts paid off. In addition to gathering a long waitlist of potential customers, they also won MIT's $100K competition and successfully raised a Seed round from venture firms as of this writing.

Helix Carbon

Helix Carbon was developing a circular process to capture CO_2 and turn it into syngas for industrial applications, starting with the steel industry. Originally, they were using a DNA-based technology, where the DNA served as a sticky but easily detachable connector for their catalyst, kind of like a microscopic zipper. They often highlighted this innovation when communicating their solution (Figure 12.5).

Once they picked an initial Market Stepping Stone (steel plants), they started communicating less about the technology and more about the benefits of their solution for customers. In pitches, their overview of the technology was much shorter, and they focused on the whole electrolyzer rather than the catalysts or the DNA zipper (Figure 12.6). This not only made the pitch more

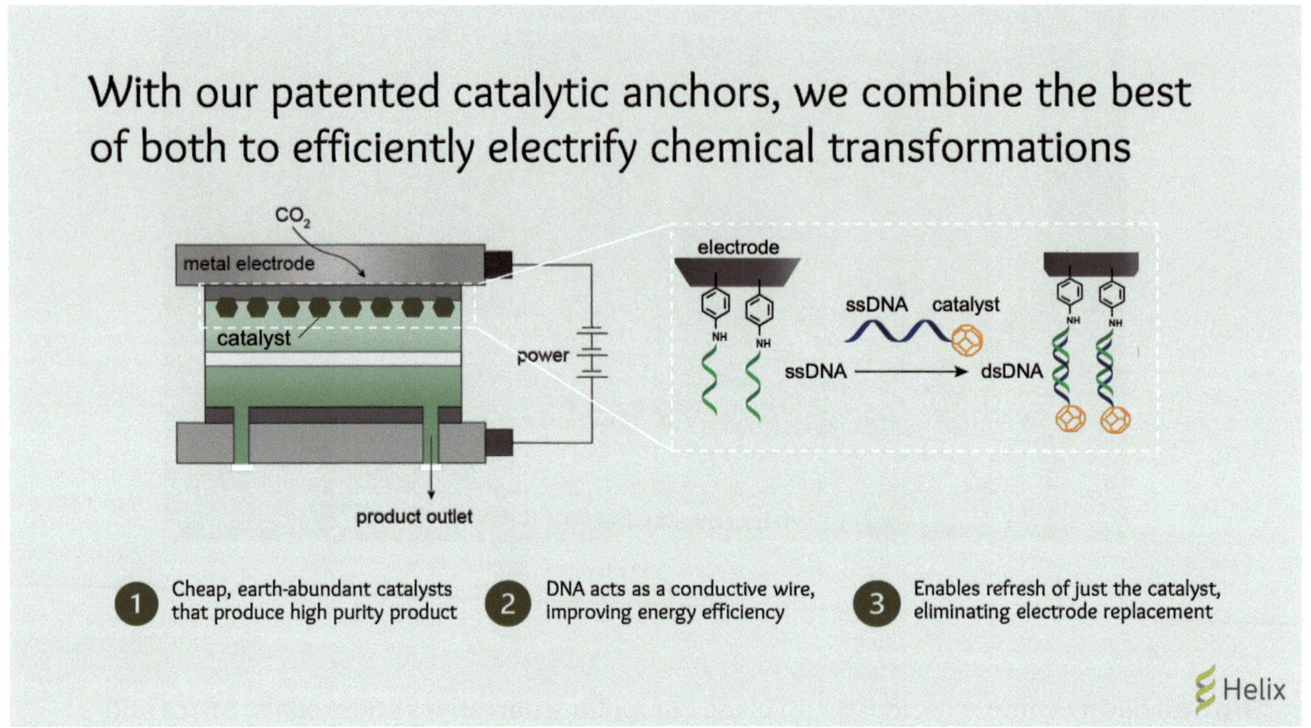

Figure 12.5: In early pitches, Helix Carbon emphasized their initial technical innovation.

customer-focused but also gave them more flexibility in their product development, which was useful because they ended up moving away from the DNA zipper entirely.

They also included a High-Level Product Specification that showed the whole system in action. Rather than highlight what was impressive in the lab, they emphasized the information they knew would resonate with customers (Figure 12.7).

A good Solution Definition not only explains the solution but also articulates why customers should want it. If done well, it will feed nicely into the Quantified Value Proposition, which we'll cover in the next step!

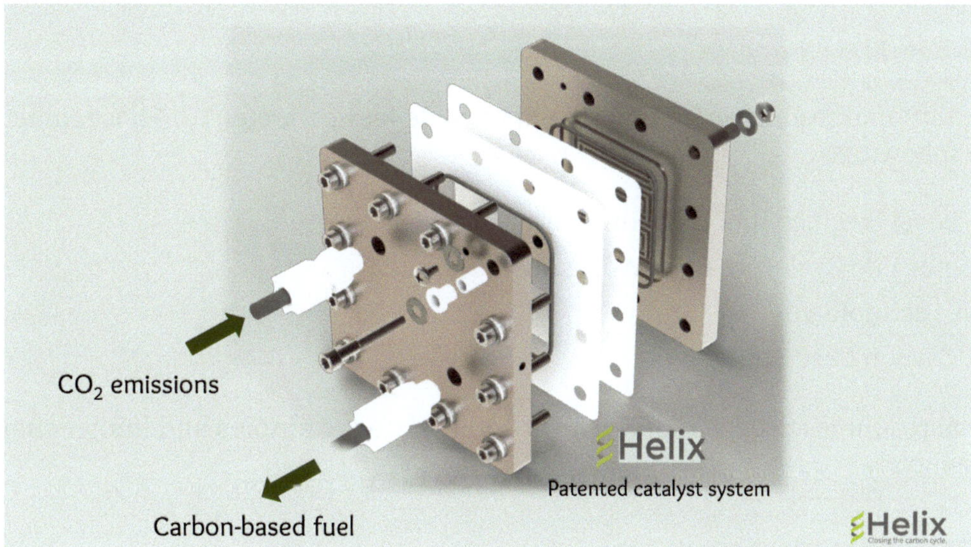

Figure 12.6: Helix Carbon's later technology overview focused on the whole electrolyzer rather than the underlying technology. Permission from Evan Haas of Helix Carbon

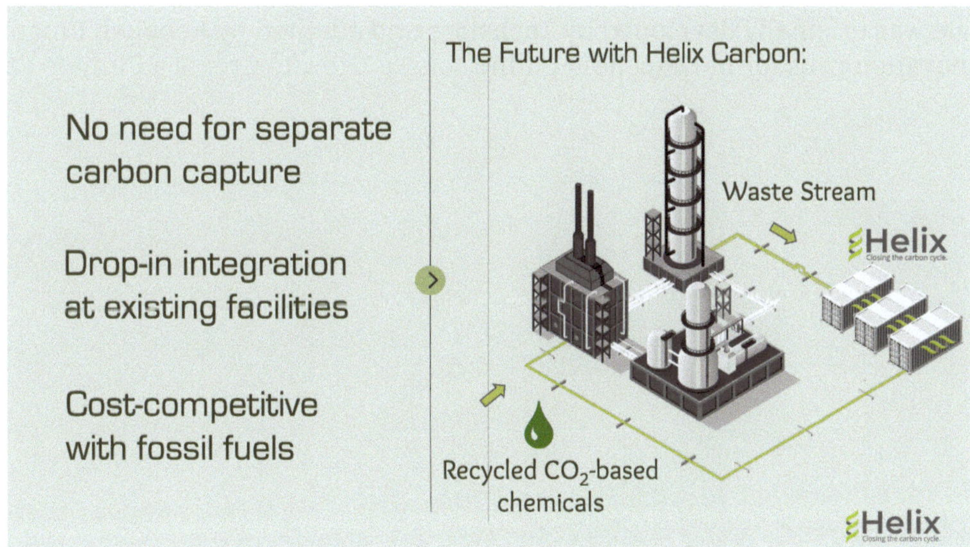

Figure 12.7: Helix Carbon's High-Level Product Specification

ADDITIONAL RESOURCES

There are additional resources for this step at www.de4cev.com/step12. These materials include the following:

- High-Level Product Specification Worksheet
- Customer Life Cycle Use Case Worksheet
- NONA Technologies Case Study
- Helix Carbon Case Study

Additional resources will be added as new and updated examples and information become available.

Notes

1. See: Michael I. Norton, Daniel Mochon, and Dan Ariely, "The IKEA Effect: When Labor Leads to Love," *Journal of Consumer Psychology*, July 2012, https://www.hbs.edu/faculty/Pages/item .aspx?num=41121.
2. This template was originally developed by Techstars and adapted by Rebekah Emanuel of Harvard Innovation Labs for her excellent online course "How to Create a Climate Venture."

Quantify Your Unique Value Proposition

In This Step, You Will

- Determine how your product will benefit your target customer in terms of the priorities they care about most.

- Formulate a simple structure and calculate quantitative metrics (in most cases) to be able to communicate this value to the customer efficiently and effectively.

- Identify the qualities of your solution and your company that provide you with a unique competitive advantage, especially relative to the status quo.

Why This Step, and Why Now?

Once you have a clear vision of your solution, you need to specify how it adds value to your customer. Do not assume the benefits will be self-evident. You need to spell them out and measure them if you can. That is why we call this step the *Quantified Value Proposition (QVP)*. Solutions can have many benefits, but the ones you highlight in the QVP should align with the customer's top priority, based on your primary market research (PMR).

This is particularly important to remember when you are measuring potential emissions reductions and other climate-related benefits. Remember that your end user and your economic buyer are probably not making decisions based on climate impact, at least not as a primary driver. This means your value proposition is probably not emissions reduction, but cost, quality, reliability, or performance.

Climate and energy ventures have an advantage in developing a QVP, which is that they have already done a quantitative analysis of their solution: the Techno-Economic Analysis (TEA).

This can be a great starting point for your value summary because it yields many informative numbers related to your solution. But just because you can quantify something, that does not make it a QVP. Ultimately, your QVP needs to align with your customer's top priorities, and it needs to be presented in the language of your customer.

Summarizing Your QVP: As-Is Versus Possible

A good way to describe your QVP is to directly compare the as-is state to the possible state. Focus on your customer's top priority. Talk with the Personas across your Decision-Making Unit about how to measure that priority quantitatively and what units to measure it in. For instance, if your customer's top priority is saving money, then your value proposition will likely be expressed in dollars (or other currency).

Next, take that quantitative measurement and, with the Persona, map out the as-is state for how they currently solve the problem. You may have already mapped this out as part of the Customer Life Cycle Use Case (part of Step 12). Use the Persona's own words when describing the as-is state, and break it down into concrete stages.

Next, define, with buy-in from your whole team, the possible state of how the user will solve this problem with your proposed new solution. Show in detail how your proposed solution will better satisfy the Persona's number one priority. Pull numbers from your TEA if you can.

The difference in value between the as-is state and the possible state is your QVP. Use the words of the customer to diagram it so they can understand that it is customized to them—or at least to their industry (Figure 13.1).

You should be highly confident your solution can attain the numbers in the possible state. If you've done any kind of scenario analysis in your TEA, use one of your more conservative scenarios. You do not want to overpromise, fall short, and lose credibility. This is especially true for climate and energy ventures, where there is a perception that greener options are more expensive and perform worse.

The Uniqueness of Your QVP

Your goal as a startup venture is to provide value to your customers in a differentiated way. If you have an easily replicable value proposition, then it's quite likely that someone else will swoop in to eat your lunch.

Quantified Value Proposition

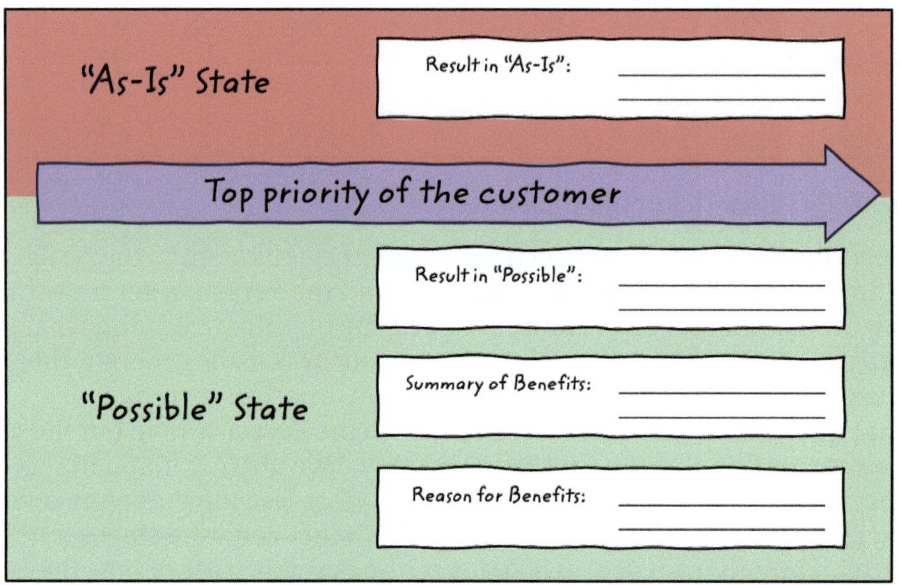

Figure 13.1: How to visually represent your QVP

Rather than framing your competitive edge as something others are not doing, try to identify what you can do better than anyone else. This internal capacity is called your Core, and it has three key dimensions:

- **Unique.** Difficult for anyone else to duplicate

- **Important.** Ties directly to your QVP

- **Grows.** Increases in strength over time relative to competitors

Your Core is what enables you to uniquely produce your value proposition with much greater effectiveness than any competitor. It is that single thing that will make it very difficult for the next company to be successful. It could be a very small part of the overall solution, but without it, your competitors don't have anything comparable.

One of the most overused and incorrect terms used when defining a Core is *first-mover advantage,* as most companies that are first to market end up losing to a later entrant that outperforms them. First Solar is the largest solar manufacturer in the United States, but they were not the first, and Tesla was certainly not the first company to sell electric vehicles. First-mover advantage can help a company with a well-defined Core, but it cannot win the market simply on its own. It must be translated into something like securing key customers, suppliers, or distributors; land rights for energy projects; positive networking effects; proprietary data the best talent in a certain area; or something equally important.

The Toughest Competitor of All: The Status Quo

Often, your largest obstacle will be convincing customers to make a change from their status quo. People and organizations have an enormous amount of inertia when it comes to change. They already have habits that are hard to break. In the energy sector, the status quo has long been fossil fuels, and many climate and energy ventures offer some alternative to this. It is important to compare your solution to the fossil option and not assume that the energy transition is a given.

Comparing your product to the status quo ensures that you have a valid and real market. Don't assume your customers will change. You must give them a compelling reason to do so. Regulatory or social pressure might tip the scales in favor of more climate-friendly options, and you can consider those factors, but the customer ultimately needs to choose your solution because it is in their best interest.

Related to this is another mistake. There are often multiple climate and energy ventures pursuing the same Big Prize using similar technology, especially in hot areas like hydrogen, carbon management, and electrification. You might be tempted to spend a lot of time on beating these other ventures, rather than delivering a product that meets the customer's needs. However, the fastest route to growth comes from getting people to overcome inertia.

In the end, if you have a good Core and people convert from the status quo to a new solution, then the market for climate-friendly alternatives will take off, and you *and* your competitors will all win big, capturing a large share of the market from the traditional fossil option. Energy is a humongous industry with plenty of room for multiple players offering similar solutions.

Charting Your Competitive Position

Once you identify your QVP and your Core, you should be able to compare yourself to competitors and the status quo and clearly demonstrate how you come out on top. One way to do this is to draw a Competitive Positioning Chart that visualizes how you and your competitors fulfill the customer's top priorities. It is simplest to do this exercise with the end user Persona in mind, but you could also do it with the economic buyer. Pick whomever you expect to be interacting with most regularly.

Charting your Competitive Position starts by identifying your customer's top two priorities and assuming that those are all that matter. You most likely will not include climate benefits in your Competitive Positioning Chart. These benefits matter for other audiences, which we will cover in later steps.

For this analysis, you will need to deeply understand your competition, including the customer's status quo. This calls for significant in-depth PMR so you can learn about the customer's alternatives firsthand.

Once you have all this information, create a simple 2 × 2 matrix and chart your company and the competitors (Figure 13.2). If you have done good PMR, your business should be positioned in the top-right quadrant. If you find yourself somewhere else, reevaluate your product compared to your competition.

Next, review this chart with your target customers and get feedback, refining it until it accurately describes your product and the competition relative to the Persona's top two priorities.

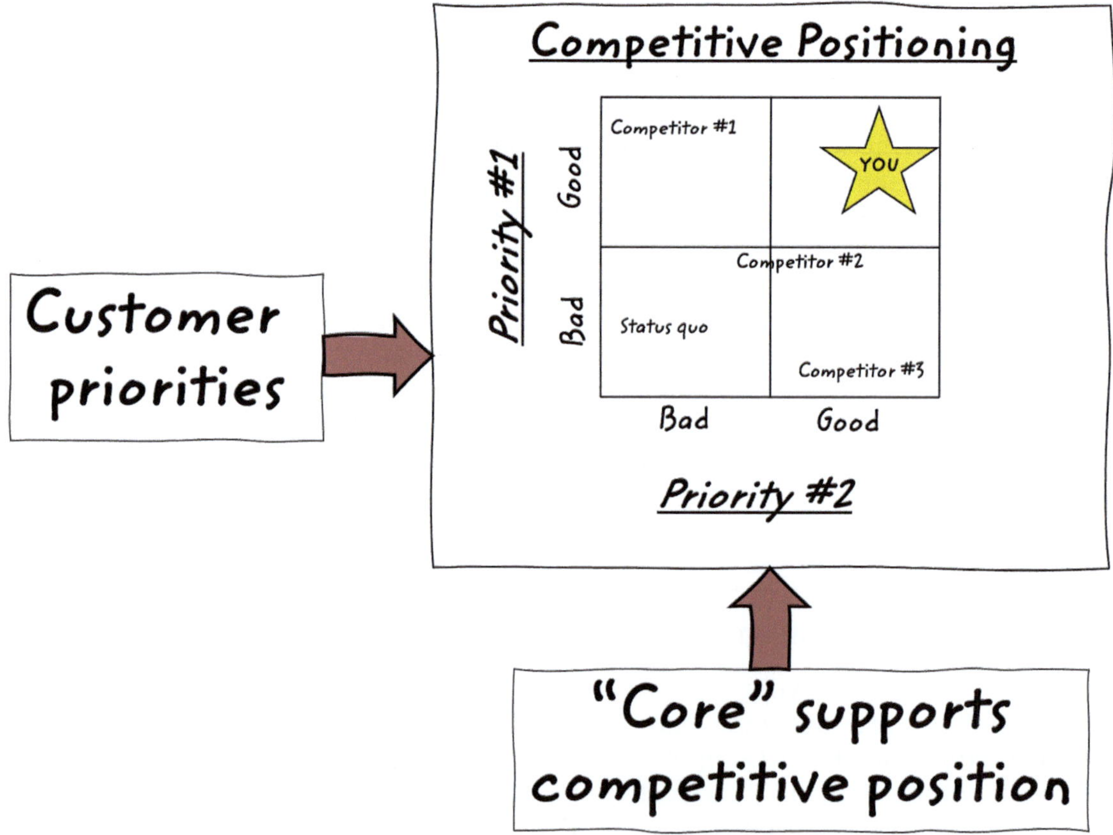

Figure 13.2: Competitive Positioning Chart, displayed as a 2 × 2 matrix

Can Intellectual Property Drive Competitive Advantage?

One common starting point when entrepreneurs try to define their Core for the first time is to say that it is a patent.

A patent is an exclusive right granted for an invention. However, to get a patent, you must fully document and disclose all the technical information about the invention to the public in a patent application. And if the patent is approved, you will only get protection for a limited time to block others from implementing that idea.

While patents can be great sources of value to a company, they have limitations. By fully disclosing all the details of your idea, you're providing a recipe for others to duplicate it, or to use it as a guideline for how to implement the underlying idea while not violating your specific patent. Also, the onus is on you to enforce your patent, which can be costly and time-consuming with no guarantee of success. You will spend your time hiring lawyers to litigate and stop competitors, instead of making your company's fundamentals stronger, and you may ultimately fail due to subtleties that arise in the process of litigating the patent protection. Finally, US patent protection lasts for only 20 years from the filing date, so its value decreases over time. This does not fit the definition of a Core, which should increase in value. Great companies are created in the marketplace, not the patent office.

The value of patents depends heavily on your industry. In the energy industry, patents can be helpful in ensuring the success of a product or a new company, but patents alone are insufficient. They tend to be static, and markets are dynamic. Developing your company's capabilities is generally better than a patent—but it is best to have both. For instance, teams with high levels of capability in an area will continually produce innovative goods, overwhelming competitors built solely around patents.

Output from This Step

Describe your QVP using the template in Figure 13.1. Make sure that it is clear and simple to understand. It should be presented in the language of the customer, tied to one of their top priorities, and explicitly compared to the as-is state. It will probably not relate directly to the climate benefits of your solution.

After you have articulated your QVP, work with your team to identify your Core and then chart your Competitive Position using the diagram in Figure 13.2.

EXAMPLES

AeroShield

As we described in Step 7, AeroShield completed multiple levels of Market Segmentation before focusing on the window components of residential doors. Nailing the value proposition was especially important for them to sell to window manufacturers. The residential window market in North America is an oligopoly, meaning that it is dominated by a few large players. Those players are competing for the same residential buyers, so they have a lot to gain by differentiating themselves from one another with unique new technology.

In quantifying their value proposition, AeroShield initially focused on three things: transparency, insulation, and price (Figure 13.3). Windows made with AeroShield's material were as transparent as glass, they were 50% more insulating than double-pane windows, and they had three times faster payback than triple-pane windows—in other words, they were much cheaper. When the AeroShield founders pitched their venture, they summarized their value proposition in a memorable and concise way: triple-pane performance in a double-pane form factor and price.

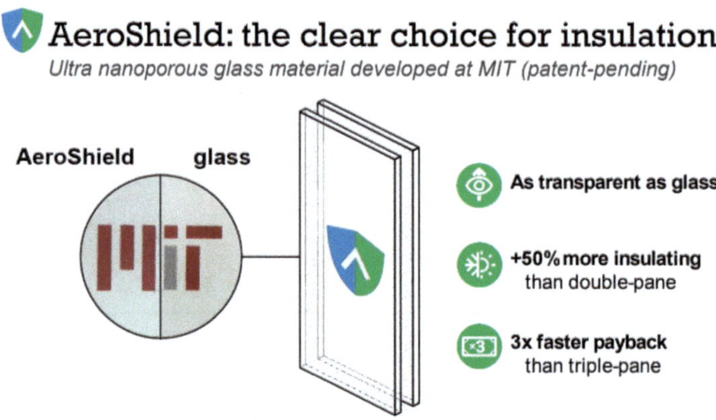

Figure 13.3: AeroShield's QVP

Note that AeroShield did not label themselves as a "green" option. Sure, there are climate benefits implicit in the improved insulation, but AeroShield did not need to call them out. AeroShield's intended customers were window manufacturers, and what those customers cared most about was selling more windows. What end users cared about was getting functional windows and saving money on their energy bills.

Orange EV

Kurt Neutgens and Wayne Mathisen realized there was a big opportunity in electrifying a very specific type of vehicle: yard trucks, which move trailers and containers within a confined area, such as warehouses, ports, or rail yards.

People running ports and warehouses are not necessarily climate champions, so you wouldn't expect them to be early adopters of electric vehicles (EVs), but Wayne and Kurt knew the selling point wasn't the environmental benefit. EVs were simply better for the job.

Yard trucks start and stop all the time, they move very short distances, and they get hitched and unhitched with heavy loads multiple times per day. All that activity puts a lot of wear and tear on the vehicle, especially the transmission. Because of the way electric motors operate, EVs don't need a transmission. They can also be cooled with air rather than liquid, further simplifying the system. And unlike traditional yard trucks, they don't need diesel fuel, just electricity, which is much cheaper.

Due to these advantages, Kurt and Wayne offered their customers an extremely compelling QVP that had nothing to do with climate: 10× less down time with a less-than-3-year payback period, stemming from $50–$90k annual savings on fuel, maintenance, and repair (Figure 13.4).

Figure 13.4: Orange EV's QVP.
Permission from Wayne Mathisen of Orange EV

Note that this QVP isn't just about costs. The sticker price of Orange EVs was higher than their diesel counterparts, though total cost of ownership was lower. A big part of the value came from the reduction in downtime. Because of all the repair, the diesel yard trucks were often offline 25–30% of the time. Orange EVs were only out of service 2% of the time. Customers could potentially get by with fewer trucks, and those savings weren't even factored into the payback period.

The business of electrifying yard trucks was clearly valuable to customers, but it was not necessarily defensible from competitors. However, Orange EV was able to develop a strong two-part Core that gave them a distinct competitive advantage. The first part of their Core was their technology, which was a product of Kurt's engineering expertise as well as his team. The second part of their core was their unique business model. They sold directly to customers and directly serviced the vehicles for their entire lifetime. Bigger players were not set up to do that kind of hands-on support. For diesel trucks, all the maintenance requests would have been overwhelming. But due to the lower maintenance needs of electric yard trucks, Orange EV could make it work.

Larger manufacturers tried to launch their own electric yard trucks, but all of them failed. One competitor even launched four different models, none of which gained much traction.

Orange EV's success demonstrates the power of a well-crafted QVP that aligns with customer priorities, driven by a defensible Core that grows over time.

ADDITIONAL RESOURCES

There are additional resources for this step at www.de4cev.com/step13. These materials include the following:

- QVP Worksheet
- Core Worksheet
- Competitive Positioning Worksheet
- AeroShield Case Study
- Orange EV Case Study

Additional resources will be added as new and updated examples and information become available.

Build Out Enterprise Financials

In this Step, You Will

- Create detailed quantitative projections that tell a compelling story about the future of your venture and its pathway to greatness.

- Build a realistic revenue plan that firms up your ideas about your business model, pricing, and customer acquisition timeline.

- Tally up the potential costs that you will incur to develop your solution and bring it to market, as well as the various costs associated with building your product and running your company.

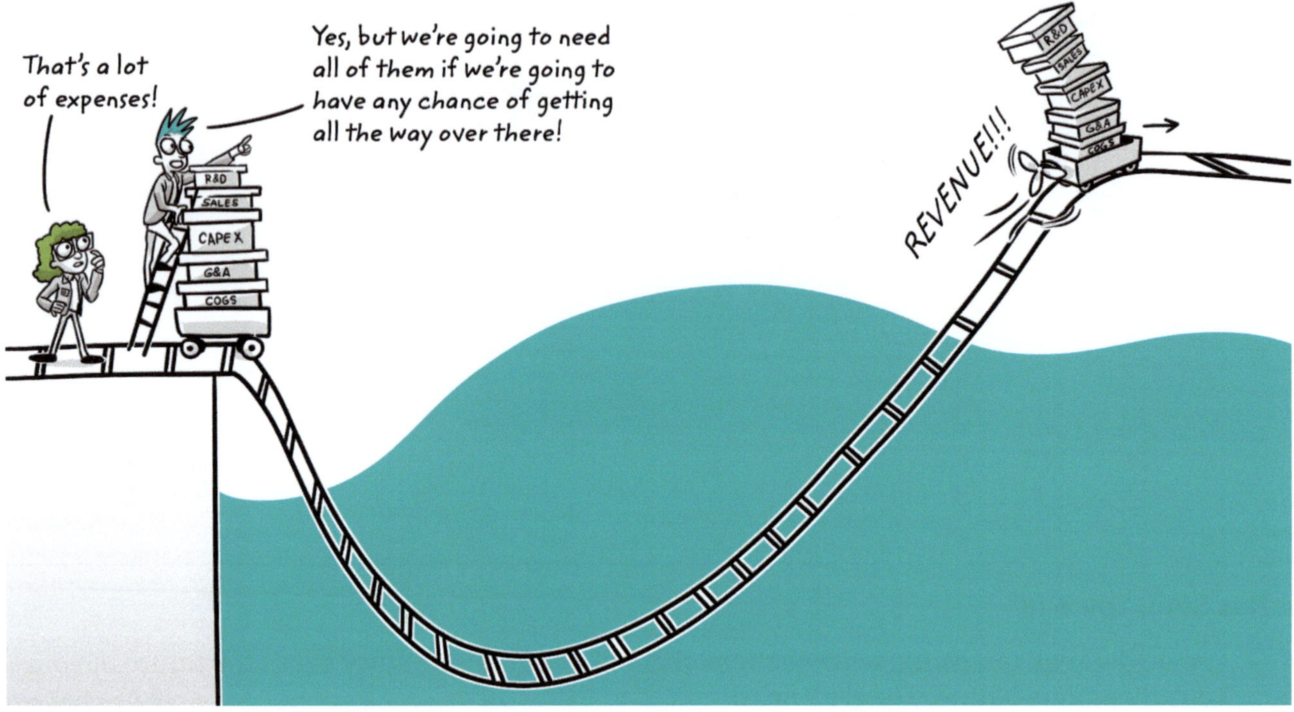

Why This Step, and Why Now?

We have now covered the core elements of the customer theme of our framework. By this point, you should have solid answers to the questions of "Who pays? For what? Why and how?" Based on those answers, you should have enough information to start building out a financial model, which is an estimated projection of your venture's revenues and expenses at least five years into the future. You will eventually track these numbers in a document called an income statement or a profit and loss statement. You will also need to develop other financial documents for your company, like a balance sheet (which tracks your assets and liabilities) and a cash flow statement. These are important, but we won't go into them in much detail in this book.

Your Enterprise Financials will help you assess the overall profitability of your company, building off what you have already done in your Techno-Economic Analysis (TEA). They will also help you decide how much money to raise and when (we will cover this further in Step 17). At a high level, your Enterprise Financials should tell a compelling quantitative story about your company's future, one that will resonate with your team internally and with other stakeholders externally. You will draw directly from this narrative in Steps 15 and 16.

We should note that we are compressing so much content from other *Disciplined Entrepreneurship* books into this one step that it's practically criminal. We will cover the essentials in this step, but if you want more information on any of the topics covered, we strongly recommend checking out the related steps in *Disciplined Entrepreneurship: Expanded and Updated.* A forthcoming book (due out in 2026) will go deeper on this topic: *Finance for the Disciplined Entrepreneur.*

We also recommend the excellent financial modeling content in *Disciplined Entrepreneurship: Startup Tactics* (Tactic 12).

The Basic Set-Up

There are three major parts of your financial model: revenues, cost of goods sold (COGS), and expenses. Once you have an estimate of each, you can subtract COGS from revenues, and the result is your gross profit. You subtract your expenses from that, and the result is earnings before interest, taxes, depreciation, and amortization (EBITDA), a key measure of profitability. Things get a bit more complicated once you start accounting for things like debt finance, taxes, and depreciation of assets.

The revenue side of the equation will come from what you have learned so far about your customers, with some additional updates around your business model and pricing. The COGS side will start with your TEA and then include expenses like staffing and equipment. Keep in mind that, like your TEA, your Enterprise Financials evolve with your venture.

Your projections should look forward at least 5 years, possibly even 10 or 15, depending on how long it will take for your solution to reach large-scale profitability. Entrepreneurs in the information technology sector chafe at the idea of projections beyond five years. However, the time horizons have to be much longer in climate and energy because it generally takes longer for these ventures to start to deploy.

Building a Revenue Plan

The top line of your financial model is revenue, which is a factor of price and quantity. You will start building your Enterprise Financials by estimating how many customers you will have, what they will buy from you, and how much they will pay.

Business Model

Before you can make assumptions about price and quantity, you need to understand what you're selling and how you're selling it. Go through each of your Market Stepping Stones and reevaluate which business model you will use to capture value in that market, building on your analysis from Steps 9 and 10. Focus on your Beachhead Market, because you have the clearest idea of those customers based on your Personas (Step 11). It will be useful to do additional primary market research (PMR) with your Personas to ask questions that validate your business model.

Here are the key questions you should seek to answer:

- Knowing what you know now about your Persona, would they be willing to buy your solution with this business model?

- What business model does your competition use?

- Does this business model match how the economic buyer purchases other products and services? If not, is this an area where they would be not merely willing to try something new but excited to innovate? If the answer to both these questions is no, then you might want to rethink your business model, especially if your customer is a large corporation in the energy industry.

- What is the unit of goods or services that you are charging them for? And how frequently are they paying for it?

- What additional revenue streams do you expect, if any?

Pricing

People have been setting prices as long as they have been selling, and it has never been easy. For detailed information on pricing, see Step 16 of *Disciplined Entrepreneurship*.

Many climate and energy ventures sell commodities, in which case the common economic wisdom would be to sell at or slightly below market price. That may work at the macro level, but the world of entrepreneurship happens at the micro level, where things are bumpier. Have you ever seen gas stations across the street from one another selling the same commodity at different prices? Similar deviations happen for climate and energy commodities. For instance, published commodity prices apply to very large transactions, but buyers who need small quantities often pay a premium. This is why it can be a good idea to seek out customers with small-batch demand for your early Market Stepping Stones.

Timing, location, and many other variables factor into commodity prices. You won't need to deal with all these variables in your initial Enterprise Financials, but do more research than a simple web search.

Your price is likely to change for each of your Market Stepping Stones because your costs will decrease as you develop your technology, enabling you to potentially sell to larger buyers with commodity-driven pricing. Fortunately, it is much easier to lower your prices over time than to raise them. However, do not set prices purely based on cost. Consider the value that you are creating with your solution and the prices your customers pay for alternatives. Are customers saving money as part of your Quantified Value Proposition? If so, try to capture some of that value in your pricing. You should openly discuss pricing with your Personas to get a sense of what seems reasonable.

BEWARE THE GREEN PREMIUM

In many cases, the environmentally friendly option is more expensive than the traditional option. This price differential is called the *green premium*, a term popularized by Bill Gates.

We have emphasized that climate and energy solutions can only scale if they offer advantages in cost, reliability, or quality in addition to climate benefits. However, many climate and energy solutions still need to charge a green premium, at least in the early days. One reason is that they are early-stage technologies, so they are still at the top of the technology cost curve. The TEA might show an ability to eliminate the green premium in the long run, but it takes years to get there.

Another reason for the green premium is that some climate and energy solutions add a step to an existing process. For instance, it costs money to install a technology that captures carbon dioxide from a smokestack, while releasing CO_2 into the air is free. This is true even if the carbon capture technology only costs a dollar. Of course, there is a climate cost to CO_2, but that cost is distributed across society and not paid by the emitter. Many policy initiatives aim to rectify those externalities by taxing emissions or by providing tax credit for CO_2 removal. These are examples of ways that policy can counteract the green premium or turn it into a discount.

You can plan to charge a green premium in your early days, especially if you have identified specific enthusiasts and early adopters who are willing to pay it, but if you are depending on a green premium indefinitely, your Enterprise Financials are likely to raise some eyebrows.

Customer Projections

The simple formula for revenue is price multiplied by quantity. We just talked about price, so now let's talk about quantity. In your Enterprise Financials, you need to project your number of customers for each time period, as well as what they will buy. One of the most common mistakes we see is being overly ambitious with these estimates in the early months or years. Remember that climate and energy ventures must plan for long timelines, high costs of technology development, and customers with long sales cycles. It can be reasonable to have few or no customers in the first one to two years.

Do not try to sound impressive by projecting high numbers right away, because you will lose credibility. Make reasonable projections that align with your Market Stepping Stones and your technology development pathway. It takes a lot of work to develop a good reputation as an entrepreneur who meets their commitments, but it can take just one bad forecast to blow it up. Under-promise and over-deliver. This principle becomes especially important as your company grows, as the market matures, and if your forecasts are made public.

Try to avoid hypotheticals wherever possible. Your initial customers should be real prospects within your Beachhead Market whom you've already identified. For more on building a strong lead list, read Step 9 in *Disciplined Entrepreneurship: Expanded and Updated*.

Add Up Your COGS and Other Expenses

Now that you have a revenue plan, let's talk about the less fun side of the equation: COGS and other expenses. Together, these two categories constitute all the costs that you incur to develop your solution and bring it to market, plus the costs associated with building your product and running your company. You probably do not have very many actual expenses at this point, and most will be based on assumptions. Of course, your assumptions must be as reasonable, ethical, and well-informed as possible, but everyone who looks at a startup financial model knows that it is essentially a work of realistic fiction. Make your best guess and revise as needed. The best possible resource for this task is other climate and energy founders, especially those who are a year or two ahead of you.

Keep in mind that your financial model should be a living document. As the company matures, update your data and assumptions with real numbers and more realistic estimates.

COGS

COGS includes all direct expenses—such as materials, labor, and production overhead—incurred to produce each additional unit of a product. COGS should be fairly straightforward to calculate, because you already did most of the heavy lifting in your TEA. Go back to your TEA and calculate all the costs directly associated with making one unit of output. Make sure to account for labor, over-head costs, energy, and feedstocks. You can think of it this way: any expenses that increase as you produce more units should be part of COGS. Any expenses that stay the same, no matter how many units you produce, should not be part of COGS.

This can be tricky for climate and energy ventures because COGS varies based on your business model. Let's say you have developed a device that produces low-carbon electricity. If you are selling the entire device, then COGS would include the cost of the materials to make the device. However, if you own the device and sell the electricity, then the device would be a capital expenditure, which we'll cover in a moment. Your COGS in that case would be whatever feedstock you use to produce the electricity (plus labor, etc.).

Staffing

Estimate all the hires you plan to make in the first five years (and possibly beyond). We will go into the practical considerations of expanding your team in Step 22. For now, you are just putting together an early estimate of a staffing plan. Note that staffing is not a category of its own, and your labor costs will fit into other expense categories. We already mentioned how you need to account for manufacturing labor as part of COGS. However, it's useful to keep track of your staffing in one place to get a sense of your overall head count, which will be a key driver of your spending.

If you're building deep tech, most of your early hires will be engineers who will help you develop your technology and prepare it for on-site deployment with your customers. You may also need team members in business development (to start building your customer pipeline), operations (to help manage your internal processes), and other areas. Just be wary of growing the team too quickly.

Your staffing plan will account for a big chunk of your overall expenses, but there are other operating expenses as well. These fall into three key buckets: research and development (R&D), marketing and sales (M&S), and general and administrative (G&A).

Operating Expenses: R&D

R&D costs are expenses related to building a solution, or piece of one, that is not sold to a customer, including labor.

For deep tech, expect major R&D costs. You may face a long timeline before selling your solution to customers, so many of your early materials costs will fall under R&D. Lab equipment is trickier to categorize, because it might also be a capital expenditure. As a rule of thumb, if the purchase is entirely used up or depreciated within a year, then it's an operating expense. If it provides value over multiple years, then it is a capital expense.

Operating Expenses: M&S

M&S costs are associated with acquiring customers and selling them your product. So far, we have not covered a lot about the customer acquisition process, but you will need to make some assumptions about this process to get an estimate of your M&S expenses. If you need an introduction to customer acquisition or a refresher on these topics, refer to the corresponding steps of *Disciplined Entrepreneurship: Expanded and Updated*.

An important consideration for climate and energy ventures is that, when it comes to customer acquisition, most of your revenue will come from a few large customers with a high Lifetime Value, so you need to spend a lot of time finding them and cultivating relationships. As a result, many climate and energy entrepreneurs erroneously focus narrowly on the process of selling to these customers, rather than on networking and relationship building to reach that point, often over a span of several years.

Operating Expenses: G&A

This last category of operating expenses is G&A, which is fairly straightforward. It encompasses many of the costs associated with running any business. Here are a few items that are specifically relevant for the climate and energy sector:

- **Intellectual property (IP).** The costs of managing IP fall under G&A.
- **Regulatory.** Team members working on government relations or any other expenses related to policy (see Step 8).
- **Insurance.** All companies need to be appropriately insured, particularly ventures that are planning to build a pilot within someone else's facility. Your customers will insist that you have a strong policy for general liability insurance before installing anything on their property.

Capital Expenditures (CapEx)

Capital expenditures are long-term investments in assets (i.e., more than one year). These items go on your balance sheet, not your income statement, but they can be major cash drains, so it is important to keep track of them. General wisdom is that startups should avoid CapEx as much as possible, but it is often unavoidable in deep tech. It is extremely difficult to build something at infrastructure scale without incurring a fair amount of CapEx. Ideally, you should find a customer who can foot as much of this bill as possible, because their cost of capital will be lower than yours. Your TEA might show that it is economically favorable for you to own and operate a lot of the CapEx in the long run, but it makes sense to avoid it in the short term (if you can) because your cost of capital as a startup is extremely high.

Pulling It All Together

As we mentioned at the start of this step, Enterprise Financials are more than numbers on a spreadsheet. They are a story you can tell about the future of your venture, and that story should be believable and compelling to stakeholders, especially investors.

You can usually summarize your financials with a chart of your cash flow or profit over time. For innovation-driven enterprises (IDEs), the trend line follows a J-curve, where the venture loses money for a while before eventually reaching exponential growth. Due to the high price of poker for climate and energy ventures, the J swoops even lower than for many other IDEs, and it takes much longer to get to positive cash flow (Figure 14.1).

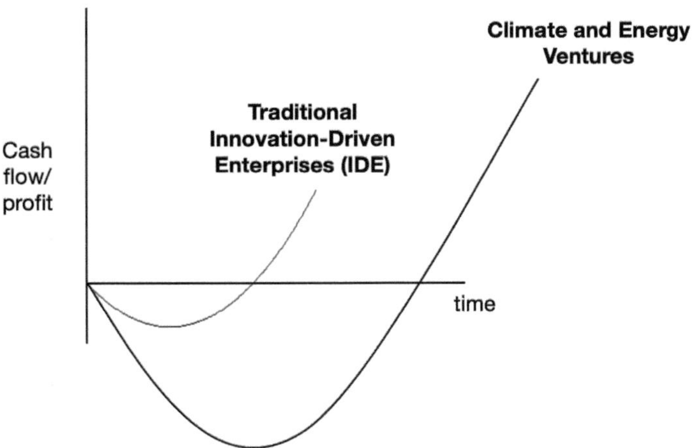

Figure 14.1: The J-curve for traditional IDE versus climate and energy ventures

Once you have a decent financial model, you should be able to answer some of the following questions:

- When will you start making revenue?
- When will your cash flow be positive (higher revenue than COGS and other expenses)?
- What is the key metric (usually number of units sold to produce the necessary revenue and profit) to measure your path to cash flow positive?
- When do you expect to expand to each of your Market Stepping Stones?

- What are the key inflection points that change your trajectory?
- What do you need to do to reach those inflection points?
- Whom do you need to add to your team to accomplish those things?
- What other resources do you need?
- How much capital do you need to raise from external sources and when? (We'll share more on this in Step 17.)

Output from This Step

In a spreadsheet, build a financial model for your venture that includes the following tabs (at a minimum):

- Assumptions
- Revenue
- COGS
- Staffing
- Operating expenses
- CapEx
- Summary income statement

Provide a high-level overview of your Enterprise Financials by making a graph of revenue and profit over time (at least five years).

EXAMPLE

MacroCycle

Stwart and Jan-Georg recognized that building and scaling a totally new method of recycling would require a lot of time and money. Building out their Enterprise Financials helped them chart their long-term pathway to scale.

Using their TEA as a starting point, they summarized all their internal and external assumptions in a single tab of their financial model spreadsheet to give their investors and others an idea of the key levers driving profitability and scale (Figure 14.2).

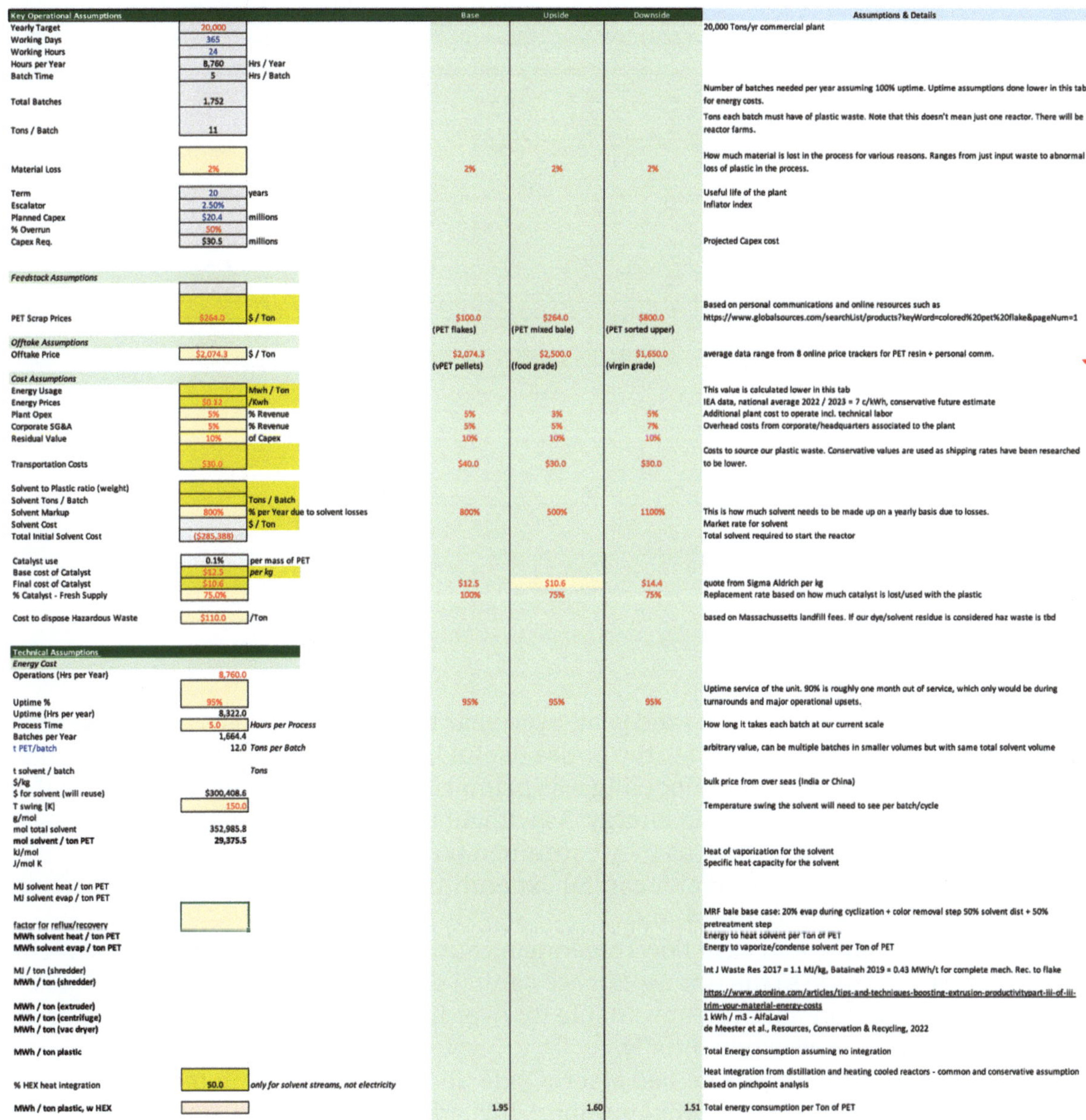

Figure 14.2: MacroCycle's key operational and technical assumptions: at the far right, they have added notes explaining the basis of various assumptions where needed (some assumptions have been changed or removed because the information is confidential).

Proforma 20,000 Tons/yr Plant-level Cashflow

Inflator		100.0%	102.5%	105.1%	107.7%	110.4%	113.1%	116.0%	118.9%	121.8%
Year		0	1	2	3	4	5	6	7	8
Date		31-Dec-26	31-Dec-27	31-Dec-28	31-Dec-29	31-Dec-30	31-Dec-31	31-Dec-32	31-Dec-33	31-Dec-34
Revenue										
Production Input (Tons)			20,000	20,000	20,000	20,000	20,000	20,000	20,000	20,000
Production Output (Tons)			19,600	19,600	19,600	19,600	19,600	19,600	19,600	19,600
rPET Price ($/Tons)			$2,233.8	$2,289.7	$2,346.9	$2,405.6	$2,465.7	$2,527.4	$2,590.6	$2,655.3
Total Revenue			21,891,520	44,877,616	45,999,556	47,149,545	48,328,284	49,536,491	50,774,903	52,044,276
			1st year ramp up period, 50% efficiency							
Expenses										
Cost of Feedstock			($5,412,000)	($5,547,300)	($5,685,983)	($5,828,132)	($5,973,835)	($6,123,181)	($6,276,261)	($6,433,167)
Cost of Solvent	higher		($2,340,183)	($2,398,687)	($2,458,654)	($2,520,121)	($2,583,124)	($2,647,702)	($2,713,894)	($2,781,742)
Cost of Catalyst	lower		($162,975)	($167,049)	($171,226)	($175,506)	($179,894)	($184,391)	($189,001)	($193,726)
Cost of Energy	higher		($3,665,400)	($3,757,035)	($3,850,961)	($3,947,235)	($4,045,916)	($4,147,064)	($4,250,740)	($4,357,009)
Cost of Waste Removal			($45,100)	($46,228)	($47,383)	($48,568)	($49,782)	($51,027)	($52,302)	($53,610)
Cost of Transportation			($615,000)	($630,375)	($646,134)	($662,288)	($678,845)	($695,816)	($713,211)	($731,042)
Fixed Opex (labor, etc.)	lower		($1,094,576)	($2,243,881)	($2,299,978)	($2,357,477)	($2,416,414)	($2,476,825)	($2,538,745)	($2,602,214)
Total Costs	higher		($13,335,234)	($14,790,555)	($15,160,319)	($15,539,327)	($15,927,810)	($16,326,005)	($16,734,155)	($17,152,509)
Process OPEX / ton			($404)	($472)	($483)	($495)	($508)	($521)	($534)	($547)
Total costs / Ton			($680)	($755)	($773)	($793)	($813)	($833)	($854)	($875)
Total EBITDA			$8,556,286	$30,087,061	$30,839,238	$31,610,219	$32,400,474	$33,210,486	$34,040,748	$34,891,767
EBITDA Margin			39.1%	67.0%	67.0%	67.0%	67.0%	67.0%	67.0%	67.0%
Margin / Ton			$436.5	$1,535.1	$1,573.4	$1,612.8	$1,653.1	$1,694.4	$1,736.8	$1,780.2
Residual Value										
Total Residual Asset Value			$0	$0	$0	$0	$0	$0	$0	$0
Turnaround Cost									$ (10,000,000)	
Cashflows to Investors		($30,810,388)	$8,556,286	$30,087,061	$30,839,238	$31,610,219	$32,400,474	$33,210,486	$24,040,748	$34,891,767
Capex per Ton		($1,540.52)								
IRR		70.4%								
IRR Through Useful Life		70.4%								
Return on Capital		23.44x								
Years Payback		1.00x								
		($22,254,102)	$7,832,959	$38,672,197	$70,282,416	$102,682,890	$135,893,376	$159,934,124	$194,825,891	

Figure 14.3: MacroCycle's cash flow model for a single plant

Based on these assumptions, they plotted year-over-year revenues and costs at the level of a full-scale plant and projected financials for the entire useful life of the plant, which they estimated to be over 20 years (Figure 14.3). Their modeling was primarily based on the technology itself, with the main cost drivers being materials and energy. As with all their initial estimates, they would need to make updates to these numbers as they continued building the venture.

After adding hiring estimates and major capital expenditures, they had a 10-year projection of their company-level financials (Figure 14.4).

When they plotted revenue and cash flow (revenue minus expenses), they got a typical J-curve, though it was a little wiggly due to the timing of large capital expenditures (Figure 14.5). This chart showed that the venture would not be net profitable for over five years, but once it became profitable, it had the potential to grow exponentially.

Building out Enterprise Financials helped MacroCycle understand where to focus to reach scale and profitability. Almost all their initial numbers turned out to be wrong, but they would not have been able to move forward without some sort of model to work from.

124.9%	128.0%	131.2%	134.5%	137.9%	141.3%	144.8%	148.5%	152.2%	156.0%	159.9%	163.9%
9	10	11	12	13	14	15	16	17	18	19	20
31-Dec-47	31-Dec-48	31-Dec-49	31-Dec-50	31-Dec-51	31-Dec-52	31-Dec-53	31-Dec-54	31-Dec-55	31-Dec-56	31-Dec-57	31-Dec-58
20,000	20,000	20,000	20,000	20,000	20,000	20,000	20,000	20,000	20,000	20,000	20,000
19,600	19,600	19,600	19,600	19,600	19,600	19,600	19,600	19,600	19,600	19,600	19,600
$2,721.7	$2,789.7	$2,859.5	$2,931.0	$3,004.3	$3,079.4	$3,156.3	$3,235.2	$3,316.1	$3,399.0	$3,484.0	$3,571.1
53,345,383	54,679,017	56,045,993	57,447,143	58,883,321	60,355,404	61,864,289	63,410,897	64,996,169	66,621,073	68,286,600	69,993,765
($6,593,996)	($6,758,846)	($6,927,818)	($7,101,013)	($7,278,538)	($7,460,502)	($7,647,014)	($7,838,190)	($8,034,144)	($8,234,998)	($8,440,873)	($8,651,895)
($2,851,285)	($2,922,567)	($2,995,632)	($3,070,522)	($3,147,285)	($3,225,968)	($3,306,617)	($3,389,282)	($3,474,014)	($3,560,865)	($3,649,886)	($3,741,133)
($198,569)	($203,533)	($208,622)	($213,837)	($219,183)	($224,663)	($230,279)	($236,036)	($241,937)	($247,986)	($254,185)	($260,540)
($4,465,934)	($4,577,582)	($4,692,022)	($4,809,322)	($4,929,555)	($5,052,794)	($5,179,114)	($5,308,592)	($5,441,307)	($5,577,340)	($5,716,773)	($5,859,692)
($54,950)	($56,324)	($57,732)	($59,175)	($60,654)	($62,171)	($63,725)	($65,318)	($66,951)	($68,625)	($70,341)	($72,099)
($749,318)	($768,051)	($787,252)	($806,933)	($827,107)	($847,784)	($868,979)	($890,703)	($912,971)	($935,795)	($959,190)	($983,170)
($2,667,269)	($2,733,951)	($2,802,300)	($2,872,357)	($2,944,166)	($3,017,770)	($3,093,214)	($3,170,545)	($3,249,808)	($3,331,054)	($3,414,330)	($3,499,688)
($17,581,322)	($18,020,855)	($18,471,376)	($18,933,161)	($19,406,490)	($19,891,652)	($20,388,943)	($20,898,667)	($21,421,134)	($21,956,662)	($22,505,578)	($23,068,218)
($561)	($575)	($589)	($604)	($619)	($634)	($650)	($666)	($683)	($700)	($718)	($736)
($897)	($919)	($942)	($966)	($990)	($1,015)	($1,040)	($1,066)	($1,093)	($1,120)	($1,148)	($1,177)
$35,764,061	$36,658,163	$37,574,617	$38,513,982	$39,476,832	$40,463,752	$41,475,346	$42,512,230	$43,575,036	$44,664,411	$45,781,022	$46,925,547
67.0%	67.0%	67.0%	67.0%	67.0%	67.0%	67.0%	67.0%	67.0%	67.0%	67.0%	67.0%
$1,824.7	$1,870.3	$1,917.1	$1,965.0	$2,014.1	$2,064.5	$2,116.1	$2,169.0	$2,223.2	$2,278.8	$2,335.8	$2,394.2
$0	$0	$0	$0	$0	$0	$0	$0	$0	$0	$0	$3,052,500
$35,764,061	$36,658,163	$37,574,617	$38,513,982	$39,476,832	$30,463,752	$41,475,346	$42,512,230	$43,575,036	$44,664,411	$45,781,022	$49,978,047
$727,027,450	$763,685,613	$801,260,229	$839,774,211	$879,251,043	$909,714,795	$951,190,141	$993,702,371	$1,037,277,407	$1,081,941,818	$1,127,722,840	$1,177,700,887

(A "-10000000" callout is printed above the column for 31-Dec-52 in the final subtotal row.)

Figure 14.3: (Continued)

	Year 1	Year 2	Year 3	Year 4	Year 5	Year 6	Year 7	Year 8	Year 9	Year 10
Profitability Strategy										
Revenue	2024	2025	2026	2027	2028	2029	2030	2031	2032	2023
JV Tons Production	1	2	35	70	10000	20000	20000	70000	100000	150000
JV Ownership	100%	100.00%	100%	100%	50%	50%	50%	50%	50%	50%
PET Price	$2,234	$2,290	$2,347	$2,406	$2,466	$2,527	$2,591	$2,655	$2,722	$2,790
JV Revenue	$2,234	$4,579	$82,142	$168,391	$12,328,644	$25,273,720	$25,905,563	$92,936,207	$136,085,160	$209,230,934
Licensing Tons Production	0	0	0	0	0	0	20	70	150	250
Licensing Revenue	$0	$0	$0	$0	$0	$0	$8,756,608	$30,648,128	$65,674,560	$109,457,600
Total Revenue	$2,234	$4,579	$82,142	$168,391	$12,328,644	$25,273,720	$34,662,171	$123,584,335	$201,759,721	$318,688,534
Costs/Investment										
Employee Cost	($800,000)	($1,575,000)	($3,307,500)	($6,945,750)	($12,155,063)	($19,144,223)	($26,801,913)	($31,659,760)	($36,936,386)	($42,661,526)
Employee Benefits	($240,000)	($472,500)	($992,250)	($2,083,725)	($3,646,519)	($5,743,267)	($8,040,574)	($9,497,928)	($11,080,916)	($12,798,458)
COGS Per Ton	($680)	($755)	($773)	($793)	($813)	($833)	($854)	($875)	($897)	($919)
COGS (Total)	($680)	($1,509)	($27,072)	($55,498)	($4,063,217)	($8,329,594)	($8,537,834)	($30,629,481)	($44,850,311)	($68,957,353)
CAPEX	($200,000)	$0	$0	$0	($16,000,000)	$0	($50,000,000)	$0	($50,000,000)	$0
Other Expenses	($124,136)	($204,976)	($432,760)	($908,577)	($1,793,281)	($1,660,896)	($4,669,059)	($3,589,402)	($7,143,425)	($6,220,913)
Total Costs	($1,365,497)	($2,254,740)	($4,760,355)	($9,994,342)	($37,658,891)	($34,878,814)	($98,050,234)	($75,377,445)	($150,011,935)	($130,639,169)
Cash Flow	($1,363,263)	($2,250,161)	($4,678,213)	($9,825,951)	($25,330,247)	($9,605,094)	($63,388,063)	$48,206,890	$51,747,785	$188,049,365
Investment Cash	$4,000,000	$0	$15,000,000	$0	$45,000,000	$0	$55,000,000	$0	$0	$0
Cash on Hand	$2,636,737	$386,576	$10,708,363	$882,412	$20,552,165	$10,947,071	$2,559,009	$50,765,899	$102,513,684	$290,563,049

Figure 14.4: MacroCycle's company-level financials

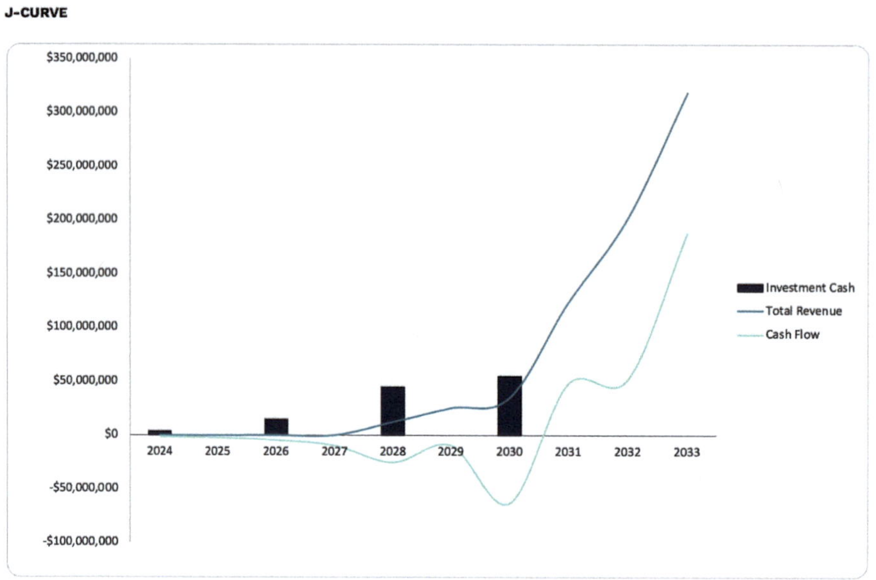

Figure 14.5: MacroCycle's J-curve, based on the company level financials in Figure 14.4

ADDITIONAL RESOURCES

There are additional resources for this step at www.de4cev.com/step14. These materials include the following:

- Enterprise Financials Worksheet
- MacroCycle Case Study
- Charlie Tillett's financial model template

Additional resources will be added as new and updated examples and information become available.

Consider the Full Life Cycle Impacts

In this Step, You Will

- Create a visual map of your Full Product Life Cycle, which includes building, operating, and ultimately disposing of your solution.

- Analyze the positive and negative impacts of your solution across the various stages of its life cycle, including the possible risks incurred by your venture.

Why This Step, and Why Now?

In Step 12, we introduced the idea of a Customer Life Cycle Use Case, but as we think about your long-term pathway to scale, we must understand the even broader Value Chain, which extends from the supply of materials through to disposal or reuse of the finished product. These aspects are important from an impact perspective, but they are also critical strategic considerations that could make or break your venture in the long term.

Understanding your life cycle impacts can also help you uncover and avoid unintended negative consequences. Even if your solution has clear climate benefits, other elements of your business model and operations may cause harm. Companies often don't consider their impacts on people and communities until it is too late to easily change their practices. Well-communicated positive impacts can attract support for your venture from customers and other stakeholders, but unaddressed negative impacts can lead to major problems for your venture through lawsuits, bad publicity, or supply chain shortages.

Academics and professionals use a tool called a *life cycle assessment (LCA)* to quantify the use of energy and materials across the life cycle of a given product or solution. There are established methods of doing an LCA, set by groups like the International Organization for Standardization (ISO). As an early-stage startup team, you probably do not have the resources to do a full LCA. Instead, we are going to pose some questions for you to consider as you plan your pathway to scale, building off the financial modeling that you did in the previous step, and we'll focus on the practical considerations for managing your impact.

Map Out Your Full Product Life Cycle

Before analyzing your solution's life cycle impacts, you must develop a thorough understanding of the Full Product Life Cycle. Do this by visually mapping out each step that goes into building, operating, and disposing of your product. You probably already have some of these steps laid out in your Techno-Economic Analysis (TEA) as well as your Customer Life Cycle Use Case. However, you need to expand the map to include the full Value Chain, including the following categories:

- **Raw material acquisition.** What are the raw materials that make up your solution? Where do they come from? Do they need to be mined, harvested, or produced?

- **Transportation.** How do materials or other components move from one place to another? Do they need to cross international borders? Are there obstacles to transportation? Can you use established infrastructure, or is it necessary to build new infrastructure?

- **Processing.** What does the processing look like at each phase? What material inputs are needed? What energy inputs are needed? Does the manufacturing capacity already exist? If so, where?

- **Sale.** Where do customers purchase your solution? How does the solution get to the customer? Is it installed on-site?

- **Use.** How does the customer use your solution? What are the inputs and outputs while it is in operation? What is the useful lifetime of the solution?

- **End of life.** What happens to the components of your solution when they are no longer useful? Is there already infrastructure for disposal? Can any of the components be recycled or reused?

These categories will likely repeat multiple times throughout your Full Product Life Cycle. For instance, in Step 9, we described the Value Chain for solar photovoltaic panels. In that Value Chain, an important raw material is quartz sand. There are at least five intermediates between sand and a working photovoltaic panel. Each one requires processing in a different facility, as well as transportation, so each intermediate comprises at least two phases in the Full Product Life Cycle.

Keep in mind that there are many raw materials that go into a given product. The solar panels in our example are not composed of pure silicon. They also include materials like aluminum, copper, and silver, each with their own set of links in the Value Chain, making it more of a value web.

Given the complexity involved, you are not going to be able to map every single phase of your Full Product Life Cycle with full precision, and you won't interact directly with most of the actors in the Value Chain or convince them to adopt your solution. That is why it is okay to map the non-customer parts of your Full Product Life Cycle using secondary research. The goal is to get a high-level understanding of the many external factors that will interact with your solution so that you can identify and address potential impacts and risks.

Analyze Your Full Product Life Cycle Impacts

Once you have mapped out your Full Product Life Cycle, you need to figure out the biggest risks and impacts across the various stages. We can break down life cycle impacts into five categories: supply chain, end of life, greenhouse gas (GHG) emissions, environmental justice, and climate resilience. For each category, we have identified some key questions to help you address potential risks.

Supply Chain

Your supply chain is where you source key inputs to your solution and their inputs, going back all the way to the raw materials. Some parts of the supply chain are standard, but others might be specialized. Even reliable supply chains can be disrupted when there is a major global event.

Supply chain risk is a particularly important concern for climate and energy ventures. Next-generation energy technologies frequently rely on rare earth minerals and other hard-to-source materials. The current supply chains for these materials are limited, and they are often fraught with geopolitical tension or unethical practices. Due to these supply limitations, the supply does not currently match the eventual demand. But don't give up. There are many stories of entrepreneurs overcoming great logistical and political challenges to bring their solutions to scale.

It is also important to account for the scale of material passing through supply chains. All told, the mass of materials needed to produce renewable energy is at least two orders of magnitude lower than the mass of materials needed to produce fossil fuel-based energy.[1] That's because the inputs are mainly used in the up-front construction of these next-generation technologies, and after that, they are not needed again until components are replaced. Meanwhile, feedstocks need to be sourced and burned continuously to keep fossil fuel systems operating.[2]

Questions to consider:

- How limited/abundant are your raw materials?
- How difficult are they to obtain?
- Where in the world are they coming from?
- How volatile is the price?
- Are there potential ethical concerns with how these materials are sourced?
- How dependent is your supply chain on geopolitical relationships?
- Are there intermediates that require specialized manufacturing processes?
- How might your supply chain become disrupted?
- Does your product require any materials that are difficult to obtain or manufacture? Will the supply of these materials be affected by geopolitical tensions?

End of Life

The end of life of your solution is a stage that comes with its own unique set of impacts and risks. Some governments have enacted laws to broadly hold companies accountable for the end-of-life stage of their products. This concept is known as extended producer responsibility, and there are general policies in place in countries like Germany, Sweden, France, and Japan, as well as several US states. And, of course, there are countless jurisdictions with laws governing how to handle hazardous waste.

It is important to have a plan to account for your solution's end of life to avoid running afoul of the government, to minimize harmful impacts, and to potentially extract value from components and by-products when they are no longer useful to your venture.

Questions to consider:

- What will happen to your equipment and other materials at the end of their useful life?
- Do any components of your solution require special disposal?
- What waste products does your solution generate, and what will happen to that waste?

- What would be the impact on people and the environment if waste from your solution were not properly discarded?
- Can any waste be recycled or reused?
- Is anyone willing to pay for the stuff you consider waste?

GHG Emissions

We will cover GHG emissions at length in Step 16, so we will not go into too much detail here. Of all your life cycle impacts, emissions are the category that you will most likely need to assess quantitatively, not just qualitatively. Your goal should not necessarily be to eliminate all emissions immediately but rather to have a material net positive effect.

Go through each stage of your Full Product Life Cycle and identify potential sources of emissions. Make sure to consider emissions created at all stages of the life cycle, not only the emissions that come directly from your solution. Also, consider places in the life cycle where GHGs are removed or captured.

Questions to consider:

- Does your solution directly emit GHGs?
- Which types of GHGs does it emit, and how?
- Where are GHGs emitted elsewhere in the life cycle? Consider emissions both upstream and downstream in the Value Chain.
- Are GHGs captured at any point in your Full Product Life Cycle?

Environmental Justice

Environmental justice is the concept that everyone—regardless of race, class, or status—deserves access to a safe and healthy environment. When an activity creates local pollution or other negative impacts in the immediate vicinity, the people who suffer the most are usually people who are already vulnerable and marginalized within society. This has been especially true in the energy industry. As a climate and energy venture, you should be wary of creating local environmental problems as you seek to solve global ones. Do not assume that what is best for the planet is also best for local communities, although this is often true.

List all the stakeholders who will be affected by your solution throughout its life cycle. This is the part of your life cycle impact analysis where it is most important to do primary research. Talk to the people within the communities where you will be building your solution. Understand their concerns, and bring them on board as allies and part of your extended Decision-Making Unit. They may not be involved in the initial decision to purchase your solution, but they do have veto power. A project may completely shut down in response to public backlash, and it can get off the ground much faster if the local community is on board.

Questions to consider:

- What are the possible positive and negative impacts for each of the stakeholders across your Full Product Life Cycle?

- Do the stakeholders have agency to change these impacts?

- Where are you choosing to locate your facilities?

- How are you engaging local communities?

- Have you spoken to the stakeholders (or people who represent their interests)?

- Who are you hiring and how are you developing your workforce? (We will cover this further in Step 22.)

- How will your product affect the accessibility and affordability of goods like energy or materials across all segments of society?

Climate Resilience

Climate and energy ventures may seek to address climate change, but that does not spare them from experiencing its effects. It used to be common for people to think of mitigation (limiting GHGs) and adaptation (adapting to a warmer world) as separate domains, but the world is already experiencing extreme impacts of climate change. You will need to adapt to these impacts to increase your venture's performance and longevity.

Climate and energy solutions often involve heavy physical infrastructure, so it is especially important to be attuned to the weather risks of the present and the probable futures ahead. Because the climate was stable for so long, we assumed it would stay the same. This assumption is embedded in building codes, engineering standards, and other norms and regulations that play a huge, usually unexamined role in infrastructure and industrial projects of all types. Whereas following those past norms and regulations, and not doing anything more, was good business practice in the past, it is now a negligent assumption. If you sell a product only for it to fail because you failed to plan for higher temperatures, the customer will rightly complain. Thankfully, assessing climate risk isn't that hard technologically if you have a process to do it.

Think about the specific location where you might build your first full-scale version of your solution. Do you know what would happen if the average temperature there shifted upward by

2°F (1.1°C)? What would happen if the number of extremely hot days or annual rainfall were to increase by 10%? What if a major storm or wildfire hit? You should have answers to these questions because conditions that were once highly improbable are now within the realm of possibility.[3]

At this stage in the process, you probably have not yet built your full-scale solution, making it the perfect time to plan. You should think through the possibilities now so you can take action, rather than waiting until something goes wrong. By then, it will be too late.

Questions to consider:

- Once your solution is up and running, how would your facilities be affected by increases in temperature?
- How would your facilities be affected by an extreme weather event like a very strong storm?
- How would your operations be affected by changes in rainfall (which includes experiencing much more rainfall than usual, much less rainfall than usual, or higher-than-usual variability)?
- How might the infrastructure elsewhere in your Value Chain be affected by extreme weather and other change in climate?
- Could climate change make any of your inputs more expensive or harder to obtain?
- How would changes in the climate affect the routes in the transportation stages of your Full Product Life Cycle?

Mitigating Risks and Impacts

So far, we have given you a framework for thinking about risks across your Full Product Life Cycle, but we have not told you how to mitigate them. Here are a few general strategies:

- **Processes and protocols.** By embedding risk management into your organization's routine, you can catch potential issues early and prepare to handle challenges.
- **Planning.** The cheapest and most effective risk mitigation strategy is having a plan for what you will do if things go wrong. It's far easier to draft this plan before a crisis occurs, rather than while it's happening.
- **Swaps.** In an ideal world, you could swap a risky location or technology for a less risky alternative. In the real world, there are always trade-offs, so weigh them carefully.
- **Minimization.** You might not be able to completely eliminate a certain risk, but you might be able to reduce its magnitude. For instance, you could minimize use of a risky input or reduce the physical footprint of a facility.

- **Policy.** You might be able to reduce certain risks by influencing policy. Consider low-cost, high-benefit ways to engage government at the local or national level.

- **Back pocket pivot.** If any part of the life cycle seems so risky that it has a decent chance of derailing your venture (and if no reasonable alternative is available), it might be necessary to change course completely. This could require starting over with a new choice of Market Stepping Stones (Step 10), business model (Step 9), or even Founder-Problem Fit (Step 4). This is not an action to take lightly. Every venture pivots at some point in its journey; the only question is how big and when. It's a good idea to consider possible pivots in advance.

Output from This Step

Create a visual map of your Full Product Life Cycle. Start with the raw materials and track them through acquisition, transportation, and processing for each intermediary. Draw arrows connecting one phase to the next. Continue up to and beyond your product (make sure to consider the end-of-life phase).

Once you've drawn out that map, brainstorm the potential risks associated with that system. You can summarize risks and brainstorm potential mitigation strategies using a table like the one in Table 15.1.

EXAMPLES

Active Surfaces

When Shiv Bhakta met Richard Swartwout in MIT's Climate & Energy Ventures course, he knew Richard had a possible moonshot on his hands—lightweight and flexible solar films made from a crystalline material called *perovskites*. They began working together and called their company Active Surfaces. Their plan was to integrate solar films into or onto building materials, offering an energy generation solution for urban environments where traditional solar panels are impractical. A key barrier to capturing this opportunity at scale was supply chain risk.

Most of the materials they needed were not a problem, but others were expensive or difficult to find. For instance, they needed conductive polymers called *polythiophenes*. Active Surfaces could only get polythiophenes through boutique chemical retailers, where pricing was highly variable and stock was limited. This scarcity drove up their costs and created risks for scaling their solution. To mitigate these risks, Active Surfaces began exploring vertical integration: making the polythiophenes (or alternatives) themselves. The synthesis for polythiophenes was only three or four steps, so it was relatively cheap, but it would still add extra time and complexity to the manufacturing process, and switching to alternatives would change the manufacturing processes completely.

Table 15.1: *Fictional Example of a Life Cycle Risk Mitigation Matrix*

Life cycle consideration	*Our solution depends on small quantities of unobtainium, which is rare and very hard to obtain.*
Category	*Supply chain*
Risks to the venture	*Price spike in unobtainium could increase costs so that the solution is no longer economically competitive with the incumbent. Supply shortages could halt production altogether.*
Level of risk	*High*
Potential mitigation strategies	***Processes and protocols.*** *Monitor the price of unobtainium and stock up when prices are low.* ***Planning.*** *Make a plan for how to respond if prices go up unexpectedly, and communicate it across the team.* ***Swaps.*** *Conduct research and development to explore a possible alternative that works with obtainium, which is much easier to acquire but more expensive.* ***Minimization.*** *Design the solution as efficiently as possible to minimize the unobtainium needed.* ***Policy.*** *Lobby US federal government to increase domestic supply of unobtainium in the long run.* ***Short-term action plan.*** *Keep a reserve of unobtainium as well as a buffer of cash, in case prices go up unexpectedly.* ***Pivot.*** *Switch to the obtainium-based solution and sell it to niche customers at a premium.*

They also had to think about their supply chains for critical manufacturing equipment. Richard did the first pass at the TEA when his lab shut down at the beginning of the COVID pandemic, and that was the basis of their economic projections. Since then, the costs of some key machines had doubled, due to COVID-related supply chain shortages as well as inflation. These cost changes added a lot of uncertainty to Richard's calculations, and uncertainty is not good for scaling. To stay on track, they decided to mostly buy used equipment.

Active Surfaces' experience underscores the need to assess supply chain risks early and develop proactive strategies to mitigate them.

Mantel

Cameron Halliday came to MIT with the intention to work on carbon capture, a complicated but important technology largely held back by cost. During his PhD work, he researched a method of capturing CO_2 with a material called *molten borates*, and he teamed up with Danielle Rapson and Sean Robertson to begin commercializing the technology under the name Mantel.

Unlike other carbon capture technologies, which needed heat to release CO_2, the molten borate material ran hot and its excess heat could be used for industrial applications, which could make carbon capture drastically cheaper under the right circumstances. This generated lots of interest from potential partners. In selecting projects, the Mantel team was very intentional about community relationships. They had seen peers spend a lot of time, money, and effort selecting a site and then investing millions of dollars into it, only to face opposition from the local community.

Cameron knew that a big carbon capture project in the community would easily be the subject of many town hall meetings, and he wanted it to be discussed in a positive light, rather than a negative one. There was a view that carbon capture was an excuse to continue fossil fuel production rather than investing in clean energy. Cameron's view was that any technology that could make electricity cheaper and less carbon intensive was worth pursuing. Ideally, he wanted the conversation to be less about global issues and more about local benefits. He aimed to generate excitement about innovation and job creation, and he made a point of engaging with site workers, unions, and other local leaders.

Cameron had come to realize that Mantel needed to capture not only carbon but also hearts and minds.

ADDITIONAL RESOURCES

There are additional resources for this step at www.de4cev.com/step15. These materials include the following:

- Life Cycle Impacts Worksheet
- Risk Mitigation Worksheet
- Active Surfaces Case Study
- Mantel Case Study

Additional resources will be added as new and updated examples and information become available.

Notes

1. David Roberts, "Minerals and the Clean-Energy Transition: The Basics," *Volts*, January 21, 2022. https://www.volts.wtf/p/minerals-and-the-clean-energy-transition.
2. Note that some low-emission technologies do use fuel, like nuclear power, hydrogen, and bio-energy, but these fuels are either extremely high-density (in the case of nuclear) or possible to regenerate in a relatively short time frame.
3. The nonprofit Probable Futures has a great set of free maps that project climate effects across the world under different warming scenarios. You can find these maps at https://probablefutures.org/maps.

Measure Your Climate Value Proposition

In this Step, You Will

- Understand who cares about your potential climate benefits and why.
- Quantify your net climate impact.

Why This Step, and Why Now?

While climate impact is not a top priority for most customers, it can still be valuable to them. You will also encounter some important stakeholders who *do* rank climate as a top priority, so you need to measure your potential climate impact. We can call this measurement your Climate Value Proposition (CVP), which adds to your Quantified Value Proposition (QVP) from Step 13. Make no mistake; your CVP should also be quantified and rigorous. We could just as well call it your Quantified Climate Value Proposition, but that's bit of a mouthful.

Who Cares About Climate?

A thorough climate accounting takes a lot of work to do well, so it is worth knowing who will care about your analysis.

Customers

Customers rarely buy products and services for climate reasons alone, but climate can be a motivator to move away from the status quo. Even when a new solution has a strong value proposition in terms of cost or performance, newness can be a disadvantage. Your CVP can tip the scales by convincing customers to try your solution instead of sticking with the status quo.

In some circumstances, your customers might not care about climate for its own sake, but they may be highly incentivized due to taxes, credits, or other policy changes. This is called a *Window of Opportunity* in Disciplined Entrepreneurship lingo. However, it's best not to depend entirely on policy, because it can change with each election.

Another Window of Opportunity occurs when companies are motivated to adopt climate-friendly options due to customer demand or competitive pressure. Many companies work toward voluntary sustainability goals. Sometimes these activities are highly ambitious, and other times they're exaggerated via a marketing game called *greenwashing*. It is up to discerning individuals and organizations to flag which claims have merit and which are misleading.

Increasingly, CVPs are becoming a point of pride for customers. Many people are reluctant to pay for climate impact but eager to brag about it. That might make you cynical, but how often have *you* made a major expense or sacrifice for climate reasons alone? For most people, the answer is never, and that's okay. If we are going to solve the problem of climate change, we need to accept that climate considerations are never going to be the only variable. It is your job as a climate entrepreneur to make your climate-friendly option as attractive as possible. Lead with your QVP (Step 13) and communicate your CVP as an additional benefit.

Investors

Climate venture capital is a subset of the wider venture capital industry that strongly considers climate impact. Some firms have explicit expectations about the CVP. For instance, Breakthrough Energy Ventures invests only in technologies "with the potential to reduce greenhouse gases, at scale, by at least a half a gigaton every year." Prime Coalition and its spinout fund Azolla Ventures use a similar metric in their investment decisions. Clean Energy Ventures invests in companies that can cumulatively reduce 2.5 gigatons of emissions between the time of investment and 2050. These firms usually have their own tools to measure climate impact, but you should be able to tell *your* version of this story and back it up with evidence. We will cover much more on raising capital in Steps 18 and 21, but for now, keep in mind that your CVP may end up being a critical pillar of your financing strategy.

Employees

A climate-oriented mission can be an important driver for your venture to attract and retain the best talent. You still need to offer competitive wages, benefits, and a positive work environment, but CVP can offer a key recruiting advantage. We will discuss more on expanding your team in Step 22.

You

You yourself are a stakeholder who cares a lot about climate. In Step 4, we helped you figure out your Founder-Problem Fit. Climate impact is probably a major reason you started the venture, so your CVP should resonate with you too. Don't lose sight of this.

How Do You Measure Your CVP?

Based on your Climate TAM, you should have a fair amount of confidence that your solution will make a positive difference for the planet. Now, you will calculate a more specific estimate of that impact. Measuring your CVP is challenging, because it is often based on a hypothetical vision of the future.

Your CVP projects a possible future state. Like in your Techno-Economic Analysis (TEA) and Enterprise Financials, it is valuable to use numbers to appreciate the relative scale of benefits and drawbacks of a given solution, and for comparison. However, it is important not to fall into the trap of false precision. Just because you calculated numbers, that does not mean they are correct, and they are certainly not exact. The idea is not to get to the right number, but rather the right order of magnitude.

There are three key components of the analysis:

- Baseline
- Additionality
- Full Life Cycle Emissions

Baseline

David Miller of Clean Energy Ventures uses a "two worlds" thought experiment to help founders get started with calculating their CVP: Think about what the world would be in 30 years if your venture never existed, and what the world would be in 30 years if your company were as successful as you hope it to be. The difference between those two worlds is your cumulative impact. Just like a QVP, a CVP compares a possible state to an as-is state (or "as-will-be" for a CVP since it's looking at a future state).

The first of those two worlds, the one without your solution, is called your baseline. It is also known as "business as usual." The simplest way to estimate this piece of your CVP is to use an established third-party source like the International Energy Agency (IEA) or the Intergovernmental Panel on Climate Change (IPCC). These groups regularly publish projections about future climate and energy systems, usually including a range of possible scenarios. If you use these projections, conduct your analysis with a mix of aggressive and moderate scenarios, and make sure you understand the underlying assumptions. Any projection of the future, even one from experts, is essentially guesswork. Keep that in mind.

Additionality

The next piece of the puzzle is additionality, which means emissions that are reduced exclusively due to your solution and nothing else in the system. In the two worlds thought experiment, this is the world where your solution is successful. Climate and energy systems are complex, so it can be hard to establish a direct cause and effect for one component, but it is important to try to quantify those effects rather than overestimate them.

Here are four possible routes to achieving additionality:[1]

- Making a high-emissions product more efficient
- Improving the output or performance of a low-emissions product
- Speeding up deployment of low-emissions options
- Directly replacing a high-emissions product

Full Life Cycle Emissions

The last consideration is quantifying the emissions that come from your solution over its full life cycle. You already started to tackle this in Step 15.

Start by calculating the greenhouse gases (GHGs) directly emitted (or removed) in each step of your process or solution. Use your TEA as a starting point. If your solution includes a process with GHG emissions as a by-product, you should be able to calculate the emissions based on the underlying chemistry of the reaction.

After estimating direct emissions, it may be helpful to calculate indirect emissions, including electricity used from the grid and the rest of the Value Chain. You can use third-party estimates, but be as accurate as possible. For instance, *someday* electricity may come from 100% renewable sources, but consider more realistic short-term scenarios.

If you are developing software or another enabling technology, also estimate the life cycle emissions for the solutions you are enabling because that is where most of your impact will come from.

Bringing It All Together

The following equation combines all three components of your CVP:

$$\text{Emissions reduction (in year } x) = \text{Baseline emissions } \textit{without} \text{ your solution (in year } x)$$
$$- \text{ net emissions } \textit{with} \text{ your solution}$$
$$(\text{net emissions per unit} \times \text{number of units at year } x)$$

$$\text{Where net emissions} = \text{lower-emissions scenario that is specifically unlocked with}$$
$$\text{your solution (additionality)} - \text{additional emissions created}$$
$$\text{by your solution (Full Life Cycle Emissions)}$$

Note that different GHGs have different contributions to warming. For instance, methane can be over 80 times more potent than CO_2 in a 20-year time frame. To account for these differences, the best standard for measuring emissions is to put everything relative to CO_2 using a metric called CO_2 equivalent (CO_2e), so that you're comparing apples to apples.

Timing is another important factor. For instance, methane is shorter lived than CO_2 so the differential goes down from over 80 to 28 over a 100-year time frame. If you're able to achieve emissions reductions in the near term, rather than the long term, that is an important part of your CVP!

Remember: the goal is not to arrive at a definitive measurement of your climate impact but to tell a compelling story that helps others to understand the potential impact you can achieve.

Many climate and energy ventures do not describe their CVP with this level of detail. Instead, they go with a simpler message like, "Coal is bad, and our solution replaces coal, so our solution must be good." This very basic narrative can serve certain purposes, but many investors and industry groups require a thorough quantitative approach. If you want to make your strongest possible case to them, you need to bring your own evidence.

What About Other Climate Benefits?

So far, our approach to measuring CVP has focused on emissions reduction as the key metric, but that leaves out the other areas of climate impact like emissions removal, global heat management, and adaptation. We have focused on emissions reductions because there is a clear variable to measure and several existing methodologies. Extending these methodologies to other forms of climate impact is fairly straightforward for emissions removal. The key metric is still emissions, but you measure what you remove rather than what you reduce. It can be harder to figure out what to measure for heat management and adaptation.

One possible metric is temperature change. The advantage of framing CVP in terms of temperature is that it more accurately captures the state of the geophysical system. Carbon dioxide emitted today can stay in the atmosphere and create a warming effect for decades (or even centuries), so measuring emissions doesn't fully capture the time dimension. Reducing emissions today has a much greater effect than reducing emissions in 20 years.

Another possible approach would be to frame your CVP in terms of avoiding harm from climate change, but there is no standard definition for "harm" and certainly no standard measurement for it. You could measure lives saved, but that leaves out the harm caused by injury, emotional stress, and property damage, not to mention the harm done to nonhuman groups like plants, animals, and ecosystems. You could also measure harm in terms of economic losses, but this runs the risk of reducing complex systems to their economic value.

It's up to you to figure out the best metric to communicate your particular CVP, but whatever metric you choose, you can still use the same concepts of baseline, additionality, and life cycle to quantify your impact. Just adjust the basic equation as needed:

[Emissions/warming/harm] avoided (in year x) = Baseline [emissions/warming/harm] *without* your solution (in year x) – net [emissions/warming/harm] *with* your solution (in year x)

Where net [emissions/warming/harm] = lower-[emissions/warming/harm] scenario that is specifically unlocked with your solution (additionality) – additional [emissions/warming/harm] created by your solution (Full Life Cycle Impacts)

Output from This Step

Come up with estimates for your baseline scenario, additional benefits, and additional harm. Then, use the equations in this step (or a more sophisticated methodology) to calculate your CVP.

Record all of your assumptions and be prepared to share and defend them with the stakeholders who care about climate impact. Showing your work is essential for this exercise. Similar to your Enterprise Financials, the narrative is more important than the number.

EXAMPLES

NCX

Max Nova and Zack Parisa realized that traditional methods of forest management were highly manual and time-consuming, remaining largely unchanged for about 100 years. They began offering landowners a suite of precision tools for measuring and managing forests.

Forests are also a major carbon sink, so selling carbon credits for this service created a huge revenue potential for forest owners. Max and Zack eventually pivoted their company to build a platform connecting carbon buyers to forest owners.

NCX's key innovation was their CVP. Since they were a platform for buying emissions removal, their CVP was closely tied to their QVP for customers. The traditional method of measuring emissions removal was to use a long-term static baseline based on the likelihood of a forest being harvested. For instance, a forest owner could sign a contract to store 110 tons of carbon for 100 years; if the baseline were 100 tons of carbon, they could sell 10 carbon credits (for the additional 10 tons above the baseline). However, a lot could happen in 100 years. The local mill could shut down, or the demand for that type of wood could decline, changing the baseline. Max and Zack realized that better accounting required a dynamic short-term baseline, and NCX had the technology to calculate that. Rather than asking carbon buyers to pay larger amounts for 100-year contracts with a lot of uncertainty, they asked them to pay smaller amounts for single-year contracts with baselines updated every year based on local timber markets.

To be reputable, NCX's forest carbon credits needed to be certified by a third-party organization. After a few years of booming interest in carbon credits, certifiers faced a wave of negative publicity when reporters and environmental organizations uncovered many questionable forest carbon projects. NCX defended their methodology, but their certifier dropped them. Demand for forest carbon credits dropped precipitously.

NCX pivoted once again, returning to a value proposition much closer to their original focus. They began helping forest owners track and manage their assets as part of a natural capital portfolio, thinking about these assets as an investor might consider a financial portfolio. Throughout all these shifts, Max and Zack retained a deep understanding of small forest owners as customers as well as a commitment to addressing pain points for those customers. They ran into problems when they broadened their scope to also include big carbon buyers and pushed a CVP that those markets were not ready to accept.

REsurety

A big difference between solar and wind power and other energy sources is that they only work when the sun is shining or the wind is blowing. Lee Taylor realized that due to this intermittency, energy buyers needed a new set of data on the value and risks associated with energy projects, and he founded REsurety to provide that information.

Many of REsurety's customers were buying renewable energy to meet climate targets, so CVP was very important to them. The emissions reductions depended heavily on where and when the energy was being generated. A kilowatt-hour of solar would reduce far more emissions when added to a coal-heavy grid relative to an already solar-heavy grid. In other words, energy projects needed to consider their additionality relative to the existing baseline. Sometimes, the relative difference in impact could be as high as 600%. The team at REsurety was able to provide this granular level of analysis, which they dubbed the *locational marginal emissions*.

The most ambitious customers loved this offering, because it helped them maximize and communicate their CVP. Other customers were more ambivalent because not only was it more complicated, but also it often showed that they were overstating their CVP. They preferred simpler methods that made them look better, even if some might argue that those simpler methods were a form of greenwashing. REsurety was able to grow by focusing on identifying and selling to customers who understood and valued their data products.

REsurety's story shows that some ventures can develop a powerful QVP in helping their customers measure and communicate their CVP, but this strategy requires a highly disciplined approach of finding the right customers and understanding their needs.

ADDITIONAL RESOURCES

There are additional resources for this step at www.de4cev.com/step16. These materials include the following:

- CVP Worksheet
- NCX Case Study
- REsurety Case Study
- Link to a white paper on a more detailed methodology for measuring CVP: Emissions Reduction Potential, a framework developed by Prime Coalition and NYSERDA
- Links to other tools for measuring your CVP:
  - Carbon Reduction Assessment for New Enterprises (CRANE) by Prime Coalition
  - Simple Emissions Reduction Calculator for Startups (SERC) by Clean Energy Ventures
  - Sustainable Energy System Analysis Modelling Environment (SESAME) by the MIT Energy Initiative
- Link to guidance on GHG measurement from Greenhouse Gas Protocol

Additional resources will be added as new and updated examples and information become available.

Note

1. Adapted from Scott P. Burger, Nicole Systrom, and Sarah Kearney, "Climate Impact Assessment for Early-Stage Ventures." PRIME Coalition and New York State Energy Research and Development Authority (NYSERDA), December 2017.

Make a Long-Term Capital Plan

In this Step, You Will

- Understand the various sources from which you might raise capital, along with their expectations for potential investments.

- Make a road map of which milestones you will achieve at which funding rounds, how much funding will be required to meet each milestone, and from what sorts of investors you plan to raise the necessary capital at each stage.

Why This Step, and Why Now?

Let's talk about money. Before you start raising capital, you need to have a plan because not all investor money is created equal. If you take the wrong steps early in the journey, you could end up on a path that gets you trapped in a corner, or worse yet, one that sends you irreversibly off a cliff.

When you raise money, you're selling a product, which is the equity in your company. We've previously described how to find a fit between your product and the customers who are buying it. Similarly, you need to make sure there's a fit between your company equity and the investors who are buying it.

A Long-Term Capital Plan is a strategy for how much money you need to raise, from whom, and when. Like your other strategies, it should change as you collect new information. There are several reasons that your venture will benefit from a Long-Term Capital Plan:

- **Plan your finances.** We have repeatedly talked about how climate and energy ventures have a high price of poker. You will need to raise and spend a lot of money. If you spend too quickly, your venture will not survive. The main job of a startup CEO is to make sure that the venture has enough money to stay afloat. A Long-Term Capital Plan can help that happen.

- **Align your team.** As your venture begins to grow, your team will need to split its limited time, energy, and attention. Having a clear Long-Term Capital Plan will enable you to make sure that everyone is on board with the direction of fundraising, even if they are not directly involved in the day to day.

- **Pitch investors.** Understanding how much money you need from them and why enables you to make a specific and compelling pitch to investors. It helps you to justify how much money you need and why they are the right people to provide it.

Sources of Capital

Before you create your Long-Term Capital Plan, you need to understand the potential sources of capital. Make sure you understand the purpose and expectations of financing organizations, as well as the roles of individuals within those organizations, including specific examples. Start with secondary sources, then learn more from direct conversations with investors and other founders who have gone through the fundraising process.

Here is a brief overview of some potential sources of capital for climate and energy ventures:

- **Public or private grants.** Funding from government or foundations to support the greater good, such as economic development, technological advancement, security, or climate impact. Grants do not need to be repaid but may have conditions, including detailed reporting requirements (see Step 18).

- **Recoverable grants.** A hybrid of grants and loans. This capital needs to be repaid if the venture succeeds but can be forgiven if it fails. Recoverable grants are often tied to economic development deliverables at later stages of the company. You should have high confidence of execution when considering this source of capital.

- **Donations.** Direct financial support with no repayment expectation. Some startups use crowdfunding platforms to get donations from the general public, but this is rare in climate and energy because getting started requires much more money than these platforms can usually provide.

- **Personal network.** Raising funds from friends and family, typically in exchange for equity. It requires wealthy connections, especially for climate and energy ventures, due to the high capital needs.

- **Venture capital (VC).** Firms that invest pooled funds into high-risk, high-reward startups in exchange for equity (see Step 21).
- **Angel investors.** Individual investors who provide Early-Stage Capital in exchange for equity, often quicker than VC firms but in smaller amounts.
- **Family offices.** Private firms managing wealth for high-net-worth individuals. They offer flexible funds but can be hard to access.
- **Growth investors.** Later-stage VC investors who take lower risks for smaller returns.
- **Private equity (PE).** Firms investing larger amounts in mature companies, often taking majority control.
- **Project finance.** Funding for specific projects via structured investments separate from the company's equity (see Step 24).
- **Debt.** Loans with repayment and interest, usually unavailable to startups until they mitigate risks (see Step 24).
- **Customers.** Ultimately, you want to finance your venture mainly with revenue from customer sales, but this can be tough to do up front. Some ventures scale only with reinvested revenue (bootstrapping). This strategy is challenging for climate and energy ventures because they often need substantial capital before making any revenue.

You will most likely pursue a mix of these capital sources, and the proportions will change at different stages of your venture development. Climate and energy ventures tend to start out with grants, followed by equity investments (possibly angel investors at first and then VC). The first meaningful customer revenue tends to come in about this point. Then, debt and growth capital become available as the venture scales. Sometimes, PE can acquire the company.

It is ultimately up to you to figure out what works best for your venture. That's why you need a Long-Term Capital Plan!

Leave No Milestone Unturned

Startups usually raise money in stages called rounds, rather than all at once. Investors distribute money this way to reduce their exposure to risk. Initially, they invest in small amounts and then follow up with larger investments (or other investors come in) once they are confident that the venture is less risky. This approach gives investors multiple chances to walk away or revise their assumptions.

Each round of funding is contingent on the venture reaching meaningful and achievable milestones that show it has reduced risk. For climate and energy ventures, the capital needs are often in the hundreds of millions, if not the billions, so this staging is critical. Your ability to raise larger rounds will be predicated on your demonstrated ability to deliver against the commitments of your previous rounds and build meaningful value in the company. Your milestones are the evidence of this. You must choose them carefully.

As a climate and energy entrepreneur, most of your investor-facing milestones will focus on three key themes of this book: customer, solution, and scaling. Customer-related milestones address market risk, while solution- and scaling-related milestones address technology risk and execution risk. You might also have a few milestones addressing risks related to policy, climate impact, or finance.

Your milestones are a key part of your Long-Term Capital Plan, so thoughtfully list them out. You can start with the scaling pathway that you developed as part of your Enterprise Financials. Here are some general milestones you can consider:

- Show the core technology works and validate your Techno-Economic Analysis with real data (building on what you started in Step 6).

- Develop a clear understanding of your market pathway (Steps 10–13).

- Show that the technology works at a larger scale (Step 19).

- Show commitment from initial customers (Step 20).

- Show that the technology works at a full commercial scale (Step 23).

- Show repeated customer deployment (Step 24).

Once you've listed your milestones, you will need to make a road map of which milestones you will achieve in which funding rounds, then determine how much funding will be required to meet each milestone. You will likely need to adjust your plan over time.

Eventually, your Long-Term Capital Plan might look something like the generalized example shown in Figure 17.1.

Output from This Step

Create a milestone roadmap that aligns your milestones with your intended funding rounds. You can use Table 17.1 to list your milestones in more detail.

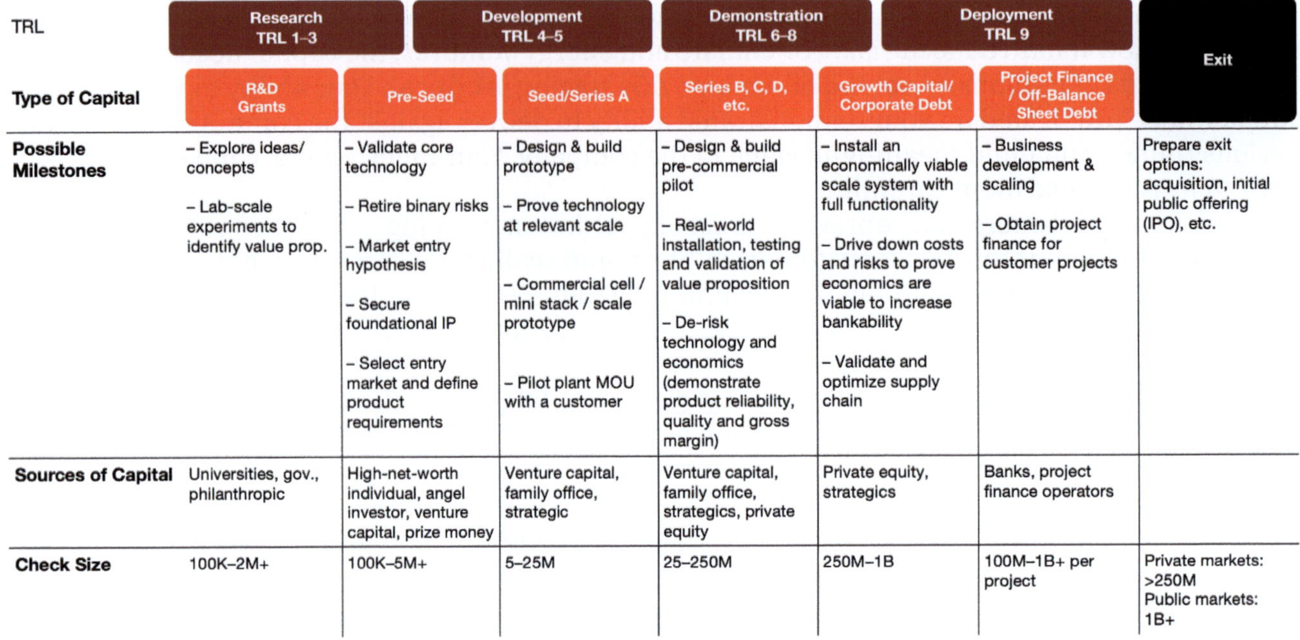

Figure 17.1: *A generalized Long-Term Capital Plan for climate and energy ventures, originally developed by Oliver Gottfried*

Table 17.1: *Milestone Matrix.*

	Milestone 1	**Milestone 2**	**And So On**
Short description of the milestone			
Type of risk addressed (customer, solution, scaling, finance, planet, or policy)			
Timing (year and quarter)			
Monthly budget (pull this from your Enterprise Financials)			
Funding round			
Possible sources of capital			

After you have established your milestones, the last part of your Long-Term Capital Plan is to estimate how much money you will need in each round of financing. Pull your best possible estimates from your Enterprise Financials, and be as conservative as possible—assume you will need more money rather than less.

Now, do some back-of-the-envelope calculations to figure out if your venture can meet investor expectations. Here are the key questions that you should seek to answer:

- Does each investor class make the return that they target?

- Does each round position the company for an increase in value in the next financing?

- Is the resulting ownership for the common and option pool sufficient? In other words, are you maintaining enough value for your founding team and your employees?

The goal here is not to predict the future. It is to create a reasonable projection that you can use as a guide and a baseline as you finance your venture going forward.

EXAMPLES

Commonwealth Fusion Systems (CFS)

The team at CFS wanted to be the first to commercialize fusion energy. When CFS started their journey, no one had come remotely close to building a fusion power plant. No one had even achieved the basic foundational breakthrough: a fusion reaction that released more energy than it consumed. Even under the best-case scenario, it would take decades and billions of dollars for the solution to reach a meaningful scale, so the founders of CFS planned for the long road ahead.

Fusion creates a high-energy state of matter called a *plasma*, and a core challenge is keeping that plasma stable. The CFS team developed a compelling design to hold plasma using highly powerful magnets. Confident they had something worth pursuing, they plotted a course to scale.

They planned to target investors that they knew could make large, patient investments, and they broke the long-term goal down into a series of phases that could be financed in series to incrementally de-risk the technology.

They started with their Big Prize: A fully decarbonized power grid by 2050, relying largely on fusion power plants. Then, they worked backwards to figure out the steps to get there, as well as the amount of money they would need at each phase.

The team jotted a rough capital plan on the back of a journal article. It looked something like this:

Step 1: Design and build magnet—$10M

Step 2: Design and build energy-generating device—$50M

Step 3: Prototype pilot plant—???

This plan was off by at least one order of magnitude on the capital needs, but the general vision was accurate. With some further strategizing, the team came up with CFS's initial capital plan, which we've re-created in Table 17.2.

Table 17.2: *CFS's Four-Phase Plan*

Phase	Name	Description	Timing	Round	Amount
I	HTS Magnet Demonstration	Build the first high-temperature superconducting (HTS) fusion magnet that can create a magnetic field with a strength of 20 Tesla.	Early 2020s	Series A	$100–500 million
II	SPARC	Build a demonstration plant capable of generating 2 to 10 times as much energy as goes into it. They referred to this as the "soonest possible" version of the ARC plant that they would build in Phase III, or SPARC for short.	Mid 2020s	Series B	$1–10 billion
III	ARC1	Build a full-scale and economically viable fusion power plant, according to the original design. The CFS team named this design the ARC, an acronym for affordable, robust, and compact.	Early 2030s	Growth Equity	$10–100 billion
IV	Full Scale	Full decarbonization with 10,000 fusion power plants across the world.	2050	Project Finance	$1–10 trillion

At the time of writing, the team is on track with this plan. They successfully demonstrated their high-powered magnet, they're now working on SPARC, and they have started the early planning for ARC. The company has over 1,000 employees, and it has raised over $2 billion.

Throughout the capital-raising process, CFS stuck to a few core principles: target investors who are the right fit, build long-term relationships, and set meaningful milestones. You might not be building something as massive as the world's first fusion power plant, but regardless of your solution, it is important to go about it with an appropriate plan for raising capital.

38 Degrees North

A Long-Term Capital Plan does not need to span across decades. Ryan Bennett founded 38 Degrees North with Jake Carney and Chris Bailey, two of his former colleagues. The trio wanted to find and support promising renewable energy projects. Their business model was to be a project developer and long-term asset owner, orchestrating the entire process of bringing an energy project from an idea to a fully operational facility. These projects cost millions of dollars and can support direct equity and debt investments into the project company, known as *off-balance-sheet financing* since the developer company doesn't sell its own shares or take on debt.

Ryan, Jake, and Chris were extremely intentional about starting the company by raising equity in the projects, rather than selling equity in 38 Degrees North. They set up joint ventures with their early partners, which were infrastructure-focused private equity companies, where they would split ownership in the projects. Their financers were able to reap the rewards of the projects (e.g., a return on their investments), while 38 Degrees North took on the risk and complexity, eventually earning regular returns as well.

The difficult part of selling equity in the projects was that the venture itself needed to stay afloat with very few resources. The three founders paid themselves moderate fees out of the projects, but the team had to keep these costs as low as possible. Now that the projects are built out, 38 Degrees North receives a significant share of the cash flow from the projects along with their partners who initially invested equity capital.

Once the team could prove that their model worked and had built up a portfolio of projects, they decided to raise equity capital at the company level. They raised a growth equity investment from S2G Ventures, which enabled them to expand their operations. Without a strong set of projects already under their belt, raising this growth equity would have been expensive and challenging.

ADDITIONAL RESOURCES

There are additional resources for this step at www.de4cev.com/step17. These materials include the following:

- Milestone Worksheet
- CFS Case Study
- 38 Degrees North Case Study
- Capital Stack Example

Additional resources will be added as new and updated examples and information become available.

Pursue the Right Non-Dilutive Funding

In this Step, You Will

- Understand where and how to find opportunities for Non-Dilutive Funding that might be available for your venture.
- Evaluate the trade-offs between the costs of Non-Dilutive Funding and the benefits.

Why This Step, and Why Now?

Non-Dilutive Funding is money that does not require a piece of equity or need to be paid back. It includes grants (public and private), fellowships, and prizes. These sources of capital can be an important part of your Long-Term Capital Plan, especially at the earliest stages, before you have raised an equity round.

There are benefits and drawbacks to Non-Dilutive Funding. One benefit is that it buys time before raising dilutive funding, where you sell equity in exchange for financing. Once you take dilutive funding, you give up equity in your venture and start a clock for when you need to deliver a return. This equity capital clock is a lit fuse that could ultimately blow up your venture if you do not create value before time runs out.

Non-Dilutive Funding also has its drawbacks. Some sources of grant funding can be time-consuming to obtain, requiring founders to navigate Byzantine application processes. There can also be strings attached that limit your future strategy. However, you can reduce effort and maximize your chances of getting funding with good timing and thorough knowledge of the process. Get help from knowledgeable mentors, if you can find them.

Taking Funding for Granted

Why would anyone just give away money, without expecting anything in return? Well, grant makers are expecting something in return, just not a financial benefit for themselves. Governments issue grants to advance solutions that they believe will benefit their citizens, and private organizations issue grants to support causes favored by their donors.

Climate and energy ventures are well placed to seek grant funding because addressing climate change is very much in the public interest. It is a classic tragedy of the commons, where everyone suffers the consequences when things go wrong, but no individual actor has responsibility for making things right. This creates a prime opportunity for governments and philanthropists to step up and help fund early-stage solutions that cannot get funding elsewhere.

Another reason that startups receive grants is to further regional economic development, which is something that nearly every venture aims to do, so think beyond climate when searching for possible grants.

There are many grant opportunities out there. It is up to you to find the ones that are a good fit. As you look for opportunities, make sure your venture aligns with the mission of the organization, and clearly address that in your application.

To find relevant opportunities, start by scouring the web, particularly government databases. Ask mentors if they know of opportunities, and ask other founders, especially those who are about one to three years ahead of you in their journey.

EVERY CLOUD HAS A SBIR LINING

In the United States, Small-Business Innovation Research (SBIR) grants are a common source of funding for climate and energy ventures, so they merit special mention. These grants support startups and small businesses developing innovative technology for commercialization across many different priority areas. They are coordinated by the US Small Business Administration and awarded by an array of different government agencies. Small Business Technology Transfer (STTR) grants are similar to SBIR grants but less widely offered and require working with a research institution.

SBIRs can be a boon to deep tech ventures because they help startups fund their early prototyping before they are ready to pursue other types of financing.

What About Prizes?

Prizes tend to have easier application processes than grants, but the judges can be time-constrained and less likely to dig deep into business fundamentals. Despite their eclectic nature, prizes can be a great source of networking opportunities and publicity, as they often involve live pitches. Even if you do not win, the process of competing for prizes can help you sharpen your pitch, build your network, and validate your venture. Despite these benefits, prize competitions can also be a distraction. Make sure not let them get in the way of actually building your business.

Prizes are not excuses to give away free money to promising startups. Organizations usually host prizes for some combination of the following reasons:

- To showcase a community or ecosystem of innovation
- To inspire future innovation in a given area
- To build a network of innovators
- To convene relevant collaborators
- To put on a good show

Before entering a prize competition, make sure you understand why it is being offered and assess whether you are a good fit.

There's No Such Thing as Free Money

Everything in life comes at a price. In the case of Non-Dilutive Funding, there are two main categories of costs. The first is the time and effort of applying. This is a cost that you are guaranteed to incur regardless of whether you are awarded funding. Think of this category as opportunity cost. The time and effort that you spend applying for Non-Dilutive Funding could otherwise be spent improving your solution or making inroads with customers. Time is your most valuable resource, and you spend some of it on every application that you fill out.

Generative artificial intelligence (AI) can help reduce the time it takes to fill out an application because grant and prize applications often follow a standard structure and format. However, like any use case of generative AI, you must spend time feeding the right information into the system, engineering the right prompts, and reviewing the outputs.

The second cost of applying for Non-Dilutive Funding is the set of limitations or stipulations that might be attached to the funding. This is most relevant for grant funding. For instance, some grants require your venture to remain based in a certain geographic area or focused on a certain industry. There also might be restrictions on your future funding or scaling. For instance, if your venture is based in the United States and receives grants from the US government, then you may have trouble raising funds from foreign investors. Grants may also have time-consuming reporting requirements and strict rules about how you use the funds. You can think of these limitations as alternative costs of capital. You can always turn down funds once they are awarded, but if you know in advance that a certain grant is going to be too limiting, then it is best not to apply at all.

Another element that you need to consider when deciding whether to apply for Non-Dilutive Funding is the probability of winning. For grants, you can often call up the grant manager to get a sense of what they are looking for and whether your solution is a fit. For prizes, you can get a pretty good sense of fit based on publicly listed criteria and by looking up past winners and finalists. Always assess your probability of winning as best you can before deciding to apply for funding.

There is also the possibility that you might need to travel to deliver a pitch or jump through other hoops after the initial application. This can be a benefit if it yields useful connections and experience, but it costs time and even sometimes money. If the ancillary elements seem like more of a cost than a benefit, it's probably not worth applying. If the ancillary elements seem worthwhile in themselves, then you can factor that value into your decision to apply.

When evaluating opportunities for Non-Dilutive Funding, you can classify them into four broad categories, as shown in Figure 18.1:

- **High chance of winning, low cost of applying.** Definitely apply. This is a golden opportunity, and exceedingly rare. Few sources of Non-Dilutive Funding fall into this category.

- **Low chance of winning, high cost of applying.** Do not apply (most likely). Focus your limited time and attention elsewhere. There may be exceptions when it is worth a shot, but do not get your hopes up.

- **Low chance of winning, low cost of applying.** Most prizes will fall into this category. If you can spare the time and think you can write a strong application, then go for it. And if you skip it, that's fine, too. There will many opportunities like this, and it is not worth losing sleep over a single one.

- **High chance of winning, high cost of applying.** Apply, but use caution. The most promising grants will fit into this category. It is probably worth the effort, but understand the costs for you and your team. The cost of applying is always a sure thing, but getting the money is not.

Never include Non-Dilutive Funding in your projected cash flow until it is 100% confirmed. You can include it in your Long-Term Capital Plan, but have back-up options in case a particular source of funding does not pan out.

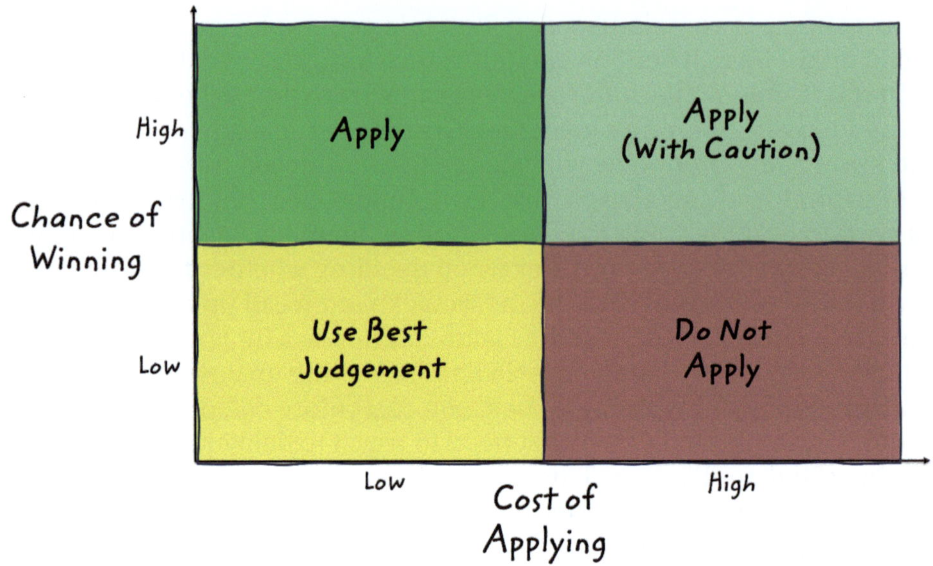

Figure 18.1: A possible matrix to evaluate Non-Dilutive Funding opportunities

Output from This Step

Build a list of potential Non-Dilutive Funding opportunities. You can use Table 18.1 to track these opportunities in a structured way.

EXAMPLES

Ayar Labs

Ayar Labs would not have existed without Non-Dilutive Funding. The company developed components of computer chips that could communicate with light rather than electricity, enabling faster and more efficient computer processing. The core technology was developed with $20 million in grant funding from the US Department of Defense, which was awarded while the effort was still a research project, not a company.

Once the company formed, Non-Dilutive Funding was similarly foundational. The team won the MIT Climate & Energy Prize (CEP), which provided $275,000. A few months later, they were

Table 18.1: *Non-Dilutive Funding Matrix.*

Funding source	What is the opportunity called?
Type of funding	Grant, prize, or something else?
Funding amount	How much funding is provided? This could be a range.
Timeline	If there's a set timeline, include that information here. What are the key steps and deadlines?
Funder	Which individual or organization provides the funding?
Funder priorities	What does the funder care about? Why are they offering this opportunity?
Eligibility requirements	What are the requirements to be considered for the funding? Is your venture eligible?
Application process	Summarize the application process. How onerous is it? What documentation or other information do you need for this application that you don't already have?
Criteria	What are the criteria that are used to decide whether or not funding is awarded? Who makes these decisions?
Reporting requirements	What kind of reporting is expected after the funding is awarded?
Limitations	What limitations would this funding place on your venture if you were to accept it? How challenging will it be for you abide by these stipulations?
Chance of winning	Estimate as best you can based on the history of the opportunity and any information you receive from the funder or past applicants. A qualitative assessment (high, medium, low) should suffice here.
Category	• High chance of winning, low cost of applying • Low chance of winning, high cost of applying • Low chance of winning, low cost of applying • High chance of winning, high cost of applying

awarded an SBIR grant of $175,000 from the National Science Foundation. With these two funding sources, they had almost half a million dollars before taking any equity financing. That was not enough for them to revolutionize the field of computing, but it was enough to get them started. Both of Ayar Labs' initial sources of capital did not require giving up equity, but the similarities end there. The processes of obtaining these funds could not have been more different.

Figure 18.2: Ayar Labs (then called OptiBit) won a total of
$275,000 in Non-Dilutive Funding from MIT's CEP.
Permission from Alex Wright-Gladstein

MIT CEP required a pitch deck and an in-person pitch. For context, MIT CEP is the "largest and longest-running competition for student-led climate & energy startups in the world." Founded by Bill Aulet and Tod Hynes in 2007, the same year as the MIT Climate & Energy Ventures course, the competition has supported hundreds of teams and awarded millions of dollars in prize money. CEP is run by MIT students, but it is currently open to student applicants anywhere in the world.

Prior to the live pitch, the Ayar Labs team ran their deck by mentors in the semiconductor and optical industry as well as anyone else they could find. Each iteration made the pitch better. By the time they went to the finals, it was close to bulletproof.

Unfortunately, a bulletproof pitch was not enough to get money from the federal government. For that, they crafted a detailed proposal and formed a relationship with the program manager who controlled the purse strings. That relationship enabled Ayar Labs to learn in advance from the funders that the technology was likely a fit for the grant.

Without Non-Dilutive Funding, Ayar Labs would have needed to raise equity capital much earlier to begin building their technology. They ultimately raised substantial venture capital money (see Step 21), but by then, they were in a far stronger position.

AeroShield

Here's an example that demonstrates how it is reasonable to continue applying for Non-Dilutive Funding even after taking other forms of capital. AeroShield's initial Non-Dilutive Funding was a $3 million grant from the US Department of Energy during their Market Segmentation process, while the project was still in the research phase.

The first funding that the team received as an actual company was a $100,000 check from the MIT CEP in 2019 (see Figure 18.3). Later that year, they also got a grant from the Massachusetts Clean Energy Center (MassCEC), which has a remit to make the state a leader in clean energy and climate tech.

MassCEC offers a range of funding opportunities, some non-dilutive and some dilutive, and the agency ended up making equity investments in AeroShield as well—first, as the lead of a $400,000 pre-seed round in 2020, and then as the lead of a $4 million seed round two years later.

AeroShield's largest funding to date came in 2024, and it was non-dilutive. They were awarded a $14.3 million grant from the ARPA-E SCALEUP program, which aims to help companies commercialize promising research.

AeroShield's story is not unusual. Having a diverse capital stack is quite common for climate and energy ventures. When seeking funding, your objective should be to find the right funding at the right time, not necessarily to maximize grant funding and then to move onto equity capital.

Figure 18.3: AeroShield winning the MIT CEP.
Permission from Elise Strobach

ADDITIONAL RESOURCES

There are additional resources for this step at www.de4cev.com/step18. These materials include the following:

- Non-Dilutive Funding Worksheet
- Ayar Labs Case Study
- AeroShield Case Study
- List of grants available for climate and energy ventures
- List of startup prize competitions with a focus on climate and energy

Additional resources will be added as new and updated examples and information become available.

Build Proof of Concept

In this Step, You Will

- Determine the key assumptions that must be true for your solution to be successful, especially on the technical side.

- Test those assumptions with an initial version of your solution that is as simple and scrappy and possible. Ideally, you should be able to make money from this initial version and begin getting feedback from customers.

Why This Step, and Why Now?

Once you have some resources at your disposal, you will need to build a version of your solution. The early versions of your solution will likely be much smaller than what you will sell at scale, and costs per unit output will be far higher. Building your full-scale solution can take many years and many millions of dollars. The goal of a Proof of Concept is to prove out your technology at a small yet meaningful scale and also to start making money from it, if you can.

Software startups thrive with rapid iteration. In Silicon Valley, there is a common mantra of "fail fast and try again." Iteration is almost always valuable, but the "fast" part can be difficult to manage, especially for hardware and deep tech ventures. If you are working on a complex physical solution, you may not be able to build or change any part of your solution in a few weeks or even months, and that's okay. However, you still need to be intentional about what you build and why, and you need to learn from your mistakes as quickly as possible.

The Proof of Concept that you build in this step should be aligned with the Market Stepping Stones that you chose in Step 10. Back then, you identified a Beachhead Market that you could reach with the simplest and fastest-to-build version of your solution. Now, we are going to tell you how to go about building that version.

Is It a Proof of Concept, a Prototype, or a Pilot?

There are many different words for an early version of a product that validates the technology and enables initial customer engagement. We have chosen to use the term *Proof of Concept* to highlight that each new iteration should prove something important about your solution. The term *prototype* suggests technical validation and features that can be replicated or even mass-manufactured in the future. The term *pilot* emphasizes on-site testing with potential customers. *Proof of Concept* captures both these aspects.

You will probably build multiple Proofs of Concept[1] as you work toward a full-scale version. Each one will validate a different aspect of the technology and bring new value to your initial customers. You've moved beyond Proof of Concept when you are building the solution at a scale that's ready for full commercial deployment.[2]

What About a Minimum Viable Business Product (MVBP)?

A concept that bears strong resemblance to Proof of Concept is an MVBP, which is Step 22 of the original Disciplined Entrepreneurship framework. Your MVBP is the most basic version of your product that a customer is willing to pay for. The difference between an MVBP and a Proof of Concept is that a Proof of Concept focuses heavily on technological viability in addition to business viability. Sometimes these two things overlap. As we mentioned, it is ideal if you can start making money from your Proof of Concept. Once that happens, the Proof of Concept will also be an MVBP, but that is not always the case.

A key area where these terms diverge is the notion of a "concierge MVBP," where a venture provides highly personalized and hands-on support to customers or users during the early stages of product development in advance of figuring out how to automate those processes. An example is having members of your team manually type in data before developing the software to do it automatically. Deep tech ventures in climate and energy often do not find a concierge MVBP useful because they're frequently selling commodities where the demand for the end product is already proven. For instance, if you are developing a novel energy generation technology, a concierge version might be to set up a big wheel and generate energy by running on it all day. That would just lead to you getting very tired, and all you would show is that people want energy, which you already knew in the first place.

Technological viability is usually the first priority, especially when producing a commodity that people are already buying, like electricity or chemicals. You first need to show that the solution functions on a basic level, and then you can show that it will deliver value to real customers who are willing to pay (see Step 20).

Testing Key Assumptions

We mentioned that each of your Proofs of Concept should, by definition, prove something. Before you begin building a Proof of Concept, you should define the Key Assumptions that you will test. Identifying and breaking down your Key Assumptions is not difficult and can be a fun exercise, but entrepreneurs tend to skip over this step, substituting intuition or research for actual testing of assumptions about technology, business, and customer behavior. Don't do that. Be disciplined.

Using your Techno-Economic Analysis (TEA) as a starting point, make a list of hypotheses that you can prove or disprove with a Proof of Concept. These assumptions can be related to either the market or the technology, but either way, they should be intentional and well defined.

Make sure that your Key Assumptions have the following characteristics:

- **Specific.** A good hypothesis should be very descriptive and rich in detail.
- **Singular.** There should only be one factor in the assumption statement. The word *and* is usually a flashing light that you need to break it up or simplify it.
- **Important.** The assumption must have enormous impact on whether your solution is successful.
- **Measurable.** Your assumption must be quantifiable so you can compare different situations without bias.
- **Testable.** If it's not testable, it's not useful.

Keep It Scrappy, Stupid

Engineers in the US Navy have long implemented one core principle in the design of aircraft and other military equipment: KISS,[3] which stands for "keep it simple, stupid." For climate and energy ventures, we suggest "keep it scrappy, stupid." You can minimize the time and expense of building your solution by making your Proofs of Concept as scrappy as possible. As mentioned, hardware and deep tech ventures cannot iterate as rapidly as software ventures, but scrappiness can help even the playing field.

Being scrappy means finding creative ways to make the most of limited resources. Buy as many materials off the shelf as you can. Only design and build from scratch the components that are absolutely fundamental to the assumptions that you are aiming to prove, or that are unavailable through any other means. Start small. Remember that a Proof of Concept should be the quickest path to proving technical viability and making early revenue. Include the minimum features necessary to test your assumptions.

If possible, use shared spaces and equipment, rather than setting up your own laboratory or workshop from the get-go. Look for technology incubators, universities, companies, and other lab spaces in your area. Greentown Labs is now the largest climate tech incubator in North America, but it started with a bunch of entrepreneurs jointly renting out an old warehouse to build climate and energy solutions that would not fit anywhere else.

Wherever you build your Proof of Concept, make sure that you are following appropriate safety protocols. Scrappiness does not mean carelessness. Moving fast is important, but so is ensuring everyone's health and well-being. Getting sued for reckless endangerment is a great way to tank your venture.

There are some situations where scrappiness is not an option. Certain climate and energy solutions are too big or too dangerous to build interim versions at a smaller scale. Consider your project needs, and be as scrappy as possible without sacrificing safety or effectiveness.

Output from This Step

List out your Key Assumptions, using the criteria we've described in this step. Then, describe the experiments and Proofs of Concept that you can use to validate your assumptions. You have already laid a lot of the groundwork for this exercise. Draw from your TEA (Step 6), your Market Stepping Stones (Step 10), your Enterprise Financials (Step 14), and the milestones you established as part of you Long-Term Capital Plan (Step 17).

EXAMPLES

Solugen

Solugen's Big Prize was to become a global chemical company that used sugar and starch as feed-stocks, instead of fossil fuels. Their Beachhead Market was float spas. Then, they moved to cleaning wipes, and after that, water treatment for oil wells. They were able to execute on these stepping stones by being scrappy and resourceful with their Proofs of Concept.

Solugen's first capital came from a prize competition called the MIT $100K. They did not win the grand prize, but they did take home $10,000 as a runner up. They spent some of the money on PVC pipe and other materials from Home Depot, and they built a janky but functional little reactor that enabled them to make their first batch of hydrogen peroxide, which they loaded into Sean's car and drove directly to float spas (Figure 19.1).

Figure 19.1: Sean Hunt stands in front of Solugen's first reactor

For their next Proof of Concept, they designed a pilot plant that was 10 times bigger (Figure 19.2). To build it, they put out a bid for contractors on an online home improvement platform, and they built the facility with just four people in total. The new plant produced enough hydrogen peroxide for the direct-to-consumer cleaning wipes, and later, it even enabled them to dip a toe in the water of the upstream oil market. Still, they were just scratching the surface of the capacity would ultimately need.

Figure 19.2: Solugen's pilot plant

Eventually, they raised millions of dollars and built a demonstration plant, which they called Bioforge1 (Figure 19.3). Within a year of completion, it was producing thousands of tons of chemicals annually. Solugen was on their way to becoming a global chemical company, and it all started with a few parts from Home Depot.

Figure 19.3: Bioforge1

Table 19.1 shows Solugen's Market Stepping Stones, matched with the Proofs of Concept that they needed to reach those stepping stones.

EQORE

The EQORE team planned to build a system that would use batteries to help manufacturers offset their expensive peaks in electricity demand. They aimed to build their solution as simply and cheaply as possible, which they would do through four Proofs of Concept.

The first was a computer simulation, which was more or less free to make. That simulation was enough for them to get a letter of intent from one of the potential customers they spoke to during primary market research.

The second Proof of Concept was a physical system they could set up on a tabletop using an inverter, some batteries, and a programmable load, costing a few thousand dollars (Figure 19.4). This helped them sign their first customer, who was willing to pay for a larger version of the system up front.

Table 19.1: *Solugen's Market Stepping Stones and Proofs of Concept*

Year	Customer	Product	Asset
2017	Float Spas	Peroxide/organic acid mixtures	PVC Reactor (7 gal)
2018	Consumers	Peroxide/organic acid wipes	Pilot Plant (70 gal)
2019	Upstream Energy	Peroxide/organic acid mixtures, blended chemicals	Pilot Plant (70 gal), toll blending partner
2020	Upstream Energy	Peroxide/organic acid mixtures, blended chemicals	Houston, Texas, and Slaton, Texas blending facilities
2021	Upstream Energy	Organic acids, peroxide, blended chemicals	Bioforge1, Houston and Slaton blending facilities

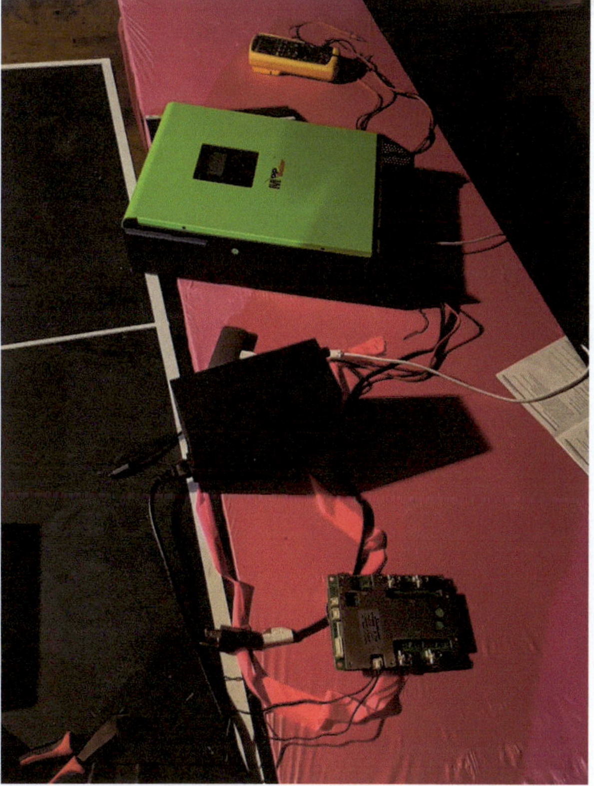

Figure 19.4: EQORE's second Proof of Concept.
Permission from Valeriia Tyshchenko Nin of EQORE

Before building the system on-site for the customer, they did pre-installation testing off site, which became their third Proof of Concept (Figure 19.5). They bought most of their equipment used from government auctions and online marketplaces. For the battery, they worked with the same one that they later would install at the site. The test system was part of their established rollout process with their pilot customer, so they purchased the battery new using the advance payment they had received for this process.

Figure 19.5: EQORE's third Proof of Concept.
Permission from Valeriia Tyshchenko Nin of EQORE

Their fourth Proof of Concept was the one they built on-site (Figure 19.6). This was the most complicated version they built, not because of the system itself but because of regulations. They needed to acquire installation permits from local authorities for safety reasons. They also needed insurance to make sure their customer would not be on the hook for anything that might get broken or damaged.

Figure 19.6: EQORE's fourth Proof of Concept.

Across all four Proofs of Concept, the EQORE team made all their decisions with scrappiness in mind, helping them get to market as quickly and cheaply as possible.

ADDITIONAL RESOURCES

There are additional resources for this step at www.de4cev.com/step19. These materials include the following:

- Proof of Concept Worksheet
- Solugen Case Study
- EQORE Case Study

Additional resources will be added as new and updated examples and information become available.

Notes

1. In case you are more familiar with the framework of Technology Readiness Levels (TRLs), what we're calling *Proof of Concept* could be anything from TRL 3 to TRL 6, maybe even TRL 7.
2. This corresponds roughly to TRL 7 or 8.
3. "What Is Keep It Simple, Stupid (KISS)?" *Interaction Design Foundation*. https://www.interaction-design.org/literature/topics/keep-it-simple-stupid.

Demonstrate Initial Market Traction

In this Step, You Will

- Identify the most promising initial customers in your Beachhead Market.
- Figure out how to turn potential customers into actual customers by getting revenue, or at least gathering strong evidence of customer interest.

Why This Step, and Why Now?

Climate and energy ventures face a three-way dilemma. Investors are hesitant to invest without customers on board, customers don't want to buy unless the technology is proven, and the technology cannot be built at scale without investor money. One way to resolve this paradox is to bring on at least one anchor customer with reliable intent to buy the technology. These customers usually end up being more than just buyers. They will likely wind up being partners in the development and construction of the pilot, lending technical expertise and possibly financing. They may also be part of large institutions that are at risk of getting bogged down in bureaucracy and inertia, so entrepreneurs must be prepared for a tricky dance.

You have already built the foundations necessary to bring your initial customers on board. At this point, you know for whom you are building your solution and what they want, and you have proved that you can build it. Now, it's time to land some customers.

Will the Dogs Eat the Dog Food?

Disciplined Entrepreneurship: Expanded and Updated describes Initial Market Traction using a fictional story about a brilliant inventor who developed a dog food formula that would be healthier and cheaper. It was lab-tested and everything looked great on paper. He raised millions of dollars to build a manufacturing plant, distribute the product, and market it to dog owners. Then, when he actually put the dog food in front of the dogs, the dogs refused to eat it.

DISCIPLINED ENTREPRENEURSHIP

REFER TO STEP

23

SHOW THE DOGS WILL EAT THE DOG FOOD

This story plays out surprisingly often across many types of solutions, including those in climate and energy. However, it's harder to test solutions that involve large infrastructure. Building just one project with huge corporate clients can take years and cost millions of dollars. Once again, we see the effects of the high price of poker for climate and energy ventures (Figure 20.1).

Figure 20.1: At the risk of egregiously mixing metaphors, a high price of poker makes it harder to figure out if the dogs will eat the dog food.

So how do we show the dogs will eat the dog food? Usually, climate and energy ventures can show this through strong buy-in from a few key customers. These early customers are more like partners, and sometimes they even invest in the company.

There is good news and bad news about these customers. The bad news is that acquiring them will be costly. You are seeking customers with a high Lifetime Value, and you should expect to pay a high Cost of Customer Acquisition. Some would call this situation hunting whales, but we prefer a metaphor that is more ecologically friendly: nurturing redwoods. This means long sales cycles with regular site visits and a lot of technical validation before these customers are willing to make a purchase.

Now, for the good news. By the time you reach this step, you probably already know your initial customers and have spoken to them for your primary market research (PMR). You might have even worked with your anticipated first customer to profile Personas across the Decision-Making Unit (DMU). That means you are already on the route to Initial Market Traction, even if there is still a long road ahead.

How to Measure Traction

Your instincts can help guide you on assessing how close your redwoods are to taking root and sprouting, but they can also lead you astray. We often hear entrepreneurs say that they are "having conversations" with a promising customer, or they have several buyers in the pipeline. These prospects might indeed be strong, but it is imperative that you gather some hard evidence about their actual level of commitment.

Here are some ways to demonstrate traction with early customers:

- **Revenue.** There is no better sign of traction than cold, hard cash. If you can provide initial product and get paid for it, that is the clearest possible signal that there is willingness to pay. Some companies will also pay in advance for promising climate and energy solutions to show investors and other customers that there is interest.

- **Letter of intent (LOI).** An LOI is a nonbinding agreement that outlines the basic terms of a potential deal between two parties. For climate and energy entrepreneurs, it is a useful tool to demonstrate early customer interest or partnership commitment without requiring a full contract.

- **Pilot.** If a customer is willing to host your solution on their premises, that shows that they are interested in it. Ideally, you should set up paid pilots where you receive revenue, but there are situations where the pilot precedes revenue, or where the pilot is not revenue ready for some reason (maybe it does not yield a useful product but is useful as a Proof of Concept).

- **Press release.** If your customer is willing to endorse your solution in a press release, then they are not just saying that it works; they are shouting it from the rooftops.

- **Investment.** Many climate and energy ventures get funded through corporate venture capital, and this is a signal from the company that they see commercial potential in what you are offering. However, it is important to realize that the venture arm of a company is likely to have very different objectives, priorities, and budget from the procurement division that would decide to buy your solution.

- **In-kind support.** If a customer is willing to allocate their own resources, it shows they see real value in your solution and want to help make it work. For example, a company might offer support from their engineers, who bring domain expertise and insights into the company's specific needs, which can help you refine your product and align it more closely with the market. However, make sure they are in it for the right reasons and be careful about sharing your intellectual property or other sensitive information with outside parties.

- **Political advocacy.** Your customers are probably even more effective than you at shaping policy because they have more resources and more experience. If they are willing to lobby on your behalf for supportive policies, that is a very good sign. It demonstrates two key things: confidence in your offering and alignment with their own goals or values.

Always Be Closing

You need to wait until the right moment to make an ask of your potential customers, but also you don't want to wait too long, and if it seems like they're stringing you along, you may need to cut them loose. The key is to constantly move forward. Drive your interactions with your initial customers toward some next step, and recognize when the process may be stagnating.

Every interaction with a potential customer or partner is an opportunity to build momentum and validate your venture. "Always be closing" doesn't mean pushing for a hard sell. It means constantly seeking ways to deepen engagement, secure commitments, and convert interest into action. Each win builds the foundation for the next.

It is also critical to have multiple irons in the fire. Do not count on any single customer to carry you to scale. Have multiple options so that you can pursue another opportunity when one falls through or gets delayed.

Output for This Step

Keep track of your most promising customer leads, indicating which ones are most likely to be your initial anchor customers. You already started to do this when you made customer projections in

your Enterprise Financials (Step 14). Then, you were making a realistic forecast, but it was still a forecast. Now, focus even more on what's real.

Record any traction that you have achieved with these customers, and identify any concrete actions you can take to build further traction. Use Table 20.1 as a guide. This is similar to the "List of 10 Next Customers" in *Disciplined Entrepreneurship: Expanded and Update*, but with a much greater focus on traction.

Remember that this information is gold. Do not share this list of customers or the information you gather with others outside your company.

Table 20.1: *Initial Market Traction Matrix.*

General info	Customer name	If you're selling to a business, put the name of the company here.
	Relevant info	Short summary of who this customer is and why they are included on the list.
	Main point of contact	If you're selling to an individual, you can consolidate this with the "Customer Name" field. Otherwise, pick the person (or possibly two to three people) within the company with whom you're most regularly in contact.
	Role in DMU	Your main point of contact should be the economic buyer or potentially the user, whoever is driving the decision. If you're not in contact with the people in either of those roles, you're not likely to gain traction with this customer.
	Title	Their official job title
	Email/phone	How to get in touch with them
Fit	Demographic	Go back to the Personas across the DMU that you profiled in Step 11. Is this person a demographic fit with what you would expect for their role in the DMU?
	Psychographic	Again, go back to the Personas that you profiled in Step 11. Is this person a psychographic fit with what you would expect for their role in the DMU? Do their top priorities match the ones that you identified earlier?
	Use case	Does this customer have a viable use case for your solution?
	Value prop	Is this customer able to realize the full extent of the Quantified Value Proposition that you determined in Step 13?
	Overall	How good of a fit is this customer for what you have to offer? Use a simple scale of 1–10 ratings or A–F grades.
Engagement	Traction achieved so far	What progress have you made in engaging with this customer? Have you been able to achieve any of the measurements of traction that we laid out earlier in this step?
	Actions to build further traction	What concrete actions can you take to build further traction? When will you take those actions?

EXAMPLES

Fervo Energy

Fervo is a great example of a venture that successfully engaged a lead customer to help launch their business. Since there was no existing market for enhanced geothermal technology or projects, the Fervo team decided to go into the business of developing their own projects and then selling low-carbon electricity.

For this business model to work, they needed to find a customer with a lot of cash, a high tolerance for risk, and a strong demand for low-carbon electricity. Their search led them to Google, which had just raised the bar on its renewable energy goals and was specifically interested in firm, clean power (versus intermittent clean power like solar and wind).

Google agreed to do a 3.5 MW project with Fervo, which is small for an energy project, but larger than any enhanced geothermal project that had ever been built.

Google was an ideal early customer for Fervo for two reasons. First, they were sophisticated enough in their understanding of power markets to properly value what Fervo was offering over the long term. Second, they were willing to engage with both a new technology and a new developer. Usually, in the power market, nobody wants to be first to adopt a new solution because that comes with risk. It's a classic example of how the early bird may get the worm, but the second mouse gets the cheese.

Google was willing to take the risk of being the first mouse, which was immensely valuable to Fervo. This initial traction was a critical signal to the rest of the market as well as to investors. It led to additional funding as well as much larger agreements with other companies, and it helped to establish enhanced geothermal as a whole new sector of clean energy supply.

Thiozen

Thiozen was working on a technology to produce hydrogen out of water and hydrogen sulfide. They targeted industrial customers that both produced hydrogen sulfide and used hydrogen because this eliminated the need for long-distance transport.

They achieved some promising traction with a large multinational corporation but, despite support from management, the corporate participants failed to complete their deliverables. Ryan realized that the corporate research and development team was more interested in the novelty of the project than it was in operationalizing it long term.

The Thiozen team learned some key lessons from this false start. One was to have multiple points of contact in different parts of the organization so they would hold one another accountable. Another lesson was to make sure the project was always tied to the bottom line. Often, climate and energy ventures can be seen as part of a long-term impact strategy, which means corporate partners do not treat them with urgency. If the company has a clear financial interest in completing the project, then everyone involved is more motivated to move quickly.

The Thiozen team then connected with Marshall Watson, who was the president of a small oil and gas company. He was also an academic, so he was excited to test out new technology. Thiozen's co-founders flew to Lubbock, Texas, and Marshall personally drove them to the site. They struck a deal with him right then and there.

Thiozen had initially been targeting the biggest names in the industry, but in the end, their first partner was basically a mom-and-pop shop. The moral of their story is that action is more important than prestige. A small player who says "yes, let's do this" is infinitely more valuable than a big player who says "no" or "maybe" or even "yes, in three years." Time is essential to climate and energy entrepreneurs, and it is not worth trading it away for the cache of a recognizable name. Ultimately, real traction will speak for itself.

Orange EV

Kurt and Wayne, the founders of Orange EV, aimed to sell electric yard trucks at ports, warehouses, and railyards. Through PMR and other research, they learned that common buyers for yard trucks were the third-party logistics providers who operate the sites where they're used. One of the biggest buyers was the logistics giant DHL.

Wayne went on DHL's website and saw they had a sustainability tab with an inquiry form, so he figured he'd give it a try. He eventually heard back from Dave Williams, a general manager for a site in Chicago who had previously done a pilot for a truck powered with natural gas. He gave Orange EV an old broken-down yard truck to use as a starting point. The Orange EV team took the entire truck apart, cleaned it up, and put it back together, replacing the diesel engine and transmission with an electric battery and powertrain.

They brought it back to the DHL yard and put it into service. At that point, it was the first and only heavy duty electric vehicle in the United States, but soon there were 17 Orange EV trucks in the Chicago area—including a second one at DHL.

It helped that policy was working in Orange EV's favor. Their electric yard truck was eligible for state and federal incentives. DHL was eager to explore incentives in California as well as Illinois, so they began placing orders for yard trucks in both states. A big advantage of working with a large international company like DHL was they had operations in many different places. Another benefit was that DHL served as a reference customer for Orange EV, which helped them build credibility with new buyers.

In early 2024, DHL announced they would be entirely phasing out diesel yard trucks by 2025, just 10 years after they bought their first electric one. As an early customer and advocate, DHL proved to be a game changer for Orange EV, by essentially building their reputation from scratch and opening the door to broader market adoption.

ADDITIONAL RESOURCES

There are additional resources for this step at www.de4cev.com/step20. These materials include the following:

- Initial Market Traction Worksheet
- Fervo Energy Case Study
- Thiozen Case Study
- Orange EV Case Study

Additional resources will be added as new and updated examples and information become available.

Pursue Early-Stage Capital

In this Step, You Will

- Build a target list of early-stage investors and use rigorous and consistent criteria to analyze their potential fit for your venture.

- Understand and systematically work through the process of going from initial outreach to ultimately closing a deal.

Why This Step, and Why Now?

If you can prove that your technology works and can demonstrate some market traction, you will be well poised to raise Early-Stage Capital to take the next step. Here, our definition of *Early-Stage Capital* is a wide umbrella that includes any early funding that takes equity (or future equity).

The process of raising Early-Stage Capital is surprisingly similar to the process of building your Initial Team (Step 5). That is because these early investors aren't just writing checks; they're essentially joining your team as critical partners. Be extremely intentional about whom you choose to partner with. Make sure they align with your Long-Term Capital Plan and that you're a good steward of their money over time.

Understanding the Investor Landscape

There are four main types of investors who often provide Early-Stage Capital: angels, venture capital (VC), corporate VC, and family offices (see Step 17). These investors have different pipelines, criteria, and expectations, so your strategy will differ depending on which ones you pursue. It is okay to court multiple types of Early-Stage Capital, as long as you are intentional about why and how you are going after each one.

Many of these investors specialize in climate and energy ventures. Different climate investors have different focus areas, so it's important to learn to tell them apart, rather than assuming a certain investor will be interested in your solution just because they have a climate focus.

The market intelligence group Sightline Climate put together a good breakdown of the categories of climate investors:[1]

- **Climate generalists** have a broad climate thesis and invest across many different categories of climate and energy ventures.
- **Vertical specialists** have a single category of focus—known as a vertical—within climate (e.g., energy, mobility, etc.).
- **Deep tech** investors focus on supporting complex innovations in science and engineering and tend to have longer time horizons.
- **Generalists** mainly invest in enterprise or consumer software but will also make opportunistic climate investments.

Not All Your Investors Need to be Climate Investors

While there are many climate investors out there, you do not need to target them exclusively. Software-based climate and energy ventures may find more value from software generalist investors who can advise them on aspects of software development and sales that are less familiar to climate investors. You should seek to find investors who are the right fit for you at the right time, in accordance with your Long-Term Capital Plan. You should also seek investors who can help you work through your current challenges and advance to the next phase.

Investors conduct thorough due diligence before they put money into a venture to unearth potential risks and make sure that the venture is investment worthy. In turn, you should conduct due diligence on your investors to make sure they are truly going to add value.

The Fundraising Funnel

Like sales, fundraising can be portrayed as a funnel where prospective investors move through different stages. At each stage, you rule out prospects, hence the funnel shape. In climate and energy, the sales process can vary, often involving a smaller pool of potential customers and long sales cycles, so the funnel can look a bit weird. The fundraising funnel follows a more traditional structure. Typically, it involves the following stages (Figure 21.1):

1. **Intro sent.** This could come from your network, an accelerator, or a warm referral. In climate and energy, leveraging mission-aligned networks or industry-specific events is critical.

2. **Initial call.** The first conversation is about gauging interest and alignment. Usually it happens over a phone or video call. Investors will want to understand what your solution is at a basic level. The work you did in Step 12 will pay off in spades here. They also care about your climate impact, market size, and traction—things like letters of intent, pilots, or early revenue are key.

3. **Subsequent meeting(s).** These go deeper into your business model, technology, and team. For climate and energy ventures, expect questions about regulatory risks, scalability, and capital intensity.

4. **Partner meeting.** If the investor is interested, they'll bring your deal to their partners. This is where alignment on return expectations and timelines becomes critical, especially for ventures with longer development cycles.

5. **Due diligence.** Investors will dig into your Enterprise Financials, intellectual property, Initial Market Traction, and Climate Value Proposition. For hardware or infrastructure-heavy ventures, they'll also scrutinize your Techno-Economic Analysis and deployment plans.

6. **Term sheet.** If diligence checks out, you'll negotiate terms. Be prepared to discuss ownership, board seats, and follow-on funding needs.

7. **Check.** Once terms are finalized, the funds are wired, and you're ready to execute your next phase.

Tracking these steps is essential because each stage represents a different probability of closing a deal. As you move through the funnel, the probability of closing increases.

For climate and energy ventures, the pipeline might include additional steps, like technical reviews or policy risk assessments, especially for deep tech or infrastructure projects. Tailoring your approach to the unique requirements of each funding source is critical to building a successful fundraising funnel.

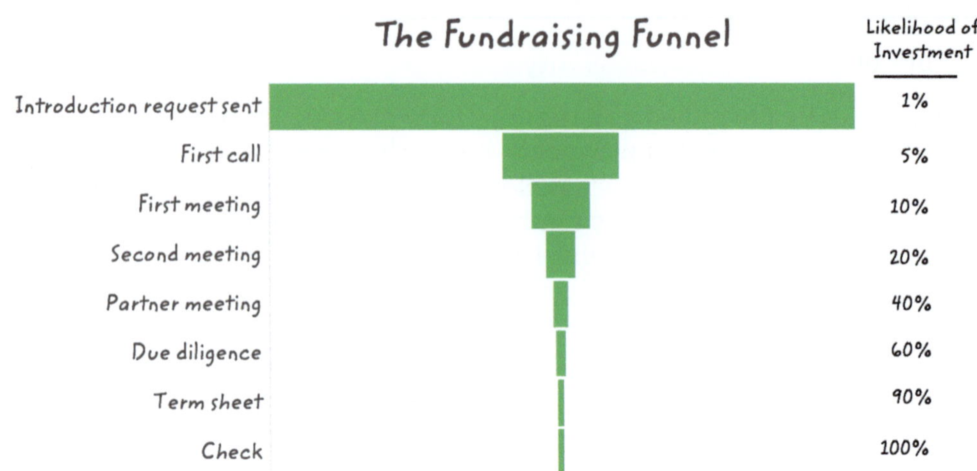

Figure 21.1: An archetypal fundraising funnel, adapted from Startup Tactics

The Importance of a Warm Intro

When it comes to early-stage funding, a well-informed plan is important, but, as the classic adage goes, "It's not just what you know, it's who you know." Investors rely heavily on their networks to filter opportunities. A warm introduction from someone they trust—whether it's a fellow investor, an accelerator, or an industry expert—carries far more weight than a cold email directly from you. The climate and energy sector is complex, and investors often look for validation from people who understand the intrinsic technical, regulatory, and market challenges.

A warm introduction can be the difference between getting a meeting and being ignored. It signals credibility, trust, and alignment before you even join the call or step into the room. It's your first chance to stand out in a crowded field.

So how do you get that warm intro? Begin building your network early. Engage with the climate and energy community—join accelerators and other ecosystem programs, attend industry events, and connect with alumni from your university. Use platforms like LinkedIn strategically, but don't underestimate the power of in-person connections. When you do ask for an introduction, make it easy for the person helping you: be clear about why you're reaching out, what you're asking for, and how it aligns with the investor's focus.

Ultimately, pursuing early-stage investment is about more than just funding—it's about building relationships that can support your venture for the long haul. Invest in your network, and your network might invest in you.

With Great Funding Comes Great Responsibility

When you raise money from investors, you have the incredible opportunity to build an exciting new business with it. You also have the responsibility to use investor money wisely. Your investors understand that entrepreneurship is about taking risks, but you must do this diligently and carefully. Under no circumstances should entrepreneurs use investors' money for purposes other than building value for their shareholders.

Output from This Step

Build a target list of investors who seem like a strong fit, now or in the future. Gather comprehensive information about each of these investors to assess fit. It is up to you to figure out the best criteria for analyzing potential investors, but we have provided some suggestions in Table 21.1. As you begin outreach with these investors, make sure to track where you are in the fundraising funnel.

EXAMPLES

Ayar Labs

Ayar Labs was having a hard time securing funding for their semiconductors. In San Francisco they expected to find a sea of VC investors eager to put their money into a revolutionary new technology that could change the future of computing. What they actually found was a rude awakening. While the foundations of Silicon Valley had been built on hardware, the zeitgeist had moved firmly to software.

Despite the many rejections, they managed to find a few investors who seemed genuinely interested in the technology. The problem was that these investors were not sending term sheets. Alex Wright-Gladstein, the CEO, knew they needed to create more of a sense of urgency to gain commitments.

One potential investor was from a foreign VC firm, and he was a superfan of a paper written by one of Ayar's founders, so he seemed particularly eager to invest. Unfortunately, Alex knew it would be near impossible to accept his money, because the initial technology development had been funded by the US Department of Defense, and there were stipulations in the licensing agreement with MIT that prohibited

Table 21.1: *Investor Fit Matrix with Definitions.*

Financial expectations (full loss of capital, partial loss of capital, concessionary returns, market returns, etc.)	What kind of return is the investor expecting?
Stage (Pre-Seed, Seed, Series A, Series B, Series C, etc.)	At what stage does the investor typically invest?
Risk tolerance (low, medium, high)	Generally, earlier-stage investors have a higher appetite for risk than later-stage investors, but this varies.
Check size (range)	How much money does the investor usually put into a company?
Return time frame/fund lifespan	Within what time frame is the investor expecting a return, if any?
Size of firm (number of people)	The number of people in an investment firm matters because it directly affects how much attention and support your venture will receive.
Focus area	Is the investor focused on climate? Do they focus on a specific vertical within climate?
Current fit	Based on the criteria above, how good of a fit is the investor for your venture right now? Use a simple scale like 1–10 ratings or A–F grades.
Future fit	Based on the preceding criteria, how good of a fit might this investor be for your venture in the future? Again, use a simple scale like 1–10 ratings or A–F grades.
Stage of the funnel	Where is this investor in your fundraising funnel? If you haven't connected with them yet, put "not yet contacted."

foreign investment. However, she had heard from other entrepreneurs that getting any term sheet would encourage other VCs to quickly counter with their own. Alex realized that receiving a term sheet did not mean accepting investment, so she told the foreign investor to send over a term sheet, and he did. When she told the other investors that she had a term sheet, she got two more of them in the next week. Ultimately, they went with the domestic firm Founders Fund for a $2.5 million seed round.

Thiozen

Thiozen's CEO, Ryan Gillis, had spoken casually with dozens of investors at MIT networking events and mentoring sessions, but he spent more than six months refining his message before attempting formal pitches. An early pitch was to John Deutch, an MIT professor who had held high-profile leadership roles in the US government in defense and intelligence.

The pitch was straightforward, and Deutch immediately understood Thiozen's appeal. He requested a written description of the venture and offered to pass it around. Ryan obliged but didn't expect much to come of it. A month later he was contacted by Max Pieri, a venture partner at Eni Next, the corporate venture arm of the Italian energy giant Eni. The Thiozen team made their pitch, which was a bit stumbling, but it was enough to keep the Eni folks interested.

Thiozen eventually entered formal diligence with Eni Next, triggering regular meetings, long lists of questions, and a renewed urgency on the Thiozen side to close the deal and get going. By the end of the year, they had a term sheet for what eventually became a seed investment of $1.7 million.

Being a structured and logical thinker, Ryan identified three things that made his fundraising efforts successful:

- **The right connections.** He had a strong network of supporters who could make warm intros.
- **The right time.** He waited to fundraise until he had refined his pitch and, more importantly, had built the fundamentals of the business.
- **The right investor fit.** Eni had been looking for a venture like Thiozen, and that is why they initiated contact, rather than waiting for Thiozen to come to them.

Spoiler Alert

Ricky Ashenfelter and Emily Malina founded Spoiler Alert to tackle the problem of food waste. Originally, they developed a software platform to help food service distributors donate excess inventory, but after struggling to get traction with customers, they pivoted to helping food brands and grocery distributors sell excess inventory to discount retail.

Before the pivot, their investors were mainly focused on food system innovation and impact. They invested because they believed in Ricky and Emily as founders and their commitment to solving the problem of food waste. They supported Spoiler Alert's initial efforts to bring on more food distributors, and when that didn't pan out, they helped to finance them through the pivot. Once Ricky and Emily switched their focus to food brands, they were able to bring on several marquee customers in the food industry, which gave them confidence that they had found a solid Beachhead Market and could deliver a strong value proposition.

It was time to scale their solution, which meant they needed more capital and support. When raising their Series A, they sought firms who knew the food space and also had extensive experience building fast-scaling software companies. Software expertise was especially critical at that point, because Ricky and Emily's biggest challenges were in building and scaling their solution rapidly enough to meet demand. They ultimately raised an $11 million round led by Collaborative Fund. Their original investors remained on the board and continued to be great champions, and the new investors were able to help them with the evolving set of challenges they were facing.

There was no such thing as an ideal early-stage investor for Spoiler Alert. Ricky and Emily needed to find the right investors at the right time.

ADDITIONAL RESOURCES

There are additional resources for this step at www.de4cev.com/step21. These materials include the following:

- Investor Fit Worksheet
- Ayar Labs Case Study
- Thiozen Case Study
- Spoiler Alert Case Study
- Links to investor databases and insight platforms
- Oliver Gottfried's guide to fundraising pitches for climate and energy ventures

Additional resources will be added as new and updated examples and information become available.

Note

1. "Who Are the Climate Tech VCs?" *CTVC*, May 5, 2023. https://www.ctvc.co/climate-capital-stack-2023/.

Expand and Lead the Team

In this Step, You Will

- Strategically expand your team by identifying the critical roles needed to achieve your next milestones while avoiding over-hiring.

- Leverage creative hiring strategies to find candidates with transferable skills, a willingness to learn, and a commitment to your mission.

- Establish scalable processes to manage and motivate a growing team, ensuring alignment with your culture, values, and ethical standards.

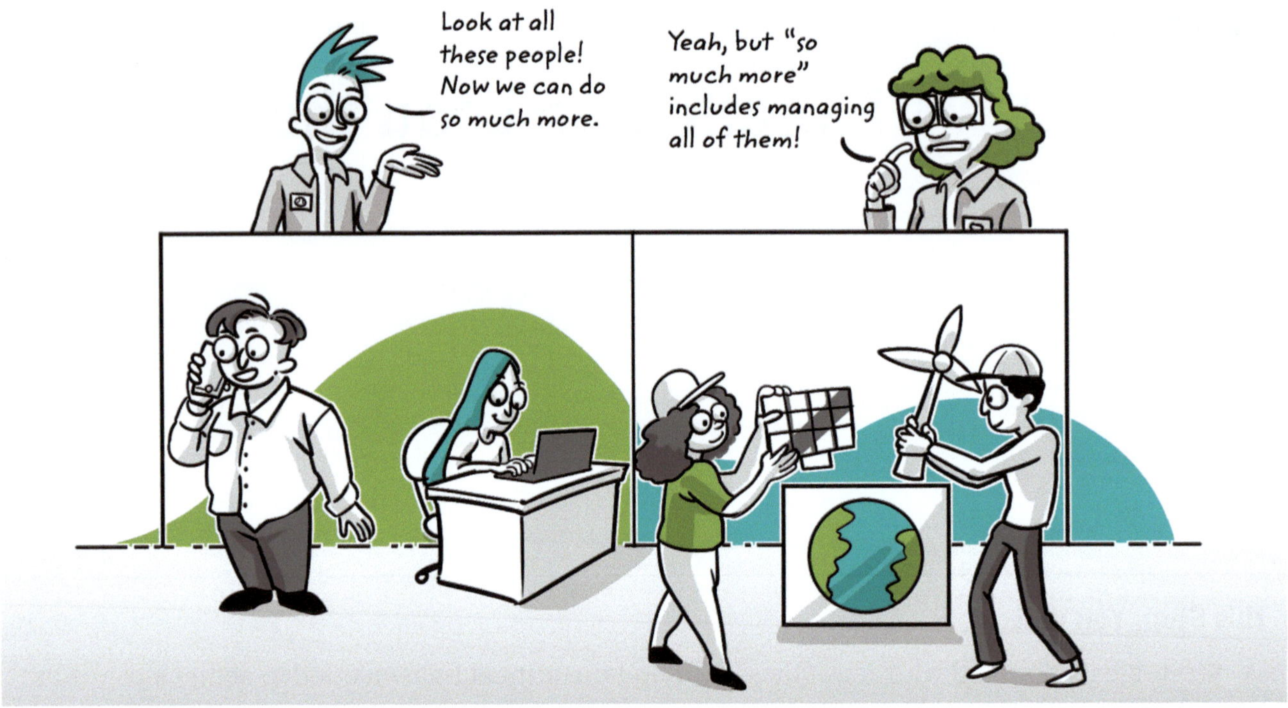

Why This Step, and Why Now?

Much of the capital that you raise will go toward expanding your team. You will need to grow your team far beyond the Initial Team you assembled in Step 5. Most of those new hires will be engineers who will help you tackle the challenges of moving your product toward commercialization. You may also need to add team members in business development to start building your customer pipeline and team members in operations to help manage your internal processes. Regardless of how you expand, you will need to develop new processes to manage and motivate a larger team. You will also need to establish the culture and ethics of the organization in a way that can be consistent yet scalable as the company grows.

After money, time is a startup's most valuable resource, and the only way to increase this resource is to add more high-performing individuals to the team. Without bringing on more people, your Initial Team will quickly max out their time and energy.

The journey to building a successful climate and energy venture is long and expensive. It is far too much for a small team to take on. You will need to grow your team to build a venture that makes a meaningful impact.

Recruiting Talent in Climate and Energy

The hiring process for startup ventures is more or less the same as for larger companies. Write a clear job description, get it out to the right networks, interview candidates, and onboard them. If your process is too far outside this standard framework, you could scare off or confuse potential hires.

Later on, you may have a people management lead or human resources team to run this process, or you may choose to work with an external recruiting firm, but for initial hires, your leadership team will likely need to handle recruiting directly. It is worth putting time and energy into this process. Hiring the right people could vault your progress forward, but hiring the wrong people could be a massive drain. A wrong hire is much more damaging to a startup than to a bigger organization.

Similar to Step 5 for your Initial Team, you need to be intentional about whom you choose to add and vet them carefully. Leverage your networks and communities as much as possible to find the right people, and make sure that you are balancing out the skills and perspectives of your existing team.

The first challenge is figuring out which positions to hire. In Step 5, we listed some roles that your Initial Team would need to take on, with the expectation that each individual would need to wear multiple hats. Now is the time to pass some of those hats to other people. Here are the first roles that you will most likely hire for:

- **Deep technical talent** who can build (and improve upon) your Proofs of Concept
- **Salespeople** who can help secure Initial Market Traction
- **Operational leaders** who can manage the team as it grows
- **Industry experts** who can speak the language of your customer Personas
- **Policy experts** who can navigate and influence the landscape of Sticks and Carrots

Your founding team may continue to take on some of these roles, while you may need to bring on multiple people for others. For instance, if you have a long way to go on developing your technology before you can start bringing on more customers, you will probably hire mostly for technical talent, while the founding team continues to take the lead on the business side. This is a common scenario for climate and energy ventures.

The Dangers of Over-Hiring

Don't over-hire. It's one of the most common mistakes early-stage climate and energy ventures make, and it can be fatal. Over-hiring can drain your cash reserves, slow decision-making, and create unnecessary complexity before your venture has found its footing.

Focus on hiring only the people you absolutely need to hit your next set of milestones. Every hire should be tied to a clear, measurable outcome—whether it's securing a pilot project, achieving a technical breakthrough, or closing your next funding round. You can always supplement your team with contractors, fractional hires, advisors, or partnerships to fill gaps without committing to full-time salaries.

Over-hiring might feel like progress, but it's often the fastest way to run out of money and lose focus.

Find Creative Parallels

When writing your job descriptions, you should keep in mind that you're likely doing something unprecedented as a climate and energy venture. You may be developing a novel technology or implementing a business model that's entirely new to the market. In many cases, you won't find people who have done exactly what you need them to do. That's true to some extent for all startups, but it's especially true for climate and energy ventures, where the challenges often involve cutting-edge science, complex systems, or highly specific regulatory environments.

The key is to focus on transferable skills and a willingness to learn, rather than an exact match. For example, if you're building a direct air capture system, you might look for engineers with experience in chemical processing or HVAC systems, even if they've never worked in carbon removal. If you're scaling a renewable energy platform, someone with experience in grid software or even fintech might bring the right skills to the table. Climate and energy ventures are inherently multidisciplinary, so finding creative parallels is often the best way to build a team capable of tackling unprecedented challenges.

Compensation Considerations

In the early days, you will most likely compensate new hires with a varying combination of cash and equity. For employees, you can set up a vesting structure over time just like you did with your co-founders in Step 5. This ensures that employees' long-term incentives align with your venture's success.

Compensation norms can vary widely depending on the role, location, and stage of the company, so it's critical to stay informed by looking at publicly available information and talking to other climate and energy founders.

Beyond cash and equity, benefits also play a significant role in attracting and retaining talent. In the United States, health insurance is non-negotiable, and a retirement plan is increasingly expected, even if you don't provide matching contributions in the early stages. Many payroll and human resources platforms now offer integrated packages for these benefits, making it easier to set them up.

Purpose Is Your Strongest Perk

Many of your early employees will be attracted and excited by the opportunity to help your venture achieve its Climate Value Proposition. This sense of purpose can drive engagement, creativity, and long-term commitment.

Your team will be more motivated when they can see the direct results of their efforts. To harness this, make the connection clear between their work and the venture's climate impact. Share measurable outcomes—like emissions reductions or renewable energy deployed—and celebrate progress, even incremental wins.

Encourage employees to bring their passion for sustainability into the workplace. This could mean hosting team discussions on climate topics, supporting volunteer opportunities in the community, or even aligning company policies with your mission—like offering subsidies for electric vehicles or carbon offsets for business travel. When employees feel that their values align with the company's actions, they can be both more fulfilled and more productive.

Make sure your team is not only inspired by the mission but also supported by equitable treatment. Passion for the cause should never be used as an excuse to underpay or overwork employees. Fair compensation and benefits are essential to retaining top talent and making team members feel valued.

Managing Your Team

Managing a team for a climate and energy venture is a balancing act. You're working in a high-stakes, fast-moving field where every decision matters to your business and the planet. To succeed, you need to create a culture that's efficient, transparent, and mission driven. Here are some tips on how to approach it:

- **Outsource intentionally.** In the early stages, your team can't do everything in house. Focus your internal resources on the core competencies that differentiate your venture. For everything else, consider outsourcing to experts, but retain oversight, ensure alignment, and address quality issues.

- **Delegate freely.** As a founder or leader, it's easy to fall into the trap of trying to do everything yourself. Don't. Delegation is necessary to empower your team to take ownership and grow. Identify the strengths of your team members and assign responsibilities accordingly.

- **Communicate openly.** To keep your team aligned, prioritize clear and consistent communication. Regular updates ensure that everyone understands the venture's goals, progress, and challenges. Transparency is especially important when navigating setbacks, which are inevitable in this space. But remember that not everyone can be in the room for every decision. Your communication style will need to change as your 5-person team grows to 15, and when it goes from 15 to 50, and so on.

- **Lead ethically.** Ethics are foundational. Be transparent with stakeholders, treat employees fairly, and ensure that your venture's actions align with its mission. Articulate your values— internally and externally—and then live by them.

Managing Your Board

Once you take funding, you become a steward of other people's money. That means those other people have essentially joined your team as shareholders, directors, and/or observers, and both you and they have a fiduciary duty to the company. Many of them will contribute to the venture by serving on the board.

Here are some tips on good board management:

- **Stay in touch.** In addition to board meetings, schedule regular one-on-one check-ins with board members to keep them in the loop, understand their specific perspectives, build rapport, and follow up on specific asks.

- **Avoid surprises.** Share big announcements in your one-on-one conversations, and then discuss further as a group.

- **Take the helm.** Your board may have some decision-making power, but your leadership team is the executive force behind your venture and understands the details of your technology and customers. You should always present the board with your proposed course of action, rather than expecting them to come up with a plan or make a hard decision.

- **Listen to feedback.** Your board's main focus will be on the long term, often thinking and planning over several years based on their experience with many different companies. Leverage your board members' insights and listen to their feedback.

- **Justify your leadership.** While your board is there to support and guide you, they've also entrusted you with the responsibility of leading the company, and they may have the ability to fire you. That means you need to consistently demonstrate why you're the right person for the job. Be prepared to explain your decisions with clear, data-driven reasoning and show that you've considered alternatives. Acknowledge challenges and mistakes but also articulate how you're addressing them. This builds trust and reinforces their confidence in your ability to steer the company toward success. At the same time, don't shy away from showing your vision and conviction. A strong leader inspires confidence not just through competence but also through passion and clarity of purpose.

Output from This Step

List the Next 10 Hires you plan to make for your venture. You can draw from the staffing plan that you made for your Enterprise Financials (Step 14), but then you need to get much more specific about whom you're looking for and how you'll find them. You can use Table 22.1 as a guide.

Table 22.1: *Next 10 Hires Matrix.*

Position title	Sum up the job in a few words.
Role on the team	Which of the key roles for a climate and energy venture could you see this person filling? For example: industry expert, technical lead, deep technical talent, customer-facing sales lead, sales support, finance lead, finance support, operations lead, operations support, and so on.
Core responsibilities	What will be the main functions of this role? What do you expect this person to accomplish?
Ideal candidate profile	What skills and experiences would you expect someone in this role to have? What would jump out to you on a résumé or online profile?
Reporting structure	Whom will this person report to?
Location	Remote, hybrid, or in person? If hybrid or in person, where will this person need to be located?
Compensation	What would be competitive compensation in terms of both salary range and equity options?
Recruiting	Where would you seek candidates for this role? List any relevant job boards, professional networks, and so on.
Possible candidates	List any specific individuals you might already have in mind for the role.

EXAMPLES

Via Separations

Via Separations was developing membrane technology for industrial separation. They used much of their $4.8 million in Series A funding on product development. The founders hired a team of scientists to create a consistent and standardized process for making the membranes so they could eventually manufacture at scale. By the time of their $38 million Series B, they were ready to install the membranes, and they needed to shift their focus to constructing the first project. They quickly learned that product development and project delivery are two entirely different skills. People who are really good at inventing things are typically not as good at installing and operating them, and vice versa.

For that first full-scale project, Via built their project delivery team as they were building the project, which proved to be challenging. To expand on a common metaphor, they were not only building the plane as they were flying it—they were also hiring the crew! However, the people they hired rose to the occasion and made the project a success. Rather than work with an outside firm to direct the project, they managed the work themselves so that they could learn as much as possible for future projects. This is not unusual for First-of-a-Kind climate and energy projects (more on this in Step 23).

Via's CEO, Shreya Dave, saw her role change dramatically as the company grew. She began to focus more on coordination, fundraising, and strategy, and less on execution. That was difficult for her, because she had been so involved in every detail of execution in the company's early days, and it was tied to her identity. However, the company had several dozen employees at that point, far more than she or her co-founder Brent Keller could manage directly. Instead, they brought on senior managers who had prior experience managing large teams.

The company's climate mission was a big draw for talent. With customers, Via highlighted that its membranes would directly generate economic value without any green premium, but with recruits, they highlighted the planetary benefits. Transforming industrial systems to save money was an interesting job, but transforming industrial systems to save the planet was an inspiring job. Shreya put it this way: "Most people here are driven by the opportunity to do something new and different and change the world."

Ayar Labs

Ayar Labs was building computing components that used light to transmit data faster and more efficiently. They got buy-in from potential customers, started manufacturing the technology, and raised money from a well-known venture capital firm. The team grew to 25 people, mostly engineers.

However, CEO Alex Wright-Gladstein's goal was to be a serial climate and energy entrepreneur, and she and her co-founders agreed that the company had progressed enough for her to move on. The three of them wanted to pick the next CEO themselves. When they met Charlie Wuischpard, he seemed like an ideal candidate. He had deep leadership experience in the industry, and he understood the potentially transformative impact of Ayar's technology. There was just one problem: they had recently gotten a term sheet from the VC firm Playground Global to lead a $24 million Series A investment round in Ayar. A new CEO was big news, and the partner at Playground Global was initially concerned. Alex assured him that she was 100% committed to the success of Ayar Labs, and she would not go anywhere if leaving could jeopardize that success.

The partner agreed to meet Charlie and was impressed. Playground Global even agreed to help with the vetting process. Ultimately, Ayar felt that Charlie's style would fit well with theirs, so they decided to offer him the job. Alex stayed at Ayar Labs for two more years in the role of chief strategy officer, and she started thinking about what her next company might be.

This time, she wanted to start with a problem, rather than a technology, and she realized that a critical unsolved problem had been right under her nose for years. When she started offering a 401(k) retirement plan to employees at Ayar Labs, she tried to add a climate-friendly option to the fund menu. It took over three years and a lot of persistence to make that happen. Why had it been so hard? After talking to a lot of the people in the 401(k) industry, she learned that it was possible to do, but someone needed to make it easy. Alex felt that she could and should be that someone, so she left Ayar Labs to start Sphere, a fintech company that makes it easy for everyone to invest in a climate-friendly way.

Alex's story is neither the sole path to success nor a cautionary tale. Her decision to transition out of the CEO role was the right one for Ayar Labs and for her personally. In other companies, the founding CEO might be exactly the right person to lead the company for many, many years. In either case, it's important to understand that the scaling phase of a climate and energy venture is distinctly different from the starting phase, and it requires a distinctly different approach to leadership. We will dive into the scaling phase in the remaining two steps of this book.

ADDITIONAL RESOURCES

There are additional resources for this step at www.de4cev.com/step22. These materials include the following:

- Next 10 Hires Worksheet
- Via Separations Case Study
- Ayar Labs Case Study
- A list of recruiting platforms geared toward climate and energy

Additional resources will be added as new and updated examples and information become available.

Build a First-of-a-Kind Project (FOAK)

In this Step, You Will

- Build a replicable foundation for scaling your solution.
- De-risk your venture for larger, more competitive capital markets by leveling up what you did in previous steps.

Why This Step, and Why Now?

A First-of-a-Kind (FOAK) project is an application of a new technology for the first time at full commercial scale. Getting to this stage represents a major milestone for your venture, and once you achieve it, you can unlock significant additional funding.

Your FOAK is more than just another Proof of Concept. It should be at or close to the full-scale version of your solution. Once you build a FOAK, you should be able to replicate it using the same processes, supply chain, permitting process, and construction techniques, all while making a profit.

You probably won't go directly from your first Proof of Concept to a FOAK. There will be various iterations in between. You will also need several rounds of fundraising and hiring, as well as substantially more market traction. All told, getting to this point will likely require going through several cycles of Steps 18 to 22, possibly in different orders or iterations.

Different FOAKs for Different Folks

Under the broad definition that we are using in this book, any climate and energy venture can have a FOAK. It's the unit of your solution that will get you to full commercial scale, whatever that looks like for you. There's no clear delineation of what size project is "big enough." That is something you'll have to determine based on the needs of your customer (drawn from your primary market research [PMR]) and the capacity of your technology (drawn from your Techno-Economic Analysis [TEA]).

However, not all climate and energy ventures need a FOAK in the specific sense of a big infrastructure project that unlocks the ability to access project finance. Some climate and energy ventures are not project oriented but rather sell individual products. In that case, a FOAK would be the development of a replicable manufacturing process for your product.

The main unifier of infrastructure FOAKs is high capital expenditure on an installation that makes something. In this narrower sense, an infrastructure FOAK could be a project (like a grid-scale energy storage project), it could be a factory (like a waste-to-materials plant), or it could be an industrial facility (like a carbon capture system).

As you plan your FOAK, it can be helpful to think ahead to what the hundredth or thousandth version of your product or project might look like and then work backwards. What are the key variables that drive the economics and the returns for the capital deployed to build this product or project? We've covered several aspects of this previously in the book. Go back to the sensitivity analysis you did in your TEA. What variables have the largest impact?

Remember, your FOAK should represent the long-term scalable version of what you're doing. For example, let's say you're building a factory to make a new renewable version of some kind of chemical or fuel. Your FOAK can't be a batch process if the large-scale version is going to be a continuous process system. Also, if you're combining two different types of technologies, then proving just one isn't sufficient.

Financing Your FOAK

Securing financing for your FOAK is one of the most challenging steps in scaling a climate and energy venture. Traditional project finance—where investors rely solely on the project's assets and cash flows—is typically off the table because FOAKs are inherently risky, unproven at scale, and often lack the long-term contracts or established benchmarks that traditional financiers demand.

Instead, you'll need to turn to the growing number of investors who understand the challenges of building a FOAK. These firms specialize in providing debt and equity for FOAK projects, taking on risks that traditional financiers won't touch. However, these investors will scrutinize both the project's assets and your company's assets, often demanding preferential terms to ensure their return on capital. Despite these drawbacks, FOAK-focused investors are often a cheaper alternative to raising more equity capital and diluting your ownership further.

The Six Categories of FOAK Risk

The key to building a FOAK is to optimize your project for the requirements of the next wave of capital providers. Think of your FOAK as your ultimate Proof of Concept. Its primary purpose is to de-risk your technology, business model, and market for larger, more competitive capital markets. This means addressing several critical categories of risk.

Technology Risk

Your technology needs be rock solid by this point. This means having working Proofs of Concept backed by strong data. You'll also need to have progressed through some level of engineering study. This ensures you've done enough design and analysis to understand the technical feasibility and risks of scaling your solution.

Customer Risk

FOAKs are capital intensive, and securing long-term commitments from customers and suppliers is critical to de-risking the project. Ideally, you'll have firm offtake agreements—multiyear contracts that guarantee demand for your product. The most secure of these agreements will span 5, 10, or even 20 years. For electricity generation, power purchase agreements (PPAs) provide this certainty, but in many other climate and energy verticals, such agreements are rare. If firm offtake isn't feasible, you'll need to educate customers on its importance or find alternative ways to demonstrate demand, such as letters of intent or smaller-scale purchase commitments.

Finance Risk

We already mentioned the challenges of financing your FOAK. Before you build, you need to have your finance sources lined up, and you need to make sure that your FOAK will meet their expectations so that those investors (or others) will back future projects.

Supply Chain and Construction Risk

Who are your suppliers, and how reliable are they? Sole-sourcing critical components can be risky, so having multiple options or contingency plans is essential.

Similarly, the construction phase of your FOAK is a major risk area. Are the contractors you've chosen trustworthy? What happens if they fail to complete the project? These are questions your investors will ask, and you need to have answers.

Also, you can't build a FOAK without a site, and it's not enough to just have a location in mind. You need to have the site identified and under some form of control, such as an exclusivity agreement or an option to lease or purchase.

Regulatory Risk

Are the regulatory frameworks for your project well defined, or are you operating in a gray area? In particular, permitting can be a major hurdle, especially for novel technologies. Mapping out the permitting process and identifying potential roadblocks early will save time and build confidence with investors.

Execution Risk

A project that looks great on paper may not play out that way in practice. You need to show a proven ability to execute and to troubleshoot effectively when things go wrong. This is hard to do with your FOAK, but it can help to bring on experienced partners.

Who's in Charge Here?

If building a large infrastructure project seems wickedly difficult to coordinate, that's because it is. Often, this coordination is managed through an external EPC (engineering, procurement, and construction) firm. The role of the EPC is a lot like a quarterback in football. They're out on the field with the other players while the game is happening, but they have a unique central position that requires them to call plays and make other strategic decisions.

At the beginning, climate and energy ventures sometimes wind up being their own quarterback. By definition, FOAKs involve technologies or systems that have never been built before, which can limit the value that established EPC firms bring to the table. Traditional EPCs are often optimized for replicating proven designs, not navigating the uncertainties and iterative problem-solving required for groundbreaking projects. As a result, many ventures choose to handle the EPC responsibilities themselves for their advanced Proofs of Concept and even their FOAK, leveraging their deep understanding of the technology and its unique challenges. This approach enables the team to maintain tighter control over the process, adapt quickly to unforeseen issues, and ensure that the project aligns with the specific needs of their innovation.

The Path to Profitability

It's important to acknowledge that your FOAK might not be profitable—and that's okay. The goal is to show a clear path to profitability and scalability. Investors need to see how you'll transition from FOAK to units 2, 3, and beyond, and eventually to a scale that attracts traditional project finance. This will likely require a mix of financing sources and a broader market that's large enough to matter.

You won't address every risk with your first project. The goal is to eliminate enough uncertainty to get to the scale-up phase. This means focusing on the metrics, milestones, and market signals that will convince later-stage investors that your solution is ready to scale.

Output from This Step

Work with your team to describe what a FOAK looks like for your venture. Even if you are a long way from building your FOAK, it is important to specify early on what it's going to be so that you have a clear goal to work toward.

Once you've described your FOAK, make a plan for how you'll get there, including how you'll address the six key areas of risk that we laid out in this step. Use Table 23.1 as a rough guide, but keep in mind that there are many aspects of risk within these six categories, and we don't have the space to list all of them here.

EXAMPLES

A Tale of Three FOAKS (Talus, Fervo, and Commonwealth Fusion Systems)

We can learn a lot about FOAKs by comparing and contrasting three good but incredibly different examples: Talus, Fervo, and Commonwealth Fusion Systems (CFS).

Table 23.1: *FOAK Matrix.*

Description of your FOAK	What does a FOAK look like for your venture? Remember that a FOAK is a replicable unit of your solution that shows you've reached full commercial scale.
Technology risk	Is your technology ready to support this FOAK? You should have a strong track record of performance by this point. If not, what more do you need to show? What are the technical milestones and Proofs of Concept standing between you and your FOAK?
Customer risk	Who will be the customers for your FOAK? Have they already signed contracts? If not, how certain are you that they are ready and willing to do so? Are they able to sign long-term contracts?
Finance risk	Do you have financing lined up? Does your FOAK match the expectations of your long-term and short-term financial partners?
Supply chain and construction risk	Who are your suppliers, and how reliable are they? Are the contractors you've chosen trustworthy? What happens if they fail to complete the project? Do you have a site secured?
Regulatory risk	What are the regulatory hurdles to building your FOAK, including permits? If you had everything else lined up, could you start building your FOAK today? If not, what would still stand in your way?
Execution risk	Have you demonstrated your ability to execute and to troubleshoot effectively when things go wrong? Do you have an EPC firm or other partners who can help inspire confidence?

Talus's technology was a modular system that made green ammonia, and their FOAK was the talusOne, which could produce approximately one metric ton of ammonia per day. Of our three examples, Talus had the lowest costs per project. Each talusOne could be built for a few million dollars (a high price tag in other contexts but a low cost by FOAK standards). Their low capital needs de-risked the business in some ways, because many investors could provide this amount of capital. However, the amount was actually too low for the big capital providers in the infrastructure space, who tended to deploy hundreds of millions of dollars at a minimum. To address this, they aggregated 10 to 20 projects comprised of their larger talusTen systems, a scale at which Talus could achieve both unit cost savings and greater financeability from traditional infrastructure funders.

Fervo's FOAK was the world's first fully functioning enhanced geothermal power plant. Building this FOAK entailed two distinct technical challenges: (1) drill better wells and (2) build a power plant to generate electricity from the steam produced by those wells. Those two pieces had each been done separately, but packaging them together was new, which increased Fervo's initial capital and EPC costs. The advantage of taking on this additional technical risk was the ability to reduce customer risk by selling power through PPAs. This business model was already highly familiar to their first customer, Google, as well as other large buyers of electricity.

CFS's FOAK is a commercial-scale fusion power plant called ARC, and as of this writing, it's still a few years away from construction. To date, CFS has raised about $2 billion, which is a massive amount of money to raise years before building a FOAK, but the potential for financial returns (and climate impact) is enormous, and the company was able to attract patient, long-term investors. Currently, CFS is focused on building a smaller Proof of Concept called SPARC, but once that's done, they want to be immediately ready to move onto ARC, so they're doing parallel processing. They've already identified a location for ARC in Virginia, and they are working on the permitting process with various authorities. If they wait to start this process until after SPARC is done, it could add an extra 5 to 10 years to their timeline. The dollars spent on permitting and siting are relatively small compared to the amount of money spent on technology development, so it is worth starting early to get things moving, even if it costs a bit extra in the long run.

These three examples illustrate the diversity of scales and approaches required to balance technology development with investor expectations. Despite differences in the size, cost, and timeline, each company has designed a FOAK that demonstrates a commercial-scale version of its technology while addressing the critical risks and milestones necessary to attract investors. When the projects are done, they will look extremely different from one another, but they all will achieve the same objective: laying a strong foundation for scaling up.

Thiozen

Thiozen's first project was a demonstration of its hydrogen production technology at a small oil and gas facility in Lubbock, Texas.

CEO Ryan Gillis figured that the project would cost $1.2 million and take about six months to build. The Thiozen team contracted an engineering firm to draw up a design, and then they passed it along to several EPC firms for bids. Out of the six firms that they contacted, they got zero bids that were compliant with their budget and timeline. Ultimately, they built the demo project themselves in five months for a budget of $750,000.

While Ryan and the team built the equipment in Massachusetts, they worked with contractors to prepare the site in Texas. They needed electrical trenches, so Ryan called the electricians recommended by the site owner. These electricians provided a quote that was six times higher than Ryan expected, but he approved it because he was in a hurry to get the project done. A few weeks later, Ryan went to inspect the site. What was supposed to be about 100 feet of cable buried underground alongside the gravel site road had somehow turned into about 800 feet of power lines (complete with eight new poles) that went to the wrong spot.

What went wrong here? Ryan had not adequately vetted the electricians before hiring them. He had traded caution for speed, and he paid the price.

Thiozen's first plant was more of a small-scale demonstration than a full-scale FOAK, but similar lessons apply, especially around working with partners. Doing the engineering in-house only works to a point. If the equipment were too large to fit on a truck bed, Thiozen would have had to construct it all on-site, and the team likely would not have been able to work around EPCs. This would have meant working with even more contractors and spending even more money, by a factor of several orders of magnitude.

Working with contractors does not mean outsourcing. A FOAK project is not something that can be completed out of sight and out of mind. For the project to be done well and at somewhat reasonable cost, all project partners need to be thoroughly vetted, and their work needs to be closely supervised.

ADDITIONAL RESOURCES

There are additional resources for this step at www.de4cev.com/step23. These materials include the following:

- FOAK Worksheet
- A Tale of Three FOAKs Case Study
- Thiozen Case Study
- Link to the Climate Tech Venture Capital (CTVC) newsletter FOAK series
- List of infrastructure-focused investors

Additional resources will be added as new and updated examples and information become available.

Scale Up

In This Step, You Will

- Access essentially unlimited capital if you fit the project finance model, address risks, and reach sufficient scale.

- Understand the targets for project finance and how they should drive your key milestones, if that is your pathway to scale.

- Consider other ways to scale up beyond the project finance model.

Why This Step, and Why Now?

The last step of our process is to show how new climate and energy ventures can put themselves on a proven and reliable pathway to bankability and global scale. It often takes many years for new climate and energy solutions to reach this stage, but once they do, they can rapidly reach new heights that are orders of magnitude higher than what was previously possible in terms of both profitability and climate impact.

From FOAK to NOAK

Scaling up looks different for different sorts of solutions. Often, it entails replicating the FOAK. Making the first full-scale version of a brand-new solution is time-consuming, expensive, and tricky to finance because it hasn't been done before. But if the solution is truly scalable, then the second of a kind should be easier, and the third of a kind should be even easier, and so on. As you build more projects, your supply chains solidify, your operations streamline, and your markets mature. Eventually, building the solution should become such a predictable and profitable enterprise that no one cares what number it is. At that point, it becomes a NOAK (nth of a kind).

The journey from FOAK to NOAK is often called the *missing middle*.[1] While venture capital and infrastructure financing dominate the energy transition landscape, there's a glaring gap in capital for companies that have outgrown the venture stage but aren't yet de-risked enough for infrastructure investment. These growth-stage ventures often struggle to secure the resources needed to scale, leaving promising technologies stuck in limbo. As an entrepreneur, you should be prepared to navigate this gap strategically. This means de-risking your technology and business model as much as possible.

The Road to Scale Is Paved with Project Finance

For infrastructure solutions, scaling up from a FOAK to a NOAK is synonymous with project finance-ability. Project finance starts with creating a brand-new company with no employees (this is the "project") and then putting millions of dollars into it. Crazy, right? Well, your startup is unproven, so the only investors willing to invest capital for an ownership stake are ones with a big appetite for risk. But if you can model the costs and revenues of an individual project, then you can provide investors with certainty about what the cash flow for the project will look like. This makes the individual project much less risky than your venture as a whole and attracts a different type of capital.

In this set-up, all the money moves through the project, so if the project borrows money, only the project needs to pay it back. The personal and professional assets of the people who own the project are not on the hook. It sounds a bit shady, but it is 100% legal, and it is the system behind many of the world's major energy projects and other infrastructure.

We can demonstrate the concept with a fanciful example. Let's say the project is an ice cream factory. If we are going to fund it through project finance, we need to remove as much uncertainty as possible:

- The people who build the ice cream factory need to be paid through preset contracts for their labor as well as for the materials that they use. That way, the construction costs are fixed and predictable.

- The people who operate and maintain the ice cream factory also need to be paid on contracts so that those costs are also fixed and predictable.

- Let's assume the ingredients in our delicious ice cream are just cream and sugar. We should have contracts in place with the suppliers who provide the cream and sugar, ensuring that we can buy these inputs at a fixed price per unit over a span of multiple years. Then those costs are fixed and predictable, too.

- We also want to have certainty on the demand side, so we need to find people who are willing to buy whatever ice cream we produce at a guaranteed price. These ice cream buyers are called *offtakers*, because they are taking the ice cream off our hands. They might eat the ice cream themselves or they might sell it to others, but either way, they are definitely going to pay us for it.

- And of course, we need to keep our ice cream nice and cold, so we will want to lock in a fixed price for electricity to run our freezers and refrigeration units.

- Critically, for all of this to work, our ice cream-making technology needs to be proven. If it winds up needing more cream than we had planned, or if it starts mysteriously putting out ice cream soup 1 year into a 10-year contract, then the whole project could fail.

Now, all our ice cream factory's financial flows are as certain as possible, so we can model them to get a clear view of the project's profitability. Each time period has a fixed and predictable set of revenues and costs. If we simply subtract the costs from the revenues, we can calculate the exact payout from our ice cream factory to its owners and investors. Boom! No more risk. This example is a bit silly because no one would ever make ice cream this way, but it helps to show very tangibly what we mean by de-risking.

Fortunately, you have already done much of the heavy lifting to build a model that translates technical performance to economic returns—it is just the next evolution of your Techno-Economic Analysis (TEA)! Remember the golden rule that internal rate of return (IRR) must be greater than the weighted average cost of capital (WACC)? You need to show that your technology will support a project that consistently makes enough profit to pay back what you owe and then some.

As you're doing this modeling, it's important for you to understand all the variables that affect your project's IRR, not just the role of your technology or solution. For example, battery cells are only part of the total cost for a grid-scale battery. You might have a way of improving the cell's efficiency, but if that reduces the life of the battery, increases the footprint, or changes some other variable, then it may not lead to an overall positive IRR.

While not all climate and energy ventures involve project finance, it is one of the most common pathways to reach massive scale. It is crucial that you understand who is ultimately paying for these projects and products. Think of project finance providers as the ultimate customer. Without them, most projects are not built.

What's the Big Deal About Debt?

One big advantage of project finance is that a project company has an easier time getting a loan than the parent company due to its predictable cash flows. But why would you want your project to take on debt in the first place? Debt is a critical tool for scaling climate and energy ventures because it enables you to bring on external capital without diluting your equity at the venture or project level. This is especially important in a sector where projects are often capital intensive. By using debt, you can finance large up-front costs while preserving ownership and control.

However, once you take on debt for your project, you are committing to a regular interest payment for many years, usually on a monthly basis. To be seen as a reliable borrower, your project company needs to make that payment in full and on time, *every* time. If you can't convince banks that your project will pay them back precisely when it needs to, then they won't touch it. But if you can convince them, then the monthly payments (known as debt service) become just another fixed and predictable cost in your model.

The Promise and Peril of New Products

In addition to accessing new financial mechanisms, you might also roll out new products as you scale up, even beyond your initial Market Stepping Stones. As we mentioned in Step 10, you should plan to sell a new solution to your existing customers or your existing solution to new customers. It is risky to attempt to build a new product and understand a new customer simultaneously.

If you are going to sell a new product, it should be related to your original solution in terms of what it does for your customer and how complicated it is to build. Many climate and energy solutions are platform technologies, where the same core process or mechanism can yield many different outputs. This means that the venture can make new products by adding onto the original technology rather than starting the whole technology development process from scratch. Given the long timelines of moving from lab to market, a platform approach is usually the only way deep tech ventures can diversify their product portfolio in the short to medium term.

Other Pathways to Scale

While project finance is a powerful tool for scaling climate and energy ventures, it's not the only option. Depending on the nature of your solution, there are other strategies that can drive significant growth and impact. Each pathway to scale has its own challenges and opportunities, and the right choice depends on your venture's unique strengths, market dynamics, and long-term goals.

Initial Public Offering (IPO)

Taking your company public can unlock substantial capital for you to scale your operations, expand into new markets, and accelerate innovation. For climate and energy ventures, an IPO can also provide credibility and visibility, attracting more customers, partners, and investors. Companies like Tesla and Ørsted have used public markets to fund their growth and establish themselves as leaders in the energy transition.

However, going public requires a proven business model, strong financials, and the ability to navigate the scrutiny of public markets. It's a long-term play that works best for ventures with a clear path to profitability and a compelling growth story.

Acquisition

Being acquired by a larger company can provide the resources, infrastructure, and market access to rapidly scale your solution. For example, if your venture develops a breakthrough battery technology, being acquired by a major energy company or automaker could integrate your innovation into global supply chains and accelerate deployment.

Acquisitions can also help ventures overcome barriers like regulatory challenges or distribution bottlenecks by leveraging the acquirer's expertise and networks. The key is finding a partner whose goals align with your mission, ensuring your solution scales without compromising its impact.

Mass Adoption

Sometimes, the most effective way to scale is simply by getting your solution into the hands of as many people as possible. This pathway relies on creating a product or service that resonates with consumers or businesses and achieves widespread use. Electric vehicles are a prime example—companies like Tesla and BYD have driven mass adoption by combining technological innovation with compelling branding and competitive pricing.

For climate and energy ventures, mass adoption often requires a combination of affordability, accessibility, and clear value to the end user. The goal is to make your solution the obvious choice for as many users as possible.

Disciplined Scaling

The most successful ventures don't stumble aimlessly into scale; they methodically build the foundation for it. This means de-risking every aspect of your solution, from technology and supply chains to customer contracts and financing structures. It also means smart and intentional timing—knowing when to push forward aggressively and when to adapt to shifting market conditions. Scaling is as much about discipline as it is about vision.

The path to scale is rarely linear and never easy. But the rewards—for people, planet, and profit—are immense. When you execute well, you're doing more than simply building a business. You're creating a solution that can transform industries and accelerate the transition to a sustainable future. The world needs scalable solutions now more than ever, and if you heed the lessons in this book, your venture can be one of them.

Output from This Step

Identify the scaling pathway that best fits your venture, considering the nature of your solution as well as the intentions of your team. Since this is the final step, reflect on how your scaled-up venture will address the main themes of this book. Remember that your objective is to reach the People-People-Planet Sweet Spot, achieving a successful synthesis of solution, customer, finance, policy, planet, and scaling (see Table 24.1).

EXAMPLES

Solugen

Solugen's co-founders, Gaurab Chakrabarti and Sean Hunt, aimed to create a global chemical company that would use sugar and starch as feedstocks, instead of fossil fuels. That was their Big Prize, and they identified four distinct stages to getting there:

- **Stage 1.** Produce and sell chemicals at a small scale.
- **Stage 2.** Finance and build the first commercial-scale plant.
- **Stage 3.** Show the risks have been addressed and access debt financing.
- **Stage 4.** Build plants all over the world.

They reached Stage 1 by selling hydrogen peroxide to float spas and then by selling cleaning wipes directly to consumers. They completed Stage 2 by building their FOAK, a demonstration plant called Bioforge1. To reach Stage 3, they would need to show that they had addressed enough risks to make Solugen a good candidate for a loan. They focused on three buckets of risk: technology, customer, and finance.

Table 24.1: *People-Planet-Profit Sweet Spot Matrix.*

Intended pathway to scale	Briefly describe the path to scale for your venture. Is it project finance, IPO, acquisition, mass adoption? Something else?
Solution	Is the solution fit for purpose?
	Have you done a TEA (Step 6)? Have you clearly defined your solution (Step 12)? Have you iterated on your Proofs of Concept (Step 20) leading up to a FOAK (Step 23)?
Customer	Who pays? For what? Why and how?
	Have you understood your customer through thorough primary market research (Step 3)? Have you thoughtfully segmented the market (Step 7)? Have you selected a reasonable set of Market Stepping Stones leading from a short-term Beachhead Market to a long-term Big Prize (Step 10)? Have you profiled detailed Personas across your customer's Decision-Making Unit (Step 11)? Have defined a unique Quantified Value Proposition that addresses your customer's salient pain points (Step 13)?
Finance	How do you finance your solution?
	Do you have a clear sense of where you'll operate in the Value Chain and how you'll make money there (Step 9)? Do you have a promising set of Enterprise Financials based on defensible assumptions (Step 14)? Have you developed a Long-Term Capital Plan (Step 17)? Do you have a plan to pursue the right Non-Dilutive Funding (Step 18) and Early-Stage Capital (Step 21)?
Policy	Is policy in your favor?
	Have you made a plan for navigating the Sticks and Carrots of policy for both you and for your customer, now and in the future (Step 8)?
Planet	If it works, does it matter?
	Do you have a large Climate TAM (Step 1) and a strong Climate Value Proposition (Step 16)? Have you identified the impacts and risks throughout your Full Product Life Cycle (Step 15)?
Scaling	How do you build it at scale?
	Have you built a well-balanced Initial Team (Step 5) and made a plan for expanding it (Step 22)? Do you have a plan for going from a FOAK to a NOAK and beyond (Steps 23 and 24)?

Solugen's market strategy exposed them to a high amount of customer risk. They signed 10-year contracts with their suppliers, but they only signed 1- to 3-year contracts with their customers. Project financiers like to see these time frames matched, so the company will not be stuck with excess inventory. However, Solugen's choice to mismatch their contracts was an intentional part of their business model. They signed short-term contracts directly with customers, rather than long-term contracts with intermediaries, which enabled them to get a higher price for their products and keep their end customers happier.

To balance out this customer risk, Solugen needed to have exceptionally low technology risk. Specifically, they needed to pass a threshold called a "golden month," in which they produced 75 tanker trucks of chemicals in 42 days at 94% yield. They achieved their first golden month at Bioforge1 in 2022. They then had five golden months in 2023. That track record was enough to secure them their first big loan: $213.6 million from the US Department of Energy Loan Programs Office (LPO).

The LPO loan enabled Solugen to begin building their second Bioforge, and by paying back the loan on time, Solugen would be able to show other lenders that they had reduced finance risk. Bankability was a critical threshold for Solugen to move into Stage 4, unlocking a whole new dimension of scale.

Horizon Wind

We've mainly been looking at emerging companies and sectors, but we also want you to learn from an example of a solution that has already scaled and undeniably reached the People-Planet-Profit Sweet Spot.

In 2005, Goldman Sachs made a bold move by acquiring a leading wind power project developer, which they rebranded as Horizon Wind Energy. At the time, the wind industry in the United States was at a critical juncture. Rising natural gas prices were driving up electricity prices. Meanwhile, wind turbine technology had advanced significantly, the supply chain was maturing, and construction expertise was becoming more widespread. These factors combined to create a Window of Opportunity for wind power to achieve scale.

Horizon Wind Energy had a strong foundation with a pipeline of 4,000 megawatts of potential projects, including four advanced projects with sites and power purchase agreements in place. At the time, project finance for wind was still in its infancy, so Goldman used its own capital to fund the development of Horizon's projects, taking on the risk of building and operating the wind farms. Horizon also secured a deal to purchase a large quantity of turbines at a fixed price, locking in a critical supply chain component and ensuring the projects could move forward.

Two years later, Horizon had grown significantly, and the market for wind power was blowing up. State governments across the United States were implementing policies that required utilities to include a certain percentage of renewable energy in their power mix. These mandates created a steady demand for wind power, and the industry was scaling rapidly. Goldman sold Horizon for over $2 billion, realizing a profit of about $1 billion.

The Horizon deal was a turning point for the wind industry. It demonstrated that wind power could be a profitable investment, attracting more capital to the sector and helping to establish wind as a mainstream energy source.

For today's climate and energy entrepreneurs, Horizon is a powerful example of finding the right intersection of solution, customer, finance, policy, planet, and scaling. The same general principles are as relevant today as they were in 2005.

We hope this example motivates entrepreneurs (and also well-capitalized investors and executives) to pursue some of the emerging sectors and companies we have highlighted in this book. The wave of wind energy was followed by solar power and now batteries. There are several other waves on the horizon—the next big winner could be you!

ADDITIONAL RESOURCES

There are additional resources for this step at www.de4cev.com/step24. These materials include the following:

- Scale-Up Worksheet
- Solugen Case Study
- Horizon Wind Case Study
- Link to Pivotal180's online crash course on project finance

Additional resources will be added as new and updated examples and information become available.

Note

1. Francis O'Sullivan and Gokul Raghavan, *The Missing Middle: Capital Imbalances in the Energy Transition*. Report, September 8, 2023. https://www.s2ginvestments.com/insights/missing-middle.

CONCLUSION

CONGRATULATIONS!!!!

You have read this entire book and now know the 24 Steps of climate and energy entrepreneurship! It should come as no surprise that actually going out and building a climate and energy venture will take a long time, much longer than it took you to read through these pages. We condensed a great deal of information into this book, spanning a wider scope than the original Disciplined Entrepreneurship framework. We needed to cover a lot of ground so that you would understand the full end-to-end process of starting a climate and energy venture. If your aim is to build a solution for people and the planet, it may take many years for you to be successful, but now you have a sense of what's in store and can plan accordingly.

Do not expect a single book to provide all the wisdom you need. The landscape of climate and energy is constantly evolving, which is a very good thing because we need solutions that are as wide-ranging and dynamic as the problems that we face in this sector. If you are serious about building a venture in climate and energy, then continue learning from the people who are in the arena with you, including industry experts, potential customers, advisors, professors, and most critically, other entrepreneurs. They will guide you toward the latest information and insight.

It's always important to remember that you are not alone in this work. The Dual Challenge of climate and energy can be daunting. We must provide ample, affordable, and reliable energy to billions of people while addressing the threat of climate change. The scale of the problems is immense, but so is the scale of the opportunity. It is a monumental and generational undertaking, and tackling it would be one of the greatest feats that humanity has ever achieved. It is also one of the best ways you could spend your limited time on Earth, striving not only to make a living for yourself but also to build a better world for everyone.

We wrote this book because we are brimming with excitement at the possibilities that exist for climate and energy ventures, so our support does not end here. We will continue to share resources on de4cev.com, including our constantly improving AI tools, which can be powerful allies to you in your journey. In many ways, these tools are more useful to have in your court than any human expert, because they contain a wider array of knowledge than any single person and they are available 24/7 to anyone with an internet connection.

Despite our limitations, we will do what we can in our capacity as flesh-and-blood human beings to keep moving the ball forward. Send us your feedback and ideas. Let us know what help you need. We want to support you. It is entirely possible to solve the vast problems that lie ahead and to capture a share of the vast opportunities, but only if we work together.

ACKNOWLEDGMENTS

As we have said multiple times in this book, entrepreneurship is a team sport, especially climate and energy entrepreneurship, because it requires such a wide range of disciplines and perspectives. The same is true of writing about climate and energy entrepreneurship. Even though we are a team of five authors, we could not have written this book without immense help from our global community.

First and foremost, we would like to extend our gratitude to the many entrepreneurs who have shared their stories with us: Alex Wright-Gladstein, Aliki Lavda, Andrés Bisonó León, Ariana Day Yuen, Bob Mumgaard, Bruce Crawford, Cameron Halliday, Carlo Tursi, Cody Friesen, Cynthia Liao, David Brown, David Dellal, Delia Rodriguez Lucas, Diego Saez-Gil, Donald Groh, Doug Moorehead, Elise Strobach, Emily Malina, Evan Haas, Hiro Iwanaga, Ines Serra Baucells, Jan-Georg Rosenboom, Jane Woodward, Jorge Nin, Juliet Rothenberg, Kevin Berkemeyer, Kurt Neutgens, Maher Damak, Max Nova, Murtuza Marfani, Neil Auerbach, Nisha Desai, Rawand Rasheed, Richard Robinet-Duffo, Ricky Ashenfelter, Ryan Bennett, Ryan Gillis, Sanchali Pal, Sean Hunt, Shiv Bhakta, Shreya Dave, Stafford Sheehan, Steph Speirs, Steve Renter, Stwart Peña Feliz, Tim Latimer, Tim Mui, Teasha Feldman-Fitzthum, Tom Atkinson, Trevor Best, Valeriia Tyshchenko, Vanessa Coleman, Victor Lesniewski, Wayne Mathisen, and Ye Tao. Your stories are the very foundation of the book, whether or not they appear explicitly as examples.

Thank you to our fantastic illustrators for bringing these concepts to life. Marius Ursache designed the cover, once again bringing his signature talents to the DE series. Nenad Kostic did the interior illustrations, continuing the DE legacy while also adding his own unique spin.

Many thanks to the team at Wiley for shepherding this project from an idea to a reality. Shannon Vargo, Leah Zarra, and Gabriela Mancuso are publishing pros who capably (and patiently) steered us through the ups and downs of the process. And Christina Verigan, Chris Snyder, Debbie Schindlar, and Julie Kerr are masterful editors who polished the roughest elements of our text and made them shine. Thanks also to Michael Friedberg, whose basketball loyalties are in question but whose business guidance is truly valued.

We also appreciate the many other people who shared their feedback and insights to make this book better, including Jacquelyn Pless, Jason Jay, Tristan Jackson, Rebekah Emanuel, David Miller, Aimee Rose, Evan Gao, Rory Burke, Alex Prather, Jeff Johnson, Liana Frey, Rohit Gawande, Neil Yeoh, Molly Bales, Mikaela Bradbury, Corey Cantor, Tiana Veldwisch, Tom Kishchuk, Luke Heeney, and Spencer Glendon.

This book is a result of far more than just the writing process. It would not exist without the 18-year track record of MIT's Climate & Energy Ventures (CEV) course. Special thanks to Jacquelyn Pless for being a vital part of the teaching team, adding her deep expertise in energy innovation, policy, and economics, as well as a much-needed dose of academic rigor.

We need to thank the amazing students from across MIT and Harvard who have made the course what it is. And we especially appreciate the students who have gone above and beyond to keep the course afloat as teaching assistants: Matt Albrecht, Phil Stephenson, Adam Rein, Vanessa Coleman, Juliet Rothenberg, Shambhavi Kadam, Adam Borelli, Kevin Berkemeyer, Ricky Ashenfelter, Liz Voeller, Michael Kearney, Victor Lafuente, Eddie Tepper, Austin Roth, Alex Prather, Evan Gao, Glen Junor, Elvis Cao, Daniel Willette, Rebecca Hutman, and Jenn Turliuk.

Many leaders from the climate and energy ecosystem contribute their knowledge and wisdom to the course as guest speakers. We cannot list all of them here, but we do want to acknowledge a few who have been a particularly integral over the years: Tim Healy, John Deutch, Ramana Nanda, Joseph Lassiter, Ernie Moniz, Steven Chu, Maryrose Sylvester, Phil Duffy, Cheryl Martin, Tom Burton, Colleen Calhoun, Jeff Johnson, Mike Reynolds, Teasha Feldman-Fitzthum, Bob Mumgaard, John Strackhouse, Spencer Glendon, Phil Giudice, Yet-Ming Chiang, Derek Warnick, Brenda Haendler, Ben Gaddy, Katie Rae, Mike Kearney, Jas Lee, Dave Eaglesham, Brian Halligan, Charles Baron, and Shreya Dave, as well as ecosystem leaders from Greentown Labs, Azolla Ventures, Lowercarbon Capital, The Engine, Clean Energy Ventures, National Grid Partners, Activate, SOSV, Energy Impact Partners, and Breakthrough Energy Ventures.

The course would not have gotten off the ground without support from the anonymous donor who started the Climate & Energy Fund at the Martin Trust Center, which also supported the Climate & Energy Prize. More recently, Breakthrough Energy Fellows provided a grant to expand the class and take it to the next level.

Both the class and the book have relied heavily on support from across the MIT community, especially the Martin Trust Center for MIT Entrepreneurship (MTC). Paul Cheek has been a tremendous asset, not only as MTC's executive director but also as an experienced author in his own right. His guidance on the book-writing process has been absolutely essential. Macauley Kenney, Jenny Larios Berlin, and Ylana Lopez have picked up a lot of slack in running programs like delta v and MIT Fuse while also providing helpful feedback. Alicia Carelli and Leslie Owens have been invaluable in finding time on busy schedules. We really need to thank everyone who was part of the MTC team while the book was being written, because they all assisted in one way or another: Amrutha Killada,

Andy Acevedo, Chris Burns, Chris Moses, Christine Hsieh, Connor Madsen, Devon Sherman Daley, Doug Williams, Emily Mooney, Emily Young, George Whitfield, Greg Wymer, Katherine Lukens, Lucia Solorzano, Maya Freed, Stephanie MacConnell, and Susan Neal. We also must recognize the late Ed Roberts, who founded the center.

Special thanks to Victoria Pisini, the most recent addition to the MIT climate and energy entrepreneurship faculty, who was instrumental in launching a new climate class at MIT while this book was being written. And thanks also to Bria Hardin-Boyer for stepping up to TA that class.

Climate and energy efforts at MIT have benefitted over the years from the unwavering support of key university leaders, particularly Susan Hockfield, Sally Kornbluth, Anantha Chandrakasan, Ernie Moniz, John Deutch, Don Lessard, Richard Lester, Melanie Kenderdine, Bob Metcalfe, David Schmittlein, Elsa Olivetti, and the many professors who have encouraged their students to take the innovations from their labs through the CEV class.

Funders have also played a key role, like Joe Nolan of Eversource who provided the catalyst funding for the MIT Clean Energy Prize, and Andy Karsner who immediately followed up Joe Nolan's commitment.

And it would all be meaningless without the students, especially the students who have led or otherwise been part of the MIT Energy and Climate Club, the MIT Climate & Energy Prize, and the many other organizations that support the MIT climate and energy innovation ecosystem.

There are so many other staff at MIT who enable all of this to happen, including security personnel like Patrol Officer Sean Collier, who was killed on a Thursday night near the CEV classroom during the Boston Marathon bombing manhunt.

We have benefitted from a wide community of supporters across the climate and energy entrepreneurial ecosystem. The dream team at the Texas Exchange for Energy and Climate Entrepreneurship (TEX-E) in Houston has provided critical connections and perspective from within the heart of the energy industry. Many thanks to David Baldwin, David Pruner, Sandy Guitar, Isaiah Hughes, Julia Johansson, and Faith Kelnhofer. David Baldwin has also been an indispensable collaborator through his leadership of Open Minds, which he founded along with Jeff Katz. That organization has advanced not only a clear definition of the Dual Challenge of climate and energy but also an evolving road map for near-term solutions, which we graciously adopted and integrated when framing this book.

Greentown Labs has been a cornerstone of the climate and energy ecosystem for almost 15 years, and we especially would like to acknowledge two of the four founding companies, Altaeros and OsComp, which came out of the CEV course. We also want to thank all Greentown's members and leaders, especially Georgina Campbell Flatter, Emily Reichert, Jason Hanna, Kevin Knobloch, Kevin Taylor, and Kevin Dutt.

Thanks also to Oliver Gottfried, Jenn Turliuk, and Daniela Gorza, who made innumerable contributions throughout the writing process and beyond.

Thanks as well to the team at Breakthrough Energy Ventures for contributing to the class in many ways: Brian Mayers, Carmichael Roberts, Chris Rivest, Christian Garcia, Christina Karapataki, Chris Poirier, Cooper Rinzler, David Danielson, Eric Toone, Gaëtan Bonhomme, Karl White, Peter Turner, Phil Larochelle, Rajeev Ram, Rodi Guidero, Sila Kiliccote, and Jim Matheson. We are also grateful for the contributions of the entire Breakthrough Energy team as well as the leadership of Breakthrough Energy's founder, Bill Gates.

Many universities have launched CEV courses, and those faculty members have been outstanding thought partners. Dave Danielson, Joel Moxley, Jane Woodward, David McColl, and Aline Schechter run the Climate Ventures course at Stanford University. Brian Korgel, Mellie Price, Molly Bales, Nora Ankrum, and Kohl Lasell are behind the course at the University of Texas at Austin. We have also learned immensely from educators across Texas: Ramanan Krishnamoorti and Marcus Stewart of the University of Houston; Paul Cherukuri and Adrian Trömel of Rice University; Joe Elabd, Jim Donnell, and Chelsea Werdel of Texas A&M University; and Philip Bouchard and Brandy Walker of Prairie View A&M University. Additionally, we want to acknowledge the global educators who are driving this work forward: Helmut Schoenenberger, Philipp Gerbert, Lars Eiermann, and Michael Viertler, who just launched a CEV course at the Technical University of Munich (TUM), and our esteemed colleagues pursuing climate and energy ventures at Tsinghua University in Beijing, China.

We also want to recognize the people and institutions who provided focused space for writing, which can be a rare commodity. Rowena Barrett lent her property in the Australian bush for a writing sprint that provided critical momentum for the rest of the process. Also, the Newton Free Library and the Waban Library Center are vital community resources for readers, writers, and curious minds of all sorts.

And last but certainly not least, we cannot forget our caring and supportive families. Without them, we would have a hard time doing just about anything. Love and thanks to Mari Ramirez, Wendy Smith, Elizabeth Hynes, Christina Cosman, Lisa Aulet, and Mike Kalin.

ABOUT THE AUTHORS

BEN SOLTOFF is the Ecosystem-Builder and Entrepreneur in Residence (EIR) at the Martin Trust Center for MIT Entrepreneurship, where he wears many hats. He's the point person for all things climate tech; he partners with universities around the world to teach climate and energy entrepreneurship, especially in places at the forefront of the energy transition, like Houston, Texas, and Queensland, Australia; and he leads the delta v accelerator, the capstone entrepreneurial experience for MIT students. He's also a co-founder of the Texas Exchange for Energy & Climate Entrepreneurship (TEX-E), which is a student-driven initiative dedicated to building tomorrow's energy and climate innovation ecosystem.

Prior to joining MIT, Ben was the Environmental Innovation Manager at the Yale Center for Business and the Environment (CBEY) and the Environmental Innovation Fellow at the Tsai Center for Innovative Thinking at Yale (CITY). In that dual role, he helped students to design, build, and launch environmental solutions.

He has also been part of several sustainability startups, and he has managed climate resilience projects around the world, including rural India.

Ben holds dual master's degrees from the Yale School of Management and the Yale School of the Environment, as well as a bachelor of science degree from Duke University.

He lives in Newton, Massachusetts, with his family. He enjoys making animal sculptures, climate fiction, and dad jokes.

BILL AULET is the Ethernet Inventors Professor of the Practice of Entrepreneurship at the MIT Sloan School of Management. Additionally, he has been the managing director at the Martin Trust Center for MIT Entrepreneurship, serving all of MIT, for the past 18 years.

Prior to MIT, Bill had a 25-year track record of success in business. He has directly raised more than $100 million in funding for his companies and led the creation of hundreds of millions of dollars in market value in those companies. He worked at IBM for 11 years, from 1981 to 1993. From 1993 to 2005, he founded and led two companies (Cambridge Decision Dynamics and SensAble Technologies) and then led a third (Viisage), which were all MIT spinouts.

As an author, he has written three books (*Disciplined Entrepreneurship: 24 Steps to a Successful Startup*, *Disciplined Entrepreneurship Workbook*, and *Disciplined Entrepreneurship: Expanded and Updated*). His books have been translated into over two dozen languages and have become award-winning US and international bestsellers. Among the various recognition he has received as an educator, in 2021, he was awarded by the United States Association for Small Business and Entrepreneurship as the Entrepreneurship Educator of the Year. His work is used in over a thousand schools and has helped educate over a million students.

Specifically, in the area of climate and energy combined with entrepreneurship, Bill has spearheaded several MIT efforts, including founding and leading the original Energy Ventures course and co-founding the MIT Clean Energy Prize as well as TEX-E. He currently sits on the board of Greentown Labs.

Bill holds a bachelor's in engineering from Harvard University and a master's degree from the MIT Sloan School of Management.

TOD HYNES is a senior lecturer at MIT, where he co-founded and teaches Climate & Energy Ventures and co-founded and advises the MIT Climate & Energy Prize. He is a senior advisor for climate and energy at the Martin Trust Center for MIT Entrepreneurship and is the chair of the board of the Woodwell Climate Research Center.

Tod is the CEO and co-founder of Maigent, a company that enables individuals to thrive in an AI-first world and automates the process of starting and running companies. Tod also founded Clymate Studios to help others help the climate. He started a wind development company before tax equity investors entered the US market, and he started XL Fleet, one of the first fleet vehicle electrification companies, which scaled across the United States and Canada and went public in 2020. From 2004 to 2008 he was the director of alternative energy at Citizens

Energy, where he launched the company's wind development business and assessed various clean energy and carbon offset development opportunities. In 2001, Tod started one of the first social networking companies, but he decided to focus on climate.

Tod holds a bachelor of science degree in management science from MIT.

FRANCIS O'SULLIVAN is a managing director at S2G Investments and is a leader of the firm's energy investing activities. Frank is also an adjunct faculty member at the MIT Sloan School and has previously served as the director of research for MIT's Energy Initiative and as co-director of the MIT Electric Power System Center. Earlier in his career, Frank was a senior consultant at McKinsey & Company.

Frank is a senior associate with the Energy and National Security Program at the Center for Strategic and International Studies in Washington, DC; he is a Distinguished Associate at the Energy Futures Initiative; and he has previously served as a board member of the American Council on Renewable Energy. Frank is a member of the governing authority of University College Cork.

He received his PhD, EE, and SM degrees from the Massachusetts Institute of Technology and his BE from the University College Cork, all in electrical engineering.

LIBBY WAYMAN is an investor with Breakthrough Energy Ventures, an investor-led fund created to accelerate the transition to clean energy and a clean economy. Libby has over 15 years of experience in clean energy and clean technology, including multiple startups and executive roles in leading energy companies.

In previous roles, Libby led clean technology innovation at GE as the global director of ecomagination innovation, served as the director of the Clean Energy Manufacturing Initiative at the US Department of Energy, and developed several technologies in the solar industry including at SunPower and Alion Energy.

Libby started her career in entrepreneurship by co-founding a business that now supplies equipment to the dairy cold chain in India. She holds a BS in civil and environmental engineering and an MS in mechanical engineering from MIT. While at MIT, Libby co-founded the MIT Energy and Climate Club and the MIT Energy Conference, and she led the student input to the formation of the MIT Energy Initiative, all of which became beacons for information sharing and analysis on energy technologies. Libby now also teaches the Climate & Energy Ventures course at MIT.

GLOSSARY

Beachhead Market An initial market that has customers who highly value what you offer, are willing and able to buy a product at your stage or from an early-stage company within a reasonable timeframe, and who can enable you to grow the business. An initial stepping stone toward bigger opportunities, culminating in the Big Prize.

Big Prize A massive global market with the potential to keep growing, and capturing a significant share of that market would have a transformative impact for people and the planet.

channel-market fit When a company identifies the most effective distribution channel to reach its target market, ensuring that the channel aligns with customer preferences and behaviors. It requires finding the right sales or marketing strategy to the audience to maximize adoption and growth.

Climate Total Addressable Market (Climate TAM) A rough estimate of the largest possible impact you could have on the climate if you focus on a given public problem. Contrasts with a traditional TAM that focuses on the private problem and its financial opportunity. (See "Problem Segmentation" for more on public and private problems.)

Climate Value Proposition (CVP) A quantified, rigorous measurement of your potential climate impact. Components of the calculation include a baseline (the future without your solution), additionality (the extent to which your solution reduces emissions), and full life cycle emissions (the emissions produced by your solution).

Cost of Customer Acquisition (CoCA) The marginal amount of costs your business will incur to acquire one more average new customer. This involves only the marketing and sales costs and not the product and development or general and administrative costs.

Core What allows your business to uniquely produce your value proposition with much greater effectiveness than any competitor.

Customer Life Cycle Use Case How your customer will interact with your solution, from initially learning about the product, to using it, to encouraging others to buy it too. A key component of the Full Product Life Cycle. (In *Disciplined Entrepreneurship Expanded and Updated*, this concept is called the "Full Life Cycle Use Case," but in this book, we call it the "Customer Life Cycle Use Case" to clarify that we are only talking about the life cycle of the solution in relation to the end user.)

Decision-Making Unit (DMU) All the people who will be involved in the decision to acquire your solution, including people who can approve or block the decision, as well as people who influence the decision.

deep tech Ventures that aim to commercialize complex science or engineering innovations, usually requiring substantial research and development as well as large amounts of money.

First of a Kind (FOAK) An application of a new technology for the first time at commercial scale.

Full Product Life Cycle Every step involved in making your solution operational, including sourcing materials, building, operating, and ultimately disposing of or reusing its components.

internal rate of return (IRR)   the discount rate at which the net present value (NPV) of all cash flows (both inflows and outflows) from an investment equals zero. It is the annualized rate of return that makes the projected cash flows of a project break even in present value terms. It is a critical measure for climate and energy ventures, as it helps determine whether a project can attract financing by comparing it to the Weighted Average Cost of Capital (WACC). If IRR exceeds WACC, the project is considered financially viable and scalable. IRR is widely used by infrastructure investors and project developers to assess and compare the potential returns of various projects and opportunities.

Lifetime Value (LTV) of an Acquired Customer The average profits you will get when you acquire one new average customer in today's dollars (or equivalent currency). This is the net present value of the gross margin that new average customer will generate for the company.

Market Stepping Stones A series of increasingly larger markets that allow you to move incrementally from the Beachhead Market to the Big Prize. Each stepping stone should give you a chance to build a bigger and better version of the solution, or possibly to implement an improved business model.

Non-Dilutive Funding Money raised for your venture that does not require a piece of equity or need to be paid back. It includes grants (public and private), fellowships, and prizes.

nth of a kind (NOAK) A later version of the First of a Kind (FOAK) that is scalable and easy to build; called "nth" because at this point, building the solution should become such a predictable and profitable enterprise that no one cares what number it is.

Persona A specific person (ideally a real person) with a name who represents a particular role within your Decision-Making Unit.

primary economic buyer The person who controls the budget and will pay you when the end user uses the product.

primary market research (PMR) The practice of observing and engaging with customers and learning from them about their world and the problems and opportunities they face. Contrasts with secondary market research, where you look at data that others have gathered and summarized.

Problem Segmentation A method to help decide what problem to target with your new venture. Start with a public problem experienced at a high level across large swaths of society, and break it down into a private problem faced by individuals or businesses who would be willing to pay to solve it.

product-market fit When your product matches what customers in a specific market are interested in buying.

Quantified Value Proposition (QVP) A quantitative description of how your product will benefit your target customer in terms of the priorities they care about most.

raison d'être Literally "reason for being." In the context of this book, a description of why you want to start a climate and energy venture.

secondary market research Information obtained from market research reports and from indirect sources like the Internet or analyst reports.

Techno-Economic Analysis (TEA) A quantitative model for determining whether a solution is both technologically viable and economically feasible.

Total Addressable Market (TAM) The annual revenue for a given market or set of markets if you achieved 100% market share. Contrasts with Climate TAM, which focuses on the opportunity to impact the climate instead of the financial opportunity.

Value Chain The full range of activities required to bring a product or service from conception to delivery to the end customer, including design, production, marketing, distribution, and support. At each stage, increasingly more value is added, and throughout the chain, ventures can identify opportunities to optimize processes or capture more value themselves. (Similar to "Full Product Life Cycle" but framed specifically around the value added at each stage.)

weighted average cost of capital (WACC) The average rate a company must pay to finance its operations, considering both debt (like loans) and equity (like investor funding).

INDEX

Page numbers followed by *f* and *t* refer to figures and tables, respectively.

THE DISCIPLINED ENTREPRENEURSHIP LIBRARY

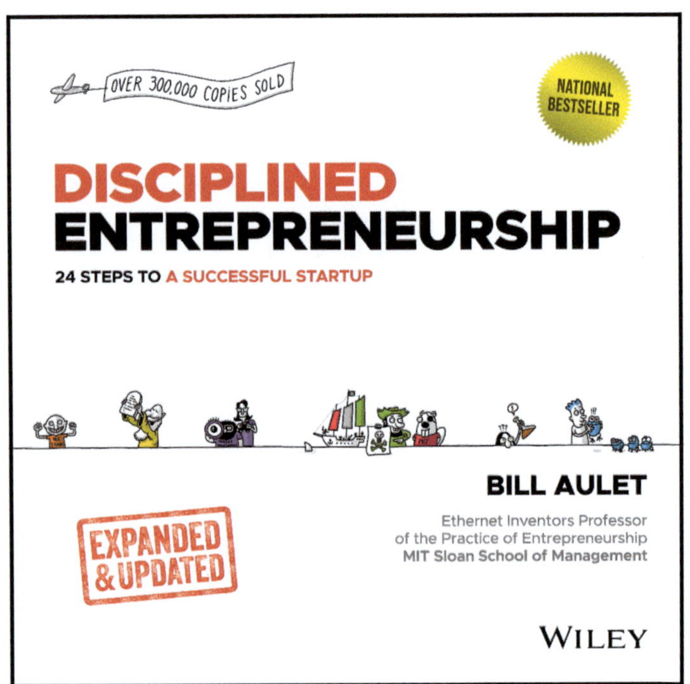

Disciplined Entrepreneurship • ISBN: 978-1-394-22251-3

Startup Tactics • ISBN: 978-1-394-22335-0